PRIVATE WORDS

Ronald Blythe has written poetry, short stories, history and literary criticism, much of it reflecting his East Anglian background. His first book, the novel *A Treasonable Growth*, was published in 1960. *Akenfield*, his remarkable evocation of rural change, much of which he had himself witnessed, appeared in 1969. It was followed by *The View in Winter*, a study of old age. *The Age of Illusion* and *Writing in a War*, an anthology, contain further personal assessments of Britain's recent past. *From the Headlands*, Ronald Blythe's collected essays, was published in 1982. *Divine Landscapes* was published by Viking in 1986 and *The Penguin Book of Diaries* in 1991. His work has been translated and filmed and has received a number of literary awards.

Ronald Blythe has also edited and introduced a number of volumes in the Penguin Classics, including *Emma* by Jane Austen, William Hazlitt's *Selected Writings*, *The Awkward Age* by Henry James and *Far from the Madding Crowd* by Thomas Hardy.

PRIVATE WORDS

LETTERS AND DIARIES FROM THE SECOND WORLD WAR

CHOSEN AND EDITED BY
RONALD BLYTHE

PENGUIN BOOKS

PENGUIN BOOKS

Published by the Penguin Group
Penguin Books Ltd, 27 Wrights Lane, London W8 5TZ, England
Penguin Books USA Inc., 375 Hudson Street, New York, New York 10014, USA
Penguin Books Australia Ltd, Ringwood, Victoria, Australia
Penguin Books Canada Ltd, 10 Alcorn Avenue, Toronto, Ontario, Canada M4V 3B2
Penguin Books (NZ) Ltd, 182–190 Wairau Road, Auckland 10, New Zealand

Penguin Books Ltd, Registered Offices: Harmondsworth, Middlesex, England

First published by Viking 1991
Published in Penguin Books 1993
1 3 5 7 9 10 8 6 4 2

The acknowledgements on pp. 308–9 constitute an extension to this copyright page

The moral right of the editor has been asserted

Printed in England by Clays Ltd, St Ives plc

For Patricia Highsmith

Contents

Contents

Introduction

The more able to be clearly viewed in retrospect, the more astonishing so much Second World War activity appears. It was a time of firsts and lasts. The Battle of Britain was a first and last, for it is surely most unlikely that armies of small aeroplanes will clash decisively on a blue field again. Equally unlikely, unless somebody manages to destroy today's world-wide telecommunications system, is it that millions of people will keep in touch via the written and not the spoken word as they did during the 1940s. The letter reached its peak of private importance then. It was a desolation not to receive them. Parted for as many as three years at a time, and more if one was an early prisoner of war, one lived for them. Watching his fellow sailors all busily writing home in the YMCA, the poet Roy Fuller observed:

> The letters are permanent
> And written with our hands
> Which crease into their lines
>
> And breathe, but are not so
> Living as these letters.
> Our hands are seas apart.

These letters – and diaries – are now half a century old and lie behind ageing lives in huge quantities. Many, each one so private, provide social history in public libraries. Letters from sons and daughters, letters from parents and lovers, letters from best friends, letters about being hurt and frightened, and about new lands, dutiful letters and letters of genius. Journals too. The authorities were none too keen on the latter, but it took more than a regulation to stop the natural diarist. This last great avalanche of private correspondence and of expressing oneself on the page generally while the earth rocked is a vast enough subject for myriad interpretations. Here is one look at it and one assessment of it. 'Just a few lines' from Keith Douglas's journal as he went into battle suggest the twin sources of the literacy which helped to create not only the brilliant achievement of writers such as himself, but also the good minor one of almost everybody who wrote home – and from home. These sources were the convention of writing a letter whenever there was something important to say, and the need to have a book to read.

> I had that feeling of almost unstable lightness which is felt physi-
> cally immediately after putting down a heavy weight. All my mental
> inquiries and arguments about the future were shelved, perhaps
> permanently. I got out my writing paper and wrote two letters,
> one to my Mother and one to David Hicks in Cairo. Although in
> writing these letters (which, of course, got lost, and were never
> posted) I felt very dramatic, the tone of them was not particularly
> theatrical ... I had asked Andrew one or two questions in the
> hope of not showing myself too ignorant in my first action [in the
> Battle of Alamein, which opened on 23 October 1942]. But it was
> fairly plain that he knew nothing himself. 'I shouldn't worry, old
> boy,' was all he would say ... When I had written my letters I
> got into the turret [of his Mark III Crusader tank] with Evan and
> tried to learn its geography. My place as tank commander was on
> the right of the six-pounder. I had a seat, from which I could look
> out through a periscope ... On the shelf, when we were in action,
> we usually kept some Penguin books, chocolate or boiled sweets.

Always letters and Penguin books, or indeed any old books: these were among the necessities of existence for serviceman and civilian at the time. That there were letters and letters, and books and trash made little difference. Everyone needed to write and loved to read. Education had been strongly formal whether it was elementary, grammar or public school, and if people could write little else, it was expected of all classes that they could put a letter together correctly. Not to be able to spell was as disgraceful as having a hole in one's sock. For millions, not to be able to read during the Depression would have blocked the only affordable means of escape. Many people had had much time on their hands between the wars and had read the penurious years away. Rural society retained the last habits of the ancient storytelling tradition. When the war came every kind of fresh experience – unprepared-for emotion, travel, violence, homesickness, the intensification of friendship, incredible boredom – discovered an often well-trained literary outlet. Had the war not happened, very few of its letter-writers and diarists would have dreamed of communicating as they did. The expression of the self through letters by men and women long-parted was often disconcerting. Things were written which would never have been said. Sometimes a stranger would begin to emerge from the post. Reunion was a constant theme but also one containing an underlying dread. After the war the self so nakedly displayed in the letters would lie at the back of the drawer, at the back of the mind.

Censorship inhibited some correspondents, others totally ignored the fact that their private lives were left open for a stranger to read. Fellow officers belonging to a mess would censor each other's letters rather like priests hearing each other's confessions, making an effort to obliterate with professionalism what they were learning about a friend. The future novelist Barbara Pym, censoring in London, pretended to be comically exasperated: '"Oh these are dull people," said the Censor in a low dragging tone. "They do not seem to realize that we are at war. They write only of trivialities and the young woman does not know her own mind. All these quotations, too, it is not natural."' The poet Arthur Waley was satirical:

> I have been a censor for fifteen weeks,
> The building where I work has four times been bombed,
> Glass, boards and paper, each in turn,
> Have been blasted from the windows.
> . . . .
> It is not easy to wash, keep warm and eat;
> At times we lack gas, water or light.
> The rules for censors are difficult to keep.
> . . . .

The Air Raid Bible alters from day to day;
Official orders are not clearly expressed.
One may mention Harrod's but not Derry and Toms;
One may write of mist but may not write of rain.

Witty posters by Fougasse, showing Hitler and other Nazis eaves-dropping on the Underground, in the pub, in the kitchen, were every-where – 'Be like Dad, keep Mum.'

While an impressive public reticence was maintained regarding troop and ship movements, the last especially, private lives soon learned to ignore the blue pencil. Although the literary and social convention of the period forbade explicitness, letters and diaries held very little back. They were written in Stephen's ink or Rowney's HB pencil on flimsy paper or aerograms, the letters often numbered to tell the recipient which had been lost on the way. Considering the nightmare conditions of delivery, the postal service was very near a miracle of trustworthiness. Writing materials were an essential item of any parcel sent to the war zones. It was the zenith of the fountain-pen. Parker pens and wrist-watches vied in popularity as twenty-first birthday presents. In 1942 Penguin Books were advertising the Penguin Pen, price 5s. 6d. It had an ebony streamlined holder with an iridium-tipped fourteen-carat gold nib, fine, medium or broad. Guaranteed five years. Paper was precious and often filled to the edge. British handwriting was still dominated by the old copperplate 'thick and thin', American was open and rounded. One reason for the immense amount of letter-writing in the services was having so much unfilled time. Long stretches of the war were, for those actually fighting in it, spent in semi-idleness. It was like film-making, with an almost intoler-able inaction between shootings. It was also spent in crowds and a dual boredom of wasteful days and hugger-mugger propinquity caused the writing of a letter to be seen as both a sane task and an acceptable retreat into privacy.

The continuous discipline of letter-writing and diary-keeping, and the solace of reading, proved to many people that they could 'write' – stories, maybe, poems, an autobiography. A novel. This phenomenon began to reveal itself early in the war when editors and publishers began to receive a flow of new work which lay outside any of the literary beginnings with which they were familiar. It was sharp, colourful and often political. The more established literary world regarded it with enthusiasm. It appeared in paperback collections like *Penguin New Writing* and *Poetry London*, and was much encouraged. Stephen Spender dedicated his *Life and the Poet*, a Searchlight Books paperback, 'to the young writers in the Armed Forces, Civil Defence and the Pacifist Organizations of Democracy, in the hope that this tribute may encourage them to write'. Similarly, the poet R. N. Currey, serving as a gunner officer, brought together in his anthology *Poems from India* a wonderful collection of work written for the most part by men (and one woman) who would not have written had not the war given them its powerful literary training. There were many forces anthologies of prose and poetry by mainly young people who had discovered how to write through the regular practice of letters.

Letters from home could be in danger of carrying to some poor chap struggling with the realities of the Western Desert or a convoy *en route* to Russia the insufferable cheerfulness propagated by radio comedians, the tabloids and some films, while those from the front, anxious not to cause worry, could be bland. The contrast between what the soldier saw and what women, mainly, were prevented from seeing bore no comparison to the situation during 1914–18, when men on leave from the trenches entered a madhouse of smiling patriotism. Robert Graves wrote of staggering around a euphoric London gradually realizing that there was no way of talking about what was actually happening in Flanders to a lady. Not so John Masefield, working in a field hospital; his letters to his wife concealed nothing, softened nothing. If the Second World War soldier–airman–sailor left out the horrors, it was because he knew there were horrors enough back home with the raids and the hardships. Illness was different. The private writing of these years reveals much illness in the forces due to stress, climate and epidemics. Death too is a frequent subject. One day the letters would stop coming – it could happen. Correspondents would dwell quite luxuriously on this probability. It was often among the calmest themes of their letters and of the poetry which sometimes extended from them. Gunner R. A. George found a body so shallowly buried that the hands stretched out of the earth, so he knelt down and covered them up.

> It seems so strange, the unexpected things,
> That one is called to do, in times like these.

The principal concern of this writing, however, is how to hold a fragmented existence together until, until ... Not ever knowing when the war would end was agony. Could a family or a friendship, or plans to change the scheme of things entire, ever last out? By mid-war the writing becomes very political and determined. It is 'get rid of Hitler and the Japs, and then!' A future other than that being arranged by the establishment is being incubated. The pre-war conditions in which millions of Britons lived, looked at from distant reaches of the Empire, or a prison, or from an ack-ack gunsite on Muswell Hill, are seen as not only evil but pointless. The act of thinking things out week by week on a writing-pad brought self-confidence and understanding. Accompanying snapshots tumbled from the envelopes showing the same face, and yet a different face. Women carried fat wodges of air letters in their handbags, men in the breast-pockets of their uniforms. Letters went on travelling. The poets found them especially poignant. Keith Douglas, on leave in Cairo, wonders whether to 'cut myself a piece of cake' with Marcelle,

> Parisienne
> always preoccupied with her dull dead lover;
> she has all the photographs and his letters
> tied in a bundle and stamped *Décédé*.

But this was never their purpose. Those who wrote them stamped them 'Life'.

Stranded from the normal, taken for granted usefulness of their lives, people often felt that they would go mad if they could not occupy themselves in what was logical, rational and wholly personal. At a time when no one was left alone, there had to be an activity which required an aloneness which could not be criticized. During these years a book, for countless individuals, became the cell into which they could withdraw from the wearing enforced sociability the times demanded. Throughout the war the call for books to be sent to ships, camps and prisoners grew ever more urgent as those who once may have just amused themselves with a tale or two now longed for that most effective escape from the boredom of their situation, the printed word. There were book drives – often abused by householders who saw a way of getting rid of otherwise indestructibly well-bound rubbish – and there was the thoughtful passing on of books, fiction mostly, which guaranteed pleasure. The paper shortage and the massive destruction of publishers' pre-war stocks during the blitz combined in making titles rare or flimsily produced. On the other hand, the great nineteenth-century novelists, sets of whose works had formed part of the circulation struggle in Fleet Street and which languished glossily in many a front room, came into their own. Their serialization on the wireless, Anthony Trollope especially, was so widely enjoyed that current notions of popular taste had to be revised.

Before the war the hopeful notion of bringing the masses 'up' was accepted as an ideal. Reading good books was the surest way to rise. That people might be well-read in different ways was disallowed. In 1934 the preface to the *Authors and Writers Who's Who* could lament:

> The trend of both literature and journalism as a whole is still towards the masses. Newspapers with a common or sensational appeal continue to gain ground and it is sensational books of a 'thriller' nature which are selling by the thousand. But it is incorrect to assume that the literary class of reader is disappearing entirely. Rather it is that the more general and superficial class of reader, spoonfed by the popular press and the circulating libraries, is growing in numbers every year.

Nearly all the weeklies, monthlies and quarterlies carried short stories and serialized novels, most of which were illustrated. The most popular 'literary' weekly was *John O'London's*, which unaffectedly propagated an emotion well known then, the love of books. But it was the public library and the commercial circulating library, such as Mudie's and Boot's (there were many others), which created a wide novel-reading public which was unconscious of being lowbrow or middlebrow because it revered and believed in its favourite authors. Life for so many was penurious and cramped, but the novel – and the cinema – brought riches and space. Reading was cheap, absorbing, consoling and exciting. Successful popular novelists were expected to maintain a steady flow. The customary price of an 80,000-word novel was 7s. 6d. – 8s. 6d. if it was 'long' – and there would be a 3s. 6d. edition once the demand for the full-price edition slackened. A number of publishers produced their own distinctive 'libraries', inexpensive, often well-bound volumes which encouraged people to build up an excellent private collection. J. M. Dent's Everyman's Library, Jonathan Cape's Travellers' Library, Nelson Classics, Oxford University Press's World's Classics and Collins's Library of Classics were among the most distinguished of these. In 1936 a young publisher named Allen Lane began issuing unbound books which he called paperbacks at 6d. each from the basement of a London church. By 1939 Penguin and Pelican Books had become the most admired and loved of all publications. For the writer it was a mark of distinction either to be reprinted by Penguin or to be commissioned to write one of their 'Specials'. By the first year of the war Penguin and Pelican were set on a course to become a formidable part of the new adult education process which would alter so much of Britain's thinking and moribund attitudes. Few publications could have been as treasured as were these extremely light and elegant books – you could pack half a dozen in a kit-bag and hardly notice their weight – and they were read to shreds from Scapa Flow to Malaya, and their influence upon the letters and diaries of these years was considerable.

During the thirties the whodunit, the best as now usually written by women, became the most boasted about leisure reading of the great. These murder puzzles set in strong class-observing situations, with their well-bred or outsider sleuths, and only just enough violence to produce a corpse or six, got a bit roughed up as a genre by the James Hadley Chase school of sex and guns. What readers wanted was the recurring hero. If a writer could invent a Captain Hornblower, a Saint, a Topper, a Whiteoaks family or a world (P. G. Wodehouse) of characters who would never run out of pages, he or she was made. The recurring hero or family or place in fiction became a comfort and reassurance, and the mores and sayings of these novels had an effect on letter-writing. Women read Ethel Mannin (romance, common sense and liberation), Sheila Kaye-Smith (romance in faithfully observed Sussex countryside), Angela Thirkell (romance and unapologetic snobbery – she was famous for describing Australia as a 'country for warrant officers'), Mills and Boon, E. M. Delafield (still very funny fictitious diary of a middle-class lady) and Naomi Jacob (romance and fighting spirit). The erotic was nearly always a big let-down. Novels such as *Lady Chatterley's Lover*, *The Well of Loneliness* by Radclyffe Hall, *Boy* by James Hanley and Joyce's *Ulysses* remained banned, while *Forever Amber*, Kathleen Winsor's sub-Defoe blockbuster, promised far more than it could give. Favourite permissible naughty reading was the pocket magazine *Men Only*. Women's magazine reading was less passionate in substance than wildly melodramatic. Or else just cosy. Many letters and diaries sternly repudiated the pictures given of foreign countries by writers such as Rosita Forbes, H. M. E. Clamp – even W. Somerset Maugham. But three novels, *The Good Earth* by Pearl S. Buck and the translations of Mikhail Sholokhov's *And Quiet Flows the Don* (1934) and *The Don Flows Home to the Sea* (1941), were to have quite a profound meaning for those British readers who were beginning to see beyond the bounds of Empire. The book clubs of the thirties also began to introduce American writers like Steinbeck, Thurber and Runyon, whose work helped to loosen the stiff style of some wartime diarists, though the chief easer in this respect was more likely to be radio shows such as *ITMA* and *Much Binding in the Marsh*. There was certainly a flood of language to carry along those obliged to write home or to communicate with themselves. It got into their descriptions and confessions, giving them extra scope for what they had to say.

If a single multifarious reason for so much wartime writing had to be chosen, it would be travel. The somewhat static boardgame which was life for the majority of people had been tipped over and the pieces thrown in all directions. Or directed to billets which had to be described to be believed. It was not just the impact of Africa or the Far East, and particularly India, but of a Nissen hut on Orkney or some blacked-out Midlands station. Journeys were drab and difficult yet absorbing, or at least something to write home about. Considering that no mention could be made of where one was going when one was on the way, or where one was when one reached a destination, the traveller in wartime had a method of showing very fully the effects of so much helpless moving about. For, unlike the regular serviceman and servicewoman, the called-up civilian could never wholly submit to being sent here, there and everywhere. Their letters and diaries thus record a struggle between necessity and resistance. But this enforced going places and its endless variety of scene – a Catterick to Arakan spectrum – drove the pen as did no other stimulus. Belonging mainly to a generation which had been brought up on the journeys of the Great War – the brief, so often one-way trip to France or the memorably beautiful voyage to Mesopotamia and Gallipoli – and on the emotion-choked embarkations from English ports of troops for the Empire wars, one of the first things which the Second World War travellers felt in their bones was that theirs were journeys without precedent. That they were not going where their fathers had gone before, even where the place bore the same name. And shifting about in Britain itself was not a homely business, not even to where one may have spent a holiday. A discomforting, hostile element had crept in. At the same time travel of any kind sprang adventures and stripped away background. One could feel excitingly free while being virtually imprisoned on a slow cold train to Inverness, or on a slow hot liner to Suez.

Travel proper had been confined to a very small group before the war. This group was chiefly made up of the officials who administrated the Empire, and included great numbers of soldiers and sailors ('Join the Navy and see the world') and the better-off who, for pleasure or health, took cruises. The only way the average young man could go abroad was to join up or emigrate to one of the colonies. For most people travel had to be a vicarious activity undertaken through novels, films and songs. To sail on a liner especially or to visit New York or the pyramids was such an impossibility that common sense kept it firmly among the stuff of dreams. They had one week's paid holiday a year and spent it traditionally at a local coastal resort or having what were called 'days out' on a 10s. rail-card which allowed a week's travelling about. During the Depression great numbers of the unemployed had virtually saved their sanity as well as their bodies by walking and cycling, camping and rambling, especially in the north. These became true travellers. They were educated by Dutt's guides, Bartholomew's maps and by Arthur Mee and H. V. Morton, and by a whole library of open-road literature. Writers like J. B. Priestley would celebrate this claiming of England as of birthright by walking it. Such travellers were rightly convinced that their explorations were as valid as those of the people who could afford to get themselves to Africa. All the same, foreign parts were never more alluring, more frustratingly unreachable. In the classroom framed prints of the Empire inculcated a global Britain. In the cinema, films such as *The Lives of a Bengal Lancer* (Gary Cooper, Franchot Tone and C. Aubrey Smith) and *Sanders of the River*, in which one sensible white man deals out *Boy's Own Paper* justice to the childish natives, made on location, became doubly thrilling because of their scenery. All the churches supported missionaries, whose infrequent furloughs laid emphasis on distance.

The Empire was both old and brazenly new, at its peak and near collapse. Less than forty years before the war Joseph Chamberlain was justifying its acquisition by declaring, 'We, as fast as we acquire new territory and develop it, develop it as trustees of civilization in the interests of the world.' And the youthful Churchill had written that, in seizing fresh lands for the Crown, 'The act is virtuous, the exercise invigorating and the result often profitable.' Empire travel, via rhetoric, fiction, film and a tremendous amount of storytelling by returned 'builders' of all kinds, created a non-parochial and, on the whole, a non-European concept of travel. Hollywood, of course, became the single, irresistible guide to the United States, where nobody expected to wander except through celluloid. Perhaps the part of the world in which people who had never travelled outside their own country best knew their way about was the Middle East. Christianity as well as the British Arabists, most notably T. E. Lawrence between the wars, had made it as familiar to them as their own backyard. Or so they thought. Wartime letters from the Holy Land to the Home Counties reveal some conflict. The highest and lowest matters have to be reconciled.

Air travel was minimal. Delta Air Lines and Pan American Airways had begun to run passenger services in the United States in 1929 and during the following decade all kinds of civil airways were functioning in Britain and elsewhere, but the principal means of getting about the world was still by liner. During the thirties the liner reached its glorious apogee in the streamlined forms of the *Bremen*, the *Normandie* and the *Queen Mary*; never before or since has travel been so luxurious. 'Liners' because they belonged to various shipping lines, the most celebrated of which was the P & O, founded by two Scots in 1837, the initials standing for the Peninsular and Oriental Steam Navigation Company. These evocative ships, shed of all their rich furnishings and packed to the gunwales with soldiers, carried armies to the battlefields. To be sailing across the Mediterranean, or in the Indian Ocean, even under such austere conditions, was for many an individual who had never before been afloat, like being admitted to take part in a legend. Minus their mock baronial halls, Versailles ballrooms, cabins like satin caves and, most of all, their hordes of servants, though not entirely their elaborate rituals, these liners managed to preserve much of their romance while on their war footing. They confirmed Kipling's claim, 'The Liner she's a lady.' Blacked out, soundlessly as possible, zigzagging and protected by their convoys, they became one of the most potent images for the wartime travellers. They may not have been 'posh' – going out to India port side to avoid the blast of Red Sea heat and returning starboard for the same reason – but they were routed where the climate would turn from winter to summer in a week or two, and where they would smell Morocco. Few in the 1940s believed that liners would not sail for ever. In peacetime they left harbour in a rain of streamers; thousands of paper umbilical cords tore to let them part from the land as the band played 'A Life on the Ocean Wave'. Now the vast shapes sneaked out furtively, led by minesweepers and dreading U-boats.

The Empire itself had to be unsinkable, too much emotion had been invested in it for it to be imperilled. But on 15 February 1942 Singapore, its major Far East bastion, fell easily to the Japanese. Sixty million pounds had been lavished on it to make it safe and formidable, with tiers of guns pointing out to sea to deter the mightiest aggressor. The

Japanese took it from behind. With the loss of Singapore the whole attitude to travel altered. In a nutshell, the certainties and probabilities of starboard-side home vanished. Letters from Burma and Malaya often reveal a sense of the writer being somehow stranded or unable to make the old connections. The landscapes, instead of colouring the prose, seem to clog and engulf it. For those at home a son or husband was, for anything they could comprehend in geographical terms, nerve-rackingly off the map. Rudyard Kipling knew the feeling when it only applied to coffee and rubber planters, and their wives.

> How runs the old indictment? 'Dear and slow',
> So much and twice so much. We gird but go.
> For all the soul of our sad East is there,
> Beneath the house flag of the P & O.

Staying Together by Air Mail

> Oh soldier lad, Oh soldier lad,
> Before the soul of things turned bad,
> She offered you so modestly
> A shining apple from the tree.
>
> Oh lonely wife, Oh lonely wife,
> Before your lover left this life
> He took you in his gentle arms.
> How trivial then were Life's alarms.
>
> Alun Lewis, 'Song'

Marriage by correspondence was to be a common fate during the war. Those parted, often for three or more years, soon realized that another form of continuity had to be established, as no relationship could stand so long a break. While at first it was natural and easy to write, it soon became apparent to many husbands and wives that letters could lead them into artificiality. It took time and either some literary ability or a pure ingenuous sincerity to push the marriage along. Once a husband was in the Far or Middle East there would be virtually no home leave for the duration. Meanwhile, the personalities of both partners would be more changed than they realized by the unusual freedoms and disciplines of the war. A glance in the mirror or a look at the situation in which they now found themselves would often confirm that they were not the people they were when they said goodbye. The war had 'done something to them', as it was said. As the months passed with no end in sight, dreams of homecoming were laced with questions and even with dread. How could two people who had for so long presented themselves on the page re-enter the realities of domesticity, small talk and bed? And what had happened to them which was not in the letters? Could they ever ask? Tom Hopkinson, warning about this particular 'cave of war memories', says that both angels and skeletons can be expected to walk out, though eventually arm in arm.

His cousins David and Diana Hopkinson were married in May 1939. She was then working for a charity which rescued Basque and German-Jewish children and he was working towards those political ideals which would implement the Beveridge Report and bring about the socialist achievements of the Attlee government. Her being partly Jewish added both an element of suffering and a shared interest in the future of Palestine to the marriage. Sir Tom Hopkinson saw these letters as 'a reflection of our gravest national crisis in its effect on two young lovers, sensitive enough to suffer deeply, but sufficiently detached to record their feelings honestly'. Their correspondence was in fact to prove a solid foundation for a long partnership, as intelligence, desire, wit, irritation, gossip, dreams and deep-down friendship, maintained on the page during years of forced separation, created a binding power which was to enrich that of the normal togetherness of marriage. Diana and David Hopkinson also recognize what an emotional and sexual torment letters can be.

1941

Diana to David, from her aunt's house, Bengal Manor

Thomas is the only man in the house with seven women, including the maids. A common enough wartime situation, I suppose, but I must arrange for him to see the gardener more often so that he knows what a man is. He is so loved here. No one wants to see him go. It will break the parlourmaid's heart. He is known in the village as 'Young Tom of Bengal', Old Tom being the gardener here, who leaves whatever he is doing if I put Thomas's pram anywhere near. Old Tom asked if he might take him to his home to show his wife and he returned with five little girls, following the pram, like maids of honour, leaving heaped nosegays of primroses and cowslips around Thomas. I feel his existence is justified by the happiness he gives to people here this anxious spring.

David to Diana

> Thomas, my baby son,
> The Bear turns over,
> Be deaf to chatter from the Besa Gun
> O kick your heels in the clover.

(The Great Bear wheels above my head each night upside-down, like this damn crazy world which parts us.)

Diana to David

Virginia Woolf has died. Apparently she committed suicide by drowning. I felt immensely sad as if a personal friend had died. Do you remember how much we enjoyed her last article in *New Writing*? I think with particular affection of *To the Lighthouse*, especially of the description of the family and their satellites enjoying a meal of *bœuf en daube* presided over by the mother who is the good genius. It gives one the feeling of warmth and a faint excitement stimulated by the presence of a familiar crowd after a day spent in sun and solitude. The whole scene glows like a sunburned cheek in the evening. I believe she is one of the writers who has enlarged my own powers of vision and expression.

David to Diana

I suppose there is no harm in telling you now that I have been living on the lowest habitable level of a ship. I can just stand upright. The engines throb behind the partitions beside us.

There is little empty space. Our kit is stacked in racks over our heads. We are supposed to sleep in hammocks slung from hooks in the ceiling. Actually after unsuccessful essays in the first few days, I have either slept on deck or in a passage. For most of the time I was one of the half dozen lucky enough to secure a mattress – but one gets used to sleeping on the boards of a deck. It is in the daytime that one gets weary of sitting, leaning, reclining on something that gets harder and harder.

Diana to David

I had a letter with your poems with a slip enclosed from the censor. 'Please warn the writer that there will be a delay in forwarding, or even risk of the letter being returned to him by the Base Censor, if he does not write more clearly.' As your writing seemed perfectly legible, I imagined he referred to the cloudy contents of the poems – suspected of being a code! ... Letters for us stand for love, longing, light-heartedness and lyricism. Letters evoke passion, tenderness, amusement, sadness, rejoicing, surprise. And none of this possible without the Army Post Office.

David to Diana, from a camp close by the Suez Canal

I have here the gentlest, freest day that one could imagine in the Army. In the camp your status alters a little each week in accordance with your supposed improvement in health or fitness. [He is convalescent.] This week I have to be at roll-call just outside my tent at 6.30. Breakfast is at 8.00 – tea, sometimes excellent porridge – always something greasy on a tin plate which one gets clean afterwards with sand. At 9.00 a little work putting up tents or tidying the camp. Then freedom for the rest of the day. Usually I read and write in the mornings and bathe in the afternoon. There is a canteen with ices and lemonade at our bathing place ... After 8.00 it is dark ... Generally we lie in our tent talking, then break off to go and hear the 9 o'clock news. A silent circle of men sits out on the sand under the stars and, amid a glow of cigarettes, the radio describes this slow progress towards the end we are all longing for.

Diana to David

Tonight I was overwhelmed by the contrast between your and my life. My companions and I with a well-cooked meal off a polished table, carnations, silver, shining glass, napkins – all the pre-war paraphernalia of a meal – and beyond the cool evening air and the lawn through the French windows; you with your tin mug, bully beef hash, dust and grit and bare boards and benches; we in the spacious drawing-room with our separate rooms to retire to for the night; you in a hut with countless others in that great heat. I want to smash up everything here and come and share your dust and dreariness.

David to Diana

You imagine too much about me and that makes the separation harder for you than me. I understand your surroundings, and you in them, so that my imagination is spared unhappy exercise about them, and so I suffer less than you do.

Diana to David

I feel when I have your praise of my letters, that if they mean so much to you, I should make them better. I should go to bed later, get up earlier to have more time for them, keep a notebook of all the things I wanted to say to you as they occur during the day, that I should write and re-write them so that they are really worthy of you and our love.

David to Diana

I think, my dear, that we shall both learn to accept our separation, but I do not expect that the sharp sudden stabs of loneliness will leave us. They may come more seldom, but they will not be blunted. But I agree there is no need of passionate assurances of our love in our letters, since we want to do nothing which might tend to dramatize something which is so natural and free and deep. And passionate words tend to dramatize. But we both know that when we have woken in the night with longing, or been blinded with it by day until tears blurred vision, that a sentence of hot, sweet love in a letter comes like an answer, even as an appeasement, to that longing, both for the one who writes and the one who reads.

Diana to David

You would have been surprised to see a group of ladies disporting themselves in your mother's drawing-room, for a Health and Beauty class – or maybe it is now re-christened 'Keep fit in wartime'. Five women were bending and stretching and waving their limbs like tame octopi all over the place. Thomas looked on, amazed, from his pram on the veranda. I don't know quite for what wartime activity we were preparing ourselves. Unless we were to follow the Air Raid Warden's admonitions when he came to demonstrate a stirrup pump.

I gave Thomas an evening's entertainment by dancing in front of him while he watched leaning over his cot. He thought it terribly funny as he does all forms of expression including singing, and he laughed a lot more when I took him in my arms and waltzed round the room with him. Oh, how I miss dancing in this war – there is still poetry and music to be enjoyed – but who will dance with me? Not you, my love – you never would – but couldn't I find a fascinating partner somewhere?

David to Diana

It is hard to think that the ultimate grimness lies ahead of us. I hope one will be able to muster one's own courage to fit in with the courage of the country ... Sweetheart, keep close to me these fateful days.

> Best of my life. Farewell, since we must part,
> Heaven hath a hand in it; but no otherwise
> Than as some curious artist takes in sunder
> A clock or watch, when it is out of frame,
> To bring it in better order.

> (*The Duchess of Malfi*)

Later. This letter is the product of two evenings in the NAAFI interrupted on both occasions for long periods of conversation. Tonight, being payday, they are playing the great army institution called 'housey-housey' or lotto. This is the officially encouraged form of gambling, just as certain brothels are officially encouraged and kept under the eyes of the authorities. Housey-housey is the most unintelligent form of gambling ever devised and the official brothels, I should imagine, the least attractive ever equipped.

... Tom and Kenneth Leys [his old Oxford tutor], both writing in the height of summer, talk of flowers, which I have missed far more than I would have expected. And in every one of your letters something about flowers creeps in. I love to hear of your daily activities, bicycling in the lanes, picking flowers in the garden, watching Thomas as he pioneers about the lawn. I go through your letters now, noting each recorded point of development in Thomas, noting how housewifely you have become, noting that you get the same dream as I do – that we are just going to meet and do not quite manage it, or that we do meet and then are at once separated.

Later. What I regretted in my last letter was not only its shapelessness but a sense that it lacked close communion with you. It seemed to be throwing off random sparks of my ideas and feelings. In your letters to me it appears that you make contact with me, sometimes almost the suggestion of a physical nearness that I can't discover for myself. You suppose in your letter 21 that where I am I cannot, except rarely, want you with me. Again and again I do want you so that I could share with you the things I see and the thoughts I have. I crave the best companionship I've ever had, but I dare not be dominated by that craving, just as I dare not let all the other cravings that I have for you get the better of me. Above all the nightmare feeling that time is slipping by and that everything lovely is eluding us. You must have discovered, like I did, that our love is like the huge mainsail of a racing yacht. It is the beautiful gigantic source of power and life. At the same time it is the supreme danger. The careless handling of the sail will tear the mast out of the vessel and leave it a hulk.

1942

Diana to David

I feel like a character in Chekov. Still young and full of aspirations and yet frustrated. And the cricket pavilion where the litter of the cricket gear, the shuttlecocks and battledores, the smiling teams from the walls and the shelf of frayed and faded novels are very Chekov. I examine the photos for some contact with you, staring at the boy in white flannels on the back row. Oh, I would like to clean out the pavilion and make it into an outdoor nursery for Thomas. A fresh start! But there are no fresh starts until this war is over.

David's cousin Tom Hopkinson was editing *Picture Post*, the celebrated photo-journalist magazine launched by Edward Hulton in 1938. In March 1942 David saw an issue on sale in Jerusalem with the naked Thomas in his bath on the cover. The issue was called 'Plan for Britain'. *Picture Post* was now engaged in its own war against the old conditions.

Diana to David

Think of our son in his bath being distributed in over a million copies all over the world. It is a terrific, exciting thought but a little overwhelming. It is a pride of place he shares with Roosevelt, the PM, Stafford Cripps, Greta Garbo and others. I have broken the news to your parents by letter. I am afraid they will be very shocked but I explained I wasn't asked about it.

David to Diana

The woman in the shop where I bought it came bustling up to me as soon as I took *Picture Post* out of the stand to scrutinize it. 'Yes,' she said, 'just came in this morning.' 'Yes,' I said, 'it's a picture of my son. I suppose I had better buy it.' She thought this was a soldier's joke and I had to go on repeating, 'Yes – really – yes', until she subsided in a mixture of surprise, embarrassment and pleasure. No one I show it to believes me. They think I am making a joke in doubtful taste.

Diana to David

A Czech friend I talked to said he thought it possible we might be entering into a new age which might be thought dark by people like us – liberal democrats – but which would satisfy the majority, as the majority only wanted peace, food enough and economic security. Freedom as such they would forego if they had these things, and forego too spiritual enlightenment and the creative arts that arose from liberty. He said he thought perhaps our day was done, at least for some long hundreds of years to come, and we should find ourselves strangely out of place in the new world, even perhaps preferring to die than to live in it. I don't know. Security and peace seem so intensely valuable, what would one forfeit to have them? For surely we have to forfeit some of the things we now hold valuable? It becomes clear that our son Thomas must grow up in a world that differs far more from our pre-war world than our world differed from the pre-the last war world of our parents.

David to Diana

Our values *have* stood up to war, so I think they will stand up to starvation, economic insecurity, or whatever the new living conditions time produces for us. Our day has not done; it has only just started. We have got news today that Cripps is in the War Cabinet. I am particularly pleased that he appears to be cast for the role of spokesman and leader. Not only knowledge-able Jews, but the men I'm with in the billet are pleased with this news. Churchill is still convincing and irreplaceable; so long as he holds the main threads in his hands he gives an impression of masterly ability. On side issues he is not the same at all.

Diana to David

I have been to the Silks Department of Harvey Nichols. This was in a way a museum because there were still lengths of wonderful French silks, rainbow taffetas, diaphanous organdies (in which you once said bridesmaids are always dressed) and brocades in sumptuous golds and blues. But few people buy these because hardly anyone wears evening dress for which they are suitable, and because most of us spend our coupons on sensible tweed and stout shoes. I got up early to buy some blue Harris tweed I had my eye on. It took a *quarter* of the year's coupons. As usual at this time I feel a great longing to buy a 39/6 hat – a little fly-away of straw with a veil and flowers bunched at the top. Of course we both know that I would look really ridiculous in it. Anyway, I am going to be very careful about not buying new clothes. I have so many good ones. There is a continual call to austerity which I think should have come much earlier. Clothing coupons are to be reduced by a third and fuel is rationed. Occasionally a wireless programme is interrupted and a lugubrious voice says, 'Have you got your electric fire on? Turn it off! It may be colder tomorrow.' There is much talk of fortress economics. That should have started after the fall of Dunkirk. People want to help so much and are prepared for something much more real in the way of sacrifices than they have hitherto made.

Wilfrid is, curiously enough, a specialist in women's dress, gained from the twice weekly dress shows in his Berlin store. Sheila and I recently asked him why it was that she and I never managed to look really smart and soignée. He didn't give us a very satisfactory answer beyond saying it was a gift some women had, and admitted it might mean spending more money and time than we chose to upon it. Also he suggested that we had a secret contempt for women who gave a great deal of attention to clothes. We denied this. Then he suggested a lack of attention to details, hair, stockings, gloves, and that we had not learnt how to put on clothes in the right way or carry ourselves in the most elegant manner. What he did *not* do was to contradict us when we said that we were *not* well dressed. In comparing afterwards, we felt rather hurt.

David to Diana

My hair is rich and plentiful just now as there is no one to order me to get it cut. It blows in the wind. I wear my army boots because it has been so wet and I can't afford to get my shoes repaired at the moment. If I am to be an officer I must have brown shoes instead of black. My battledress is very shabby, of which I am proud. The blouse is too small and doesn't meet the trousers. I usually carry my forage cap in my hands (a) because it doesn't fit and (b) because once when I was pissing it toppled off my head into the piss bucket and, although I dried it in the sun, I have never much liked wearing it since. My overcoat buttons have not been cleaned since I left England.

Diana to David

I saw an exhibition of pictures at the Leicester Gallery – work by Graham Sutherland of smouldering burnt-out gorse, and John Piper's pictures of ruins. I wanted to buy a Sutherland but Jane Rendel, who was with me, pointed out that War Savings Certificates were of more practical use to the country than pictures which one had nowhere to hang. I came upon a scene which moved me more than any of the pictures, a house that had been bombed last year with the front wall and windows still standing. Through the windows I saw a tracery of trees framed from the garden behind, so you had a strange feeling as if you did not know whether you were inside or outside. I can't explain how beautiful it was.

Later. Today I was upset by a trivial thing. I lost one of Thomas's three ration books – the one that entitles him to oranges, soap and blackcurrant juice. The other two are for main rations and 'points' for tinned food and luxuries like dried fruit. I had seen some oranges this morning at Hemel Hempstead but wasn't allowed to buy them until 2.00 p.m. according to the Ministry of Food's mysterious and seemingly quite illogical ruling, so I thought in order to give Thomas a special treat, I would bicycle down again this afternoon. Also give myself the treat of being out this rare sunny day. When I wanted to start I couldn't find the book. I had to go down without it and make a special application at the Food Office for a new one. It was all very tedious and I had a hatred of all the people and shops and silly regulations. But coming back up the long hill of Featherbed Lane – my heart melted in the sun. The threshing machine was working and there were a lot of land girls and men and soldiers working by it, and the sun was warm on my face. And for the rest of the afternoon I thought in terms of love rather than hate. And Mary had bought Thomas some lovely chocolate biscuits for his tea for which he would gladly sell his soul – only I wouldn't let him.

I have no real comfort to offer for your missing this stage of

Thomas's life. When I am specially delighted by him, the thought that you are not seeing too pierces me and indeed takes away half the pleasure in him. But there, I am left with the other half of the pleasure still, while you, poor sweet, have none. The only sort of comfort I can offer is that the essential Thomas remains whatever age you see him, that these early stages of physical changes are only the prologue of his life.

David to Diana

You write of Thomas with the full power to make him come alive for me. I suppose he is your creation like a novelist's favourite character whom he is always talking about. For you Tommy is a creation both in the word and the flesh. For me the flesh has become the word, and not the word the flesh.

Diana to David

At least it is one year of absence over. We shall never have the pain of that absence to live again. Put it away – have done with it. We have to travel on into the almost incredible second year of separation. It is like going for a horrible walk one never wanted to start on and having to go on walking further than one meant to ... Do you remember that walk up through the rain to St Gervais to the chalet? I thought it was never going to end, even with you dragging me up half the way. But it did end in wine and a hot supper and a fire to dry ourselves by and that soft sink-in bed, and each other's arms to rest in. And so my letters run on, our only bridge.

Later. The wireless has become a central element in my life. I listened to sweeping romantic ballet music last night until I wept like a sentimental girl for the past grandeurs of ballet dancing and the heady excitement connected with hot summer nights amidst an audience high up in the gallery. And walking home, through the shadowy stuffy streets of European towns with some loved companion – perhaps dancing some of the steps on the pavement and nodding to the tunes over a drink in a dazzling, noisy café. Strong heady stuff, dancing, a faint beat of desire and an intoxication with the town at night. And now it is Sunday morning and I have just washed my baby's nappies and the joint is in the oven, and the opera houses where they danced are shut or put to some grim purpose, and, yes, there is a war on, and all is harsh and sour except Thomas's cheek and the lilac outside, and our love.

Julian Huxley spoke on the *Brains Trust* last night about the various organizations which were drawing up plans for physical reconstruction after the war. They are PEP, the Town and Country Planning Committee, the 1941 Committee, several of the architectural societies and then the government planning committees. I thought I would try and collect literature from them to send to you as it might be useful material for your lectures.

David to Diana, from the Western Desert

I gave a talk this afternoon on the Anglo-Russian Treaty. It is odd to stand before an audience plugging Anglo-Russian co-operation, pointing out that future peace, our children's lives, civilization in Europe will all depend on it, and being confronted with interested but sceptical and dubious faces. I suppose they wonder what I am doing it for. Those who ask questions are generally repeating left-wing slogans of 1939 and 1940, long out of date. The others talk about it a bit among themselves afterwards, but don't risk putting to me their unfledged opinions. I am thrillingly pleased by the Treaty – the one piece of news we've had lately of certain good. All the rest is so much in the balance – I mean Kharkov, the Mediterranean and the Desert.

The desert battle is an inconceivable, monstrous horror which yet will be making many in it thrill with an unearthly inner exaltation. Casualties must have been awful and the disappointment when it became clear that Rommel, just when it seemed that he might be beaten, had got up reinforcements to force us back. I wonder if it will be over by the time you get this letter or if, in this terrible death grip, the antagonists will still be swaying backwards and forwards.

Later. These are the events on which the shape of the world's history day by day depends. And yet, though they sway me backwards and forwards, they do not dominate my daily moods. My private history in these fourteen months, its peaks and troughs, does not coincide with the graph of world events. Now fourteen months parted I feel the burden of my longing for you worse than ever before. I feel sometimes that the sustained loftiness of our feelings toward each other is hollow. An uncomplaining acceptance of fate, a belief in ourselves, a hope for the future – all this collapses, overwhelmed by an inrush of agony, despair and death-wish. This is what the army calls 'moaning'.

Later. I dreamed last night that a Jewish ATS girl came to deliver a message to me and, as she saluted, I thought, 'Can this be Diana?' But her face was in a kind of haze. Her breasts, her hips, the fall of her skirt and her legs seemed just like you, and I tried to make myself believe that the face was yours, although I really knew that it wasn't. I could see her black hair wandering out under the unbecoming hat, and that was yours. When she went away I almost cried with disappointment.

Diana to David

We are regularly visited for the collection of National Savings. All the salvage is sorted out into neat little dumps in a central position, and what is known as the WAR EFFORT is constantly kept in our minds by voluntary effort. I suspect a feudal social hierarchy is still preserved here. This comprises the Squire in the Manor (though his name is only Brown), the Vicar, who lives in the one modern house in the village, and a grand old lady in the Old Rectory next door to us, alone with six servants. We see her pass on her way to church on Sunday dressed in lilac silk with a parasol to match. The lesser gentry include a retired wing commander and wife who are *deeply* shocked that we do not play bridge. Apart from these the population is predominantly made up of farm workers and a scattering of evacuees. There is one general shop, one pub and the Post Office, which also sells a curious miscellany including Kosmic Toilet Paper and the Devil's Own Nibs advertised by a picture of a lurid devil snatching at a pen from behind a judge's ear. With our insatiable demand for postage stamps we are the ancient sub-postmaster's best customers.

Yesterday evening on my bicycle I took the road which rambles between the foothills of the downs, gently following their contours on my right all the way. Like your hills, they had fissures of shadow in them in the evening sun – gently blue fingers laid on their sides. The fields were full of harvesters and I met great carts and patient horses on the road, and as I passed sunburned workers held up the rabbits they had captured after that awful exciting few minutes when they escape from the last patch of corn. Such fullness everywhere, cottage gardens full of apples, sunflowers, hollyhocks and dahlias, and women leaning on their cottage gates. Harvest, harvest home!

I have discovered an oasis of civilization in deepest Wiltshire at Ham Spray House – ten minutes' walk up the road towards Inkpen. This is where Lytton Strachey, Carrington and Ralph Partridge lived and where Strachey died, and Carrington, soon afterwards, committed suicide. Now Ralph Partridge, wife Frances and son Burgo live there. He is a conscientious objector now, though a major with an MC from the last war. This pacifism puzzles the local gentry and isolates the Partridges from the villagers. There are dark murmurs about 'Conchies'. But they are certainly not lonely as they entertain many friends, such as Julia Strachey and Lawrence Gowing, who are local, and Raymond Mortimer from London.

The house is plain, low and dignified, with a pink washed exterior. It stands at the end of a magnificent avenue of elms. One reaches the front door through the stableyard. On the south side the garden stretches beyond a swimming pool almost to the foot of the downs, which rise very steeply through a hanging wood. There is a glass veranda which throws fascinating shadows into the rooms and round two sides of the house. The interior is wonderfully decorative, but has a slightly decaying brilliance about it. There are strange but sourly successful combinations of colour, such as rose-pink, lemon, magenta and lime-green. Among the many pictures by Duncan Grant and Vanessa Bell there was one of Lytton Strachey by Carrington, an artist then unknown to me. Strachey, his head thrown back, is holding a book between his elongated hands. He resembles a stone figure lying on a tomb. There are four-poster beds with patchwork quilts and everywhere curios such as medieval Spanish fire-irons, early English musical boxes, shell caskets and African carved wooden dolls. I admired Lytton Strachey's library, deep shelves, so quiet – the windows looking across the downs. And the Partridges said, 'Borrow any books you like!' They seem a quiet country couple. Only the beauty of the house and the slightly flaunting mannered style of decoration gave any evidence of their unusual past. He is enormous, rubicund, fair and smiling, and I admired his white tweed trousers. She is slim, dark, gypsyish and quick, and I covet her white silk petticoat, glimpsed while we changed by the swimming pool.

David to Diana

You tell me I am safe in your heart, which is a sweet and humbling assurance. You are safe in mine. The world turns for me on that axis. Your comparison of our lives now to bomb craters, somehow filled up with rubble and debris and all sorts of makeshifts, is exact. Anything may be thrown in now to fill the gaping blast hole, for life must go on and we must serve its purposes.

If I need a woman badly it is a reflection of my need for you. Nothing counts but to be *your* lover again, and I think a better lover one day in what will be a harder, but fresher, and in your words, 'a less haunted' world. I think we are very near to the turning-point of the war. I know I have always been more optimistic than you, but I do not think my optimism can now be considered irrational. It is my belief that the Nazis will not capture Stalingrad, will not cross the Caucasus, and that our air strength will be the key to the situation in the West. In bombers and in offensive fighters we shall have set up an overwhelming supremacy by the end of this year [1942]. I am often asked 'When will the war end?' If I give anything like a serious answer it is that next spring will be the earliest possible moment at which it could end in our favour, but that the close of next year is more likely.

Later, after Diana's illness and depression had caused her to write to her husband about doubts concerning their marriage, the tone of his letters alters. They are still loving but also sharp.

David to Diana

Frankly, I never have and never will agree with you about marriage. Marriage is simply a practical expression of a wish. Love is the reality, and marriage the social form adopted for it in a particular set of circumstances. In 1939–1940 our circumstances were such that marriage did fit our love. In other circumstances we might have expressed our love by dying for each other, a suicide pact, or simply by deliberate separation. You say that separation, war, loneliness, should not affect marriage. Certainly those things in our case demonstrably do not affect love, but it is blindness to deny that they must affect marriage. It would be suicidal if they didn't, because marriage, as it exists for us now, is not the suitable form or symbol for our love to adopt. In our circumstances we must have a new relationship above and beyond marriage. I don't know what it is, but I know its three strongest elements – confidence, tenderness, sympathy.

Diana to David

Your airgraph of November 10th made me feel a bit ashamed and indeed showed the uselessness of arguing and bitterness, although it saddens me that we should not be able to understand each other's attitude better. At least I think we do both *understand*, but neither of us can accept. You must not talk of suicide pacts. I want to live. I want to be your wife again.

Later. Wilfrid was intensely disturbed by the Nazis' recent drive to exterminate the Jews. He has the feeling that as the horrors of war mount up people's capability for compassion dries up. They feel when so many suffer, 'What is there that can be done about this extra bit of suffering?' Many suffer for some real or imagined cause, but the Jews for nothing they can see or understand except blind cruelty. I can hardly bear to think of it myself and it is brave of him indeed to work day after day against hopeless odds, constantly hearing the most atrocious details, meeting indifference and defeatism, but still trying to do what he can against it. This exportation of Jews from France oppresses me more than almost anything that has happened in the war. To strip men, women and *children* of every mark of identity and send them to die in great herds on some Eastern Frontier seems to me a crime beyond words.

I am reading Rebecca West's *Black Lamb and Grey Falcon*, which gives me a sense of Europe again and of European culture, and fascinating objects to be discovered there. All this helps me at a time when I am chiefly thinking of Europe as the torture chamber and graveyard of the Jews. I found the Allied Declaration about the Jews moving. Whether it can have much impression on their fate seems doubtful, but at least it keeps alive the conscience of the people outside Europe and stirs them to greater effort to release Europe. There is nothing effective one can do for the Jews except to win the war as quickly as possible, and to rescue as many of the children as possible, which can still be done in some neutral countries.

David to Diana, from Palestine

The Jews here are so extraordinarily mixed. It is possible that the perfervid Jewish nationalism may be calming down during this period of enforced calm and, possibly, that after the war the recent and ill-absorbed immigrants may return to Europe. There will certainly be ferment in the Arab countries at the end of the war. Both sides tend, I think, to regard this as an interval in their own struggle although responsible Jews and their supporters at home naturally try to put everything they can into the war effort. The Moslem peoples in Syria, Iraq and Egypt were all on the threshold of self-government. When the war came it disturbed a delicate equilibrium and put them all back into tutelage again. It is, therefore, of prime importance that our good faith in holding out hopes of independence is immediately re-established when war circumstances make it possible. In the Middle East, which must now be regarded as a *whole* and not as being made up of independent states, the Jews are a tiny fraction only and they are already rightly suspected of being able to exert an influence in England disproportionate to the size of their stake in the Middle East. I am convinced that Zionists must accept the White Paper's stipulation that no further immigration into Palestine is to be allowed until a responsible independent government is set up, and then only with the approval of that government. Such a government might be a federation of Palestine, Jews and Arabs, Lebanon, Syria and Transjordan in which predominantly Jewish areas would enjoy local autonomy. I admit that my view is influenced by anti-Zionism – the view that Jews are of greatest value within the countries where they have been long established. I am as impressed as everyone must be by the technical and cultural accomplishments of Jews in Palestine, but for an intensely nationalistic minority to seek to carve out for itself an independent state from territories to which others also have a claim seems to be inconsistent with the high ideals of peace and humanity in which civilized Europeans believe.

Diana to David

When I am washing up what remains of our lovely Wedgwood
china I think of the expression on your guilty face when you
broke a dish and looked for my reaction. I find it quite *comforting* now to remember this domestic detail of our life together.
Wedgwood china is irreplaceable. So are most kinds of china,
and lots of shops have notices up, 'No cups or saucers'. But
'Utility' china is appearing – quite good shapes though all in the
most lifeless plain white.

Reconstruction and all it might mean in healthier, happier
living for everybody does give me a sense of inspiration at times,
and there is a certain tonic effect in reading about it. I concentrate
rather on physical reconstruction although I have a growing,
passionate desire to see England a real part of Europe, taking
full part in its economic and cultural life. That seems an essential
preliminary, coming even before the world's united nations
plans.

I saw in *The Times* that the Ministry of Food had appointed
an art director to supervise the decoration of British Restaurants,
the hanging of loan exhibitions and mural paintings in them. I
don't know how many British Restaurants there are, but I
imagine well over a thousand, and many of them in places where
there is not the ghost of an art gallery.

David to Diana

Going for a walk alone I came on a rather pretty girl sitting by
herself on a stone where a footpath was crossing the open
country. We could only speak in French and she was Polish, and
had also lived in Yugoslavia. When she said with smiling resolu-
tion, '*On attend la fin de la guerre*', I felt so touched that I
couldn't go on. My halting French seemed a crude intrusion into
her privacy. She was waiting for someone who hadn't come, so
she went back to the city and I continued my walk.

Diana to David

I wish I had something like a divining rod which would tremble and spring in my hands and tell me where you are, and how you are now. All of me is reaching out to you, yet I cannot discover you. I want to stress that you have no need to fear that I am, and will be in all essentials, any different from when you left. Emotions rise and fall but love is intensified.

1943

David to Diana

On Thursday I put in a lot of work and scarcely noticed that it marked the passage of two years without you. It is better so, better not to think of these things too frequently. I try not to think that it is two years out of the small number allotted, which have vanished unblessed. Better not to dwell on anniversaries or numerical measurement of time or of happiness. It is quite enough to feel the unremitting ache without adding mathematics to make mincemeat of one's life.

Diana to David

Thomas is talking so much about you now. He even says he is going to look for you, and he makes puddings for you, and works out a crude aggrieved logic, 'Burgo's Daddy here – Tommy's Daddy not here – come back, Daddy.' Alas, it is enough to make a stone statue weep. I began explaining about Spring to him today and told him how lovely it would be. For the first time this year we went into the garden after tea and inspected the fallen elm, a massive giant lying on its side. Thomas says he is coming with Jessie's chopper to chop it up, but occasionally he exhorts it, 'Get up, tree!' This evening he got out of his bed after I had put him to sleep and came downstairs. He said, 'Another boy has got into my bed.' I asked him what he was called and where he came from. 'Called Goldilocks and comes from Palestine.' When I reported this to Winnie she said that morning, when 'helping' her to wash up at the sink, he had put a dish aside and said that it was for another little boy. Has he second sight and sees a ghost in the house, or is it the result of a fatal remark of mine that, if he was not good, I would get another little boy?

There is a lovely little iris out in the garden, iris stylosa, a big purple bloom but very delicate, like a dragon-fly, growing close to the ground. I should like to send Mother flowers as the few flowers there are for sale in London are at terrific prices. But it is now forbidden by law to send any flowers by post or rail. One is allowed to carry a moderate mixed bunch with one in the railway carriage 'at the discretion of the railway company'. A sad day for England when there are no flowers on the rack being taken up to London after a holiday in the country!

Winnie was talking about Lytton Strachey yesterday, and saying how the people in the village called him Jesus because 'he looked exactly like the photos of Jesus in the Bible'. He used to talk in a very simple friendly way which also gave them a Christlike association in their minds. One of his oddities was to offer them a cigarette by taking just one out of its packet and then putting the packet back in his pocket, which they thought *very* strange.

In February 1943 David received a copy of the Beveridge Report. Hints of its contents were creating a sensation both at home and abroad. Post-war Britain was not to be anything like pre-war Britain. Everyone would be cared for from the cradle to the grave.

David to Diana

The Beveridge ban has applied here as in England and the Army Bureau of Current Affairs pamphlet outlining the scheme is not apparently to be circulated even now. It was printed here and the Army Education Corps got copies together with an order that it was not to be used for ABCA discussions, which are compulsory, and normally led by regimental officers. Instead, it is only to be used in voluntary discussion groups organized or led by AEC personnel. We are starting two of these at once . . . They have just begun to issue special pamphlets from India which, so far, are first-rate, laying stress on rural development, and suggesting that what had been learned in the army could be translated into post-war reconstruction. Nobody seems to doubt among the Indian Army people I meet, that there will be full independence for India after the war.

In July 1943 Diana and Thomas, and their friend Maire, went on holiday to Cornwall.

Diana to David

As we anticipated that the train would be very full, and we had an eight-hour journey, we planned to travel First Class. Maire was *refused* a First Class ticket as she was a Private's wife. I bought a First Class ticket, only to find the First Class carriages were full of officers and their wives who made no effort to make room for me, although I was carrying a small child. In the event, we travelled a long way in the corridor, mixed up with exhausted soldiers asleep on their kitbags. And that was the first time I have ever bought a First Class ticket! (Though I remember you bought them on our honeymoon.) I shall write to the company about both these points. Can't you imagine me seething with righteous wrath!

Young airmen are nearly always here on the beach on their days off, leaping about, playing cricket, rather beautiful with their bronzed bodies and white shorts. And often, aeroplanes, like great white birds, appear to rise out of the sea. Convoys go by on the horizon with barrage balloons attached. We meet coast-watchers, such as I remember from the last war, peering down the cliffs. We are told they search the coves at dawn. War has transformed these remote places but not diminished their beauty. There was a storm the other night with thunder and great flashes of lightning. Thomas awoke frightened and I told him, no, it was not bombs, he need not be afraid. Cornwall stimulates his imagination; when he saw a group of fluttering little girls on the sand he said, 'They are like seagulls.' And when I lifted him out of a pool, he fingered my collar bones and remarked, 'Bones are like the stalks of flowers.' And one night when I asked him who he was talking to he replied, '*I'm* not talking. One of my hands is talking to the other.'

Diana noted the behaviour of the elderly rich during the war, that of her grandmother in particular.

Diana to David

I stayed as usual with my grandmother whose example inspired me, at least temporarily, with a braver, more resilient, attitude. Her confidence was unfailing, sustained by unusually all-embracing feelings of patriotism. When she sorted the possessions of her brother after his death, she found a medal presented to him by the Japanese government for some service he had rendered to their national art collections. She held it at arm's length and said, 'I should like to add this to the scrap metal collection but I shouldn't like anything Japanese to be found amongst the collection from this house.' I said I didn't think that mattered. She rang the bell for the butler and said, 'Remove this, Keane, please, for the metal collection. See that it is really taken away. It is Japanese.' And Keane walked out holding it rather gingerly and looking a bit scared, as if it were a small bomb.

War was the supreme enemy of one of the chief tenets of my grandmother's life – orderliness. This war upset her more profoundly than those through which she had lived before, because it brought not only danger, but disorder and dislocation of lives, old customs, privileges and pleasures. It shocked her deeply when the iron railings were uprooted from the London square where she had lived for so long. Its treasured garden was thus laid open to malefactors, and menaced by every passing dog and cat. When these railings came down she was more agitated than when all sorts of offensive ironmongery fell from the skies about her home. 'Untidy' she pronounced it. But such irritations as the blackout hardly affected her. She had always had heavy curtains, lined and inter-lined, and punctually pulled by a maid at dusk, and she never went out at night.

When I had been staying with her on an earlier occasion there was a particularly unpleasant and destructive air raid. The shattering noise penetrated even my deaf ears and I was very frightened. Keane, who was rather drunk, appeared at intervals, urging her to go down to the shelter, but she would not stir. Her only concession was to move from the front room which had long windows into the dining-room at the back. On one occasion, Keane crawled under the dining-room table for shelter but I didn't dare join him for fear of my grandmother's scorn. So we continued to sit upright until the All Clear, she knitting and I helping to wind her wool. She belonged to the knitting brigade who knitted for their menfolk at war Balaclava helmets, khaki mufflers for the Western Front and knee-length socks to be worn with shorts in the Middle East. Each movement of her hands symbolized a sword thrust at the enemy. 'We will win the war, we will win the war!' rang the rhythm of her clicking needles.

Her cook, with the support of a network of relations in her native Wales, saw that her ladyship, and her guests, were adequately fed. My grandmother was punctilious in observing wartime regulations, but it did not occur to her to inquire whether her cook used the black or blue market as long as there was some semblance of decent food to offer her guests. And when, for a change, her daughter took her out to lunch at what was deemed a good restaurant, she remarked, though the whole place had been shattered in a raid the day before, 'What, no napkins!' This was followed by, 'These plates are not china, they are earthenware and not very clean at that!' Nor was she mollified by being told that the restaurant served the best food in London, since its standards were far below those set in her own house. 'How,' she asked, 'can one serve a good meal for five shillings?' which was the maximum price allowed at that time. Her own sweet ration she distributed amongst her grandchildren and great-grandchildren. Her clothes coupons she gave to her more flighty young relations – 'So she could look nice when her (errant) husband comes home' – because she had little need of coupons herself since the clothes which had been carefully constructed by court dressmakers before the war had, like her principles, been built to last.

She listened to every news bulletin and received reports on the progress of the war from numerous young visitors and in letters. People were a bit surprised by Lady Spielman's reactions. When one of her nieces, who held high rank in the ATS, called on her, she was told that khaki did not become her, especially with all that grease-paint. Could she not find a civilian job and wear more becoming garments?

David to Diana

I adored your description of Thomas's birthday party. How delightful it must have been. I do want a little girl, 'like a seagull' as Thomas would say, in a tiny flowered frock and with a delicate skin like silk. The trouble is that if we did have another child, and it was a girl, I should love her, being there to see her grow all the time, while you would love Thomas. But perhaps we should go on loving each other so much that it wouldn't matter. I have no wish for children compared with my longing for you. If I was told that I could come to you at once provided we had no more children, otherwise only in eighteen months' time, I should choose to come now, I'm afraid. One marvellous thing is that when we do meet again it will be a second love-dream. How our friends will hate us! We shall rush about London in taxis, not be able to eat our meals, load kisses on each other in the street, never be able to get up in the mornings for love of each other, as on our wedding-day, and I shall never be able to stop touching you. How awful it will look to the outside world, brushing against your breasts, putting my hand under your skirt and all the puerile things so exasperating to other people.

Diana to David

You very often have said that during your absence you and I should make lives of our own. How far have we succeeded? You, obviously, with your work to a greater extent than I have. Mine seems such a pale, washed-out version of a life. Perhaps I have never really made the effort to build a separate life since you have been away. It has been nearly all waiting. Do you blame me for this? And yet you would rather have had it this way than that I should have built up an independent life so strong that our coming together in a joint life would have been impossible. That must have happened with many a couple separated by the war.

David to Diana

I love you to write about your physical self; sometimes a kind of puritanism comes into your letters. I know you have all the responsibility and a much harder life than mine, but if we were actually together it would be easy to carry off between us almost light-heartedly all burdens and anxieties that Thomas causes, as well as all the planning and so on. The kind of puritanism I mean embodies a mixture of impatience, over-rigid conviction, restlessness, vicarious ambition. I hate to think that you could ever become crabbed and anxiety ridden. Don't be brow-beaten by the puritans. Don't forget that you have the temperament of an artist.

Later, touring the Western Desert battlefields. At Alamein itself the coast road follows a low ridge overlooking the sea, cruelly brilliant in colour. On the other side the flat expanse of scrubby desert where only a year ago the armies had manoeuvred there is only to be seen now the wired-in minefields, a few notices, a few graves. Further on, much evidence of the Axis retreat, burnt-out planes, tanks, trucks and abandoned guns. We went off the road down to the sea, leaving our delighted driver to rummage through dumps of old vehicles. John and I bathed in shallow water where flat ledges of rock met the sea. Then we played a naked game of beach cricket with a bit of wood and small stones.

1944

In February 1944 Diana sent a letter-card to David to break the news to him that Pat Henderson, his closest friend at Oxford, had been killed in Italy. But on 3 February David sailed from Port Said, homeward bound, missing this information. Diana believed that he would have had time to come to terms with this loss by the time he reached England. On 8 February she wrote:

Lord, O Lord, how slowly the days pass now. Are you a mile, an hour, nearer me? As I clean my room, I wonder whether I am sweeping the bridal chamber. Your return has somehow a classical or biblical feeling. Ulysses? No, that isn't a fortunate analogy. I haven't twenty suitors — not even one — and I weave no tapestry except the darns in my stockings.

I've shed my hearing instrument. It was an internal instrument, always going wrong. The truth is I don't really want to hear anyone until I hear your voice, which will surely ring clear and true for me. I know this letter is fragmentary, like a conversation when one is waiting to see someone depart by train, though I am waiting for your boat to *arrive*.

They met on Hungerford Station on a bitterly cold February evening, he laughing and saying, 'My bride, my darling!' as if he had rehearsed it, she confused.

I had never seen him wearing an officer's cap and his seemed quite different from anyone else's. His strange uniform, his strangely thin face glimpsed in the dimmest light, gave me a feeling of artificiality. Even in our kisses there was something unreal. In bed there was a terrible sadness to overcome — Pat's death — before we could make love. When at last he turned towards me, we made love as if we were partners in a solemn rite, strange, speechless but familiar.

The next morning I was again overwhelmed with a sense of unreality, for I found myself alone in our room. He was not there, nor in the house, nor as far as I could see in the garden. Had he in sober truth come home at all? Or had he left again, overcome by the emotions of the previous night?

I looked towards the village for some clue and then saw him coming from the shop with a packet of cigarettes in his hand, an essential detail of his wellbeing which I had forgotten to provide. He was wearing the civilian clothes which I had so carefully laid out for him. He did not understand my worried looks, nor could I explain at once my momentary lack of faith in our reunion.

Loyalties

'London can be very pleasant,' said Phillip, turning over to lie on his back. 'These elms are fine creatures, lifting their arms to the sky. Byron must have known them, and Keats, and Shelley. W. H. Hudson, too. I saw a green woodpecker here in nineteen-twenty, during my first year in Fleet Street.'

'How can you talk about that when the world is on the brink of a war that will end in the bolshevization of Europe?'

'Did I ever tell you that my cousin Willie met Hitler at Bayreuth in nineteen-twenty-three, after the abortive *putsch*? My cousin said Hitler was the most sensitive and eager creature he had ever met, or was likely to meet. He was all idealism and hope and naked sensibility. And he had almost a mystic admiration for England. Willie, as an ex-service man, was invited by Frau Cosima Wagner to sit in her box during a performance of *Parsifal*. Hitler sat at the back, concealed from the audience. He was on the run. The music moved Hitler so much that the tears were running down his cheeks.'

'I'd have given ten years of my life to have seen Hitler. He is *everything*. Birkin [Oswald Mosley] is a clod compared to Hitler.'

Henry Williamson, *The Phoenix Generation*

The dangerous, the naïve, the thuggish, the romantics of all classes were swept up in the safety drag-net of the 18B Act when war was declared. They were arrested and taken off to be vetted and interned on the Isle of Man, for the most part. Some were to be there for the duration, others were eventually found either harmless or useful in some special way and called up or directed into curious jobs suitable for their equally curious talents. Their leader, Sir Oswald Mosley – 'Before the organization of the Blackshirt movement free speech did not exist in this country' – was also interned, along with his wife. For most of the thirties Mosley, who had begun as an inspirational left-winger, had organized and inspired Britain's Fascists, a more formidable and secretly influential group than was subsequently acknowledged when this country's sympathy for Hitler was examined by historians. Mosley was a tall, handsome, upper-class guru who regimented his followers and who taught them to revere black banners, shirts and songs. Up until Munich he received enthusiastic backing from sections of Fleet Street and his carefully staged oratory based on the Nuremberg pattern drew the mob. He proclaimed devotion to Church and Crown, and heady promises to the dwellers in the slums and dole queues. His motto was 'Action!' and many eyes were turned away when his British Union of Fascists made violent raids on Jewish streets in the East End.

After the fall of France there was in some quarters an acceptance of the inevitability of world Fascism and there was a sizeable welcoming party in Britain for the Führer in 1940–41. Some believed that the Duke of Windsor, their 'King over the water', would arrive with him. Certainly during the last years of the peace, and the heyday of the new movement, it could not have occurred to the ordinary Fascist, pressing his uniform for the Saturday afternoon strut, that eventually there would have to be an early morning knock on *his* door.

Margaret, the wife of a Fascist, describes what happened. She writes with alarming simplicity about poverty, natural leanings, gullibility and the seedy glamour of Mosley-by-Sea. She writes to apologize for her husband and to rehabilitate his character as best she can, which is honestly and sentimentally. Her narrative by its very naïvety throws a merciless light on the inadequacies of the kind of people who fall for hectic political solutions. Her beloved John was half English, half Bavarian, and was a victim of the slump. Fascism gave him something

to do – to be. It also brought him into contact with men who loved
Germany, his father's land, at a time when Germany was hated for
having started the Great War. John Vernal Charles Federl's career
after he had been cleared by the examining board on the Isle of Man
was intriguing. Then aged thirty-one, he was called up and, after
training, attached to the military police guarding the experimental
station at Shoeburyness, Essex. Soon after this, when large numbers of
German prisoners of war were expected from North Africa, he was set
to work building cages for them. When they arrived his ability to
speak German singled him out for preferment and his work as an
interpreter later on during the repatriation period was to be rewarded
with the British Empire Medal. After the war he took his family to
Austria, where he worked in intelligence. His wife's attempt to
vindicate him reflects the ambience of thirties Fascism far more tellingly
than many sophisticated accounts.

The young man who started courting me was very handsome,
blue-eyed, blond, broad of shoulder and slim of waist, and full
of Bavarian charm. He began his wooing by sending me a single
red carnation every day and, whenever we met, he would click
his heels together and kiss the back of my hand. What girl of
nineteen years old could hold out long against such flattery and
attention!

   It wasn't long before we were married and living in Worthing,
where we stayed for three years, and where our first three
children were born. It was the perfect environment in which to
bring up children as we were able to row across the water to the
beach, where we spent most of the summer swimming and
having picnics. 1937 flew by as we were so happy in our house,
and with our home life and the wonderful days by the sea. In
February 1938 we had a new baby daughter, Mary. Her birth
was just the incentive my husband needed to try and become
self-employed and start his own decorating business. Although
there were rumblings of war, no one really believed it would

come to anything, so he went ahead as planned. Unfortunately, it turned out that it wasn't a good time to have taken such a chance.

But for a while it did look as if my husband's business would be successful, as several friends and acquaintances had asked him to decorate their houses. In those days, to enable workers to buy their tools of trade, half the cost of the estimated work undertaken would be paid immediately, and the other half on completion of the painting and decorating. Until 1939 he did fairly well, just covering his overheads, but suddenly several of his customers welched and refused their final payments, saying, that as the war seemed imminent, they had no intention of wasting any more money on their houses in case they were bombed out of existence in the near future. In a way we couldn't blame them but it certainly made things more difficult for us and, as we didn't have a queue of customers forming up at our front door, my husband had no choice but to go back on the dole, and I began charring at Shoreham bungalow town every morning. During this time I was very lucky indeed to meet John Masefield, the Poet Laureate, who had one of the bungalows there. Many times my husband and myself would meet him in Shoreham, where we would have a drink together in one of the old pubs in the High Street.

A few months after the declaration of war my husband was arrested by the police, who had been given extra powers to detain people under the 18B Act which had been introduced at the outset of the war as a precaution against German sympathizers. This arose because, first of all his father was Bavarian, and then because for many years my husband had been a working member of the British Union of Fascists. Although I never actually joined, I used to go to the canteen to help out with the refreshments. I met Sir Oswald Mosley a couple of times. The first time was on a day out with our two children when we were attending a summer camp organized by members of the BUF. Our daughter Elizabeth was eighteen months old and one of the young men present asked him if he would kindly hold her while he took a photograph. Mosley was only too willing to oblige. Elizabeth squirmed, wriggled and cried to be put down, and someone said, 'You can manage to control hecklers, sir, but it doesn't look as if you can manage that young lady!' A woman standing by said, 'I wish I could change places with her – I wouldn't try to get away!'

The second time I met Sir Oswald was when he came to address a meeting on Worthing pier and he came into our canteen for a cup of tea and something to eat. He was a very slim and handsome-looking man in his early thirties, with a very friendly manner. He was well known as being a great orator. William Joyce, later nicknamed Lord Haw-Haw, accompanied him on his visit to Worthing. Unfortunately Joyce later went to Germany and during the war broadcast propaganda over the radio. He was captured by British troops when the war ended. During his trial he tried to claim Irish nationality but because his passport was British he was hanged as a traitor. Before the war he had a bungalow at Goring-by-Sea, where he held many a noisy week-end party. Sometimes we would go swimming at a small cove in Goring because it was very quiet, and I was pregnant with my first child and shouldn't feel conspicuous in front of other bathers. Occasionally William Joyce and his companions would walk slowly along the beach and stop near us to have a chat. He seemed quite pleasant. He was a rather funny little man with a scar down the side of his face, which he said was the result of a duel in his teens(!). I never felt really at ease in his presence. It was rumoured that he was rather fond of the fair sex.

When war was actually declared you could have heard a pin drop. It seemed as if everyone had been stunned into silence and a state of numbness. It was some time before the shock wore off, and then everybody began to talk at once. Then all of a sudden they began to rush home in case the bombing started. The next day we heard that many of our friends had hurried to join the armed forces.

My husband and I just lived from day to day, and wondered

what life held for us round the corner. When rationing came in we actually fared better than some of our friends. Our food was plain and simple but very nutritious and good. When meat became scarce my husband and his friend, without their wives' knowledge, found ways and means to fill the larder. Way up on the Sussex Downs there roamed many sheep and early one morning they decided to pay them a visit. Going by motor-bike, they stopped a few yards from the flock and, very silently, sidled up to the nearest sheep and grabbed its neck. Apparently if you hold a sheep by the neck it doesn't baa and all the other sheep stay silent. They cut its throat, skinned and cleaned it, buried the entrails, head and wool in a clearing among blackberry bushes, cut the carcass into joints, wrapped them in newspaper, put them in a sack, and quietly stole away. When they arrived home, they salted the meat to prevent it going rancid and stored it in a long tin bath in the shed. Next day they shared it among their friends with families in Shoreham, Worthing and Brighton. The following week there was a short article in the Worthing paper concerning the theft of a sheep on the Sussex Downs, and it was stated that whoever did the killing must have been a butcher, as it was so expertly done. My husband during his schooldays in Freiberg had helped his uncle in the slaughterhouse, and it was there that he had learned his butchering skills.

Later, as fuel became short and we began to feel the cold, my husband, again without telling me, went to the local coal depot and picked up any pieces of coal which had fallen by the wayside. One night in the coalyard he heard someone coming. It was our neighbour. This neighbour later in the war received a posthumous citation for bravery while serving in the Royal Navy. My husband received the BEM for services rendered, but not until after the war.

Tuesday 7th June 1940 will always remain in my mind as being a very dramatic day, and one of the stepping stones to our life in Austria in 1948. It was 6 a.m. when we were woken by a loud knocking at the front door. Looking out of the window, I saw four men. I opened the window slightly and asked who they were. They showed us identity cards and warrants, and I realized that they had come to arrest my husband. They were plainclothes policemen. Although we had been expecting them for several weeks, it came as a shock to know that they had actually arrived. I dressed and opened the door to let them in, and then to put the kettle on and to make us all a cup of tea. The policemen were exceedingly kind and considerate under the circumstances, and while drinking their tea said how sorry they were to do such a distasteful job, but that it was a matter of security, and until another way was found to sift the potential 'spy' from the nation there was nothing else for them but to carry out their orders under the 18B Act as pleasantly as possible.

My husband was allowed to shave and have his breakfast at leisure. He was only able to take a small attaché case with him, and this was to contain his pyjamas, pants, socks, a couple of shirts and his shaving tackle. They told me he was being taken to Brixton prison but didn't know how long he would remain there. When it was almost time for them to go, they allowed my husband to kiss the children, who were still in bed. I asked one of the policemen what I should do as my husband was to collect the dole the next morning and we didn't have any savings. I was worried sick, wondering how I was to feed the children. The policeman gave me an address to go to in Shoreham, which was about twenty minutes' walk from us.

I was shattered though when the police went on to say that our mail had been tapped for months, and that they knew that an uncle of mine had died in New Zealand, and that he had left me some money which I would be receiving in the near future. I told them that they were mistaken as I had asked the New Zealand government to keep it over there for a while as the rate of exchange was so bad. They said they knew all about that but that my orders had been rescinded by the 'powers that be', as they knew that I would be needing it! When the police car arrived and they were leaving the house, all the policemen, without exception, put some silver into the babies' hands. As my husband kissed me and left I became really scared. Remember, I was only twenty-four years old and now had to be responsible for looking after four young children, all under the age of five. I felt I wouldn't be strong enough to manage it and the only thing that helped me was knowing that hundreds of other women were in the same boat, and were probably in a worse state than I was. At least I knew that I had some money coming in the not too distant future.

On Thursday 9th I asked one of my neighbours to keep an eye on the children while I walked to the address in Shoreham which the police had given me. I was feeling very nervous and sick, and praying that this nightmare would go away. On entering the office, which was situated upstairs, I noticed a very nice-looking young man seated behind a desk. After explaining to him the hardships I was going through, he looked straight at me and said, 'Why should we help you and your family, when your husband is interned when he should be in the forces fighting for England?' My eyes suddenly stung and I knew that if I stayed any longer I would break down and cry, so I said, 'If you feel so strongly about it, what are *you* doing in such a cosy job? Why haven't you volunteered to fight?' Then I walked downstairs, unable to see where I was going as my eyes were full of unshed tears. I had reached the last step when I felt a hand on my shoulder and heard a voice which said, 'I am so sorry. Please accept my apologies and come upstairs again.' The young man wrote out a chitty which he told me to take to a grocer's shop called Lipton's, and they would give me a week's supply of food. It was quite an ordeal for me to hand over the chitty. I felt that all eyes were on me. Everyone knew that only the poorest of the poor had to have food given them. How I got home that day I'll never know. I never had to go for that means test again as my money from New Zealand arrived on the Saturday morning.

With capital in hand I was able to think things out more clearly. The first thing I did was to go out and buy a few luxuries such as soap, cigarettes, my ration of sweets, etc., in order to make up a parcel to take to Brixton prison. I also had to take my husband's suits, extra shoes, all his socks and other wearing apparel. This meant I had to carry a large suitcase. Evidently he was to be moved in a few weeks. Travelling by train from Lancing station to Victoria, and then by bus to Brixton, it took me three hours, by which time I was very tired. I felt even worse when, having travelled all that way, I was told that my husband had been moved that morning, and too late for me to be informed. I was able to leave his things with the policeman in charge. He told me that they would be sent on to his new address and that I would be receiving official notification as to his whereabouts in due course.

When I heard it was actually from my husband himself, who told me that he was now living in the Elephant House in the winter quarters of Chipperfield's Circus. He said that he and the others were being treated with consideration, had plain but adequate food, and although the working facilities were rather primitive, they were able to keep themselves and their clothes clean. I received a second letter from him six weeks later telling me that he was on the move again, this time to Huyton near Liverpool, from where he would be leaving for his final destination, the Isle of Man. It was from there that he would eventually appear before a tribunal where he would be assessed and either sent home or remain in internment for the war. His tribunal wasn't held until February 1942, nineteen months later. I was then working in a canteen and was shattered on leaving work one evening, when the light of the wintry day was almost done, to see my husband waiting for me just outside the gate. He had been suddenly called before the tribunal and told to pack and go home.

The Posting

3 July 1943. Journeying north. Everyone in the carriage is reading or writing letters. There are still four hours of rhythmic monotony and time to take stock of one's position. Geographically it is somewhere spinning up the backbone of England ... I am obsessed with the idea of parting. A chapter has finished before I had time to get to the end of the page and I am forced to start a new one with reluctance.

Keith Vaughan, *Journal*

The Newly Commissioned Mr Bruce Hollingsworth Travels North

September 1941. 5.30 p.m. Now I am in this whistling train and we have rushed past Rugby, and now Stafford. Next we contact Crewe, where I have to change. It is all a little unreal. I am standing at the door of my compartment, watching myself, and though intent and searching, I can't see very clearly. Perhaps there have been too many tunnels and the country so flat. I feel I have been on Brooklands for four hours. So I am watching myself as clearly as possible. There is my Sam Browne and by the side of him, lying coiled over, that startlingly clean new mackintosh. They look better after that cup of tea and surprisingly fresh cake which followed the interminable wait, and the girl rushing north to Southport to meet her husband whom she had thought to be at sea. These things awake echoes and interests.

But who are these people opposite me in the carriage? This man with silk hair falling from a central parting who picks his nose at intervals, and who reads *The Times* and Mary Lavelle? Of course, with that *useful* suit and smooth forehead he must be a solicitor. The other man has no expression. He looks as if he had spent his last ten years pressing buttons. And now we come to this officer, this 2nd Lieutenant in the corner and writing feverishly. At times they both look over at him. Why this carriage rocking through Staffordshire and why this trio? Wigan. Wigan is without doubt the ugliest and biggest eyesore I have ever seen, a sty filled with the pus and fester of industry. At the next station the door of our elegant and first-class carriage is rudely flung open and a shower of confetti precedes the undignified entry of a newly married couple. After them comes a bedizened and slightly withdrawn lady who looks like an emancipated Vera Hurst. She picks with elaborate care the circles and crescents, pink, mauve and blue, from our clothes, our shoes, our sleeves. When the newly married couple themselves had combed the confetti out of their hair in a silence almost tantamount to temper, we all settle down resignedly but forgivingly, myself slightly mollified by this singularly unaffectionate spectacle of a tongue-tied union.

Settling, then, in comparative peace, we reach Warrington. There the door was knocked back with a catastrophic bang by a sea of tugging hands, and in lurched another newly married pair shedding moons and stars once more all over us, and followed by the jeers and catcalls of twenty brightly dressed and be-veiled relations and friends, who leered without compassion for ten solid minutes while the train took root, apparently, in the granite of its track. As these relations and friends withdrew, a large group of other persons squeezed into our compartment with boxes, books and bags. We sat in stiff, upright positions, resentfully trespassed upon.

At last my station. The bombardier smartly saluting, having waited for half an hour, drove me off in Olive, a truck which was later to cause me anguish. Driving off, then, to Broadfield

House, a gaunt redbrick building on top of Leyland Works, where I discover the Major and half-a-dozen other officers at dinner seated round a deal table, the only other table being overladen with many assorted wine bottles. I was briefly introduced. Then once more in Olive (whom I will always avoid in future) to rattle for twenty miles to this Bungalow, where the first person seen was none other than Hollyhead! I nearly fell into his arms, and thank God it was mutual. Now our uniforms, the pride of our tailors, hang on the picture-rail. After a meal golloped down with cups of tea, I fly to bed and sink into hairy blankets with considerable delight, in spite of no sheets, no pillow and no bag. And I dream of my railway carriage filled, as it were, at the platform of every station with a dozen girls, all the dead spit of Gracie Fields.

The Last Time I Saw Paris

> To make a union with Great Britain would be fusion with a corpse.
>
> Marshal Pétain, 1940

Apprehension regarding the strength of the French will to resist Hitler was felt months before the German invasion. Britons travelling to Paris to co-ordinate war supplies and on other Allied business, such as the anonymous author who called himself 'A Metal Man', experienced a great unease in the capital. A member of the London Metal Exchange, his mission was crucial to the war effort and he was disturbed by the absence of urgency. In Britain, while there was much bewilderment by what the press was calling 'the phoney war', there was also a recognition that this was only a phase, or the 1940s equivalent of the old 'choosing the ground on which to fight' lull. In France the Metal Exchange dealer senses a kind of hopefulness of there being no need, or at any rate no great hurry, to choose ground at all. His diary gives a subtle account of those fatal months of waiting and lassitude between the beginning of the war and the fall of France, the blitzkrieg, Dunkirk, the Battle of Britain and more tumult than anyone had found possible to conceive. During the phoney war the RAF dropped millions of pamphlets on Germany to counteract Nazi propaganda, causing much amusement. The new song 'There'll Always be an England' had a premature sound. Evacuees flooded back to London and to the south coast and a strange mixture of relief, fear, puzzlement and mockery prevailed. Voices were heard asking the government to stop the war;

its declaration so soon after 1918 having been a mistake. The Metal Man viewed the anti-climactic scene nervously.

Friday, 23 February 1940. There has latterly been amazing activity on the American copper market. New York today is the centre of what remains of the world market. The non-ferrous metal situation in Germany seems to be worsening and people are wondering how much is getting to the Reich through the USSR.

Wednesday, 28 February. Pamphlet dropping by the RAF over Germany is in full swing. A number of amusing stories are being told in this connection:

One RAF pilot brought his machine back sooner than expected. His commandant inquired the reason for the early return, whereupon the pilot said, 'I thought we'd save time by throwing the pamphlets out in bundles.'

'Good God, man! Don't you realize you might have hurt somebody below?'

Mr Sumner Wells, the American observer in Europe, has arrived in Berlin. There is much speculation about the object of his visit.

Friday, 1 March. A big aluminium deal has been concluded between the Ministry of Supply and the British Aluminium Co. and the Aluminium Co. of Canada. The Ministry is to take the whole 1940 output of the former and the 1940 and 1941 production of the latter. It is intended to raise Canada's output capacity almost as high as Germany's.

Pay visit to Military Censor to have all papers and documents scrutinized and sealed. It's a kind of mild third degree.

Sunday, 10 March. At last all the tiresome preliminaries of my foreign trip are complete. Tonight I am spending at a London hotel in order to ensure my punctual arrival at Airways House. Take an evening stroll through the West End by moonlight. The great buildings, still undamaged by enemy bombs, stand out with a weird beauty. In the streets there is a moderate throng, most carrying gas-masks, but it is only a shadow of the gay pre-war crowds. Inside the hotel there is light and life. But underlying everything there is a note of expectancy. How long can this near-normality last? When will the first bombers soar overhead, let fall their bombs and start the work of ending European civiliza-tion? In the hotel, there is comfort. Only the heavy black-out curtains remind one that life is dangerous.

Monday, 11 March. There is a different atmosphere at the London aerodrome from that which prevails in peace-time. The passengers for Paris who, after various delays, have succeeded in obtaining their Exit Permits and foreign visas, now have to face further formalities and to satisfy the immigration, customs and censorship officials at the airport. They are not allowed to wander at will over the aerodrome and are kept under a genial but strict supervision. Finally, they are escorted from the heavily camouflaged aerodrome buildings to the waiting air-liner which, in its protective coat of green and brown, resembles some prehistoric monster of the slime.

Considering that England and France are at war, the journey to Paris is uneventful. The south-eastern counties of Britain are calm and pleasant in the sunshine. The Channel seems deserted but for a few vessels which are apparently trawlers. As we pass the cliffs of France, Verey lights are discharged by our pilot as a signal. We cross over Northern France, which is bathed in an atmosphere of peace. No doubt the countryside below is bristling with military secrets. The forest of St Germain drifts underneath and in a few minutes we are dropping into the Paris airport. It is only after we have landed that we notice another air-liner of the same type as our own is waiting on the ground – a tribute to the excellent camouflage adopted.

There are many signs of war-readiness in the suburbs of Paris.

There are many sandbags, criss-crossed windows and the ubiquitous word 'abri'. These notices regarding shelters state in ink the number of the street where they can be found and the number of people they are supposed to hold. The rain, however, has in most cases made it almost impossible to read these details, which is a side-light on the easy-going character of the French. As the coach draws nearer to the centre of Paris, one observes that many public monuments have been heavily protected. For instance, the huge Porte de St Denis – one of the old gates of Paris – has a complex timber structure to strengthen its great arch, whilst it is also heavily protected by sandbags. But as one enters the very centre of the city, the evidence of war becomes less marked until around the Opéra one can sometimes imagine that one is back in the times of peace.

The main boulevards in the early evening are crowded just as they used to be – in fact the crowds on the pavement round the Porte de St Denis constitute such a press that one cannot help thinking that a few bombs from a German raider would slaughter thousands of people. The fashionable cafés are filled with well-dressed ladies and gentlemen. As dusk descends it becomes evident that the black-out in Paris is very much less rigorously enforced than in London. The street lamps provide ten or twenty times more light and one can easily discern the faces of passers-by. The Place de la Concorde and the Champs-Élysées are studded with innumerable gas lamps and although their upward rays are heavily masked, the illumination provided is, in the opinion of a Londoner, excellent. Shops are also permitted to illumine their windows in what the British would consider a reckless fashion, though broad strips of coloured cellophane on the upper portions of the windows diminish the amount of light thrown into the sky. It is surprising to discover that many Parisians consider their city to be so poorly lighted that the only thing to do in the evening is to go home.

No civilians carry a gas-mask in Paris, except school children. A Parisian who was asked why the population did not carry gas-masks answered, 'Because we are not mad.' Absence of German bombing raids on London and Paris is attributed to Hitler's fear of reprisals. I was downstairs in the bar when the word was given that enemy aeroplanes were overhead; the barman looked a little nervous and this fact dispelled my initial suspicion that it was merely a stunt on the part of the management to keep the customers drinking in the bar. Actually, although we could not hear the noise, the Paris anti-aircraft batteries were then firing furiously, with unfortunate results for a number of people on the outskirts, who were wounded. Next morning at half past four, Paris was aroused by the wail of sirens, followed by the all-clear. Cynics who had their slumber disturbed by the uproar suggested that this was not really a raid at all, merely an effort on the part of the ARP to restore their prestige after failing to give a warning in the evening.

Homesickness

How do you feel after sixteen months of Army life? I asked myself. Exactly how do you feel? Stop now, I said, before I could begin to answer. You were going to reply without thinking or considering. Why not? I said. I can reply without thinking and without considering; and I can give you three answers. All of them would be correct, though none of them would describe exactly how I feel. Today it is no longer possible to be exact about the way one feels.

I could say –

I feel much better, thank you,

or

I do not feel at all, thank you,

or

I feel quite differently, thank you very much.

William Chappell, *The Sky Makes Me Hate It*

Homesickness was the most hidden, least confessed malady of the soldier. For one thing, its ravages seemed impossible to describe. And, of course, for the distant family it was a kind of compliment. Wife and children, parents and brothers and sisters were badly missed, as they thought it only right to be. It rarely occurred to them that the loyal packing of so much familiar domestic detail into their letters to the battlefields, aerodromes and ships could intensify homesickness and make the reading of them both comforting and unbearable. While there were those men who were glad to have got shot of the whole

cramped life at home or the boring missis, the majority were shocked
by the degree of suffering which homesickness brought them. Once
abroad, there could be little or no home leave and year would succeed
year without a glimpse of the beloved house with its inmates and
contents, the garden, the dog, the neighbours. Some writers confessed
in their diaries how they came to dread looking at the snapshots in
their wallets. The apple-tree or the curtains in the bedroom window
could aggravate the sickness as much as a son's face. The air mails
grew into two distinctive piles. Those from home said, 'We miss you',
those from abroad said, 'I want you.'

The homesickness of the First World War was expressed more in
terms of places than of people. In the literature which poured from the
Western Front there is a passionate longing for the Cotswolds, the
Welsh borders, certain villages and towns, the Malvern Hills – a
longing fashioned and taught by poets and composers. 'If only this
fear would leave me I could dream of Crickley Hill,' wrote Ivor Gurney.
He begs, 'Do not forget me quite, O Severn meadows.' Francis Ledwidge,
destroyed by a shellburst at Ypres, is homesick for County Meath:

> This is the song a robin sang
> This morning on a broken tree,
> It was about the little fields
> That call across the world to me.

Ivor Gurney in the trenches listens to the homesick Welsh soldiers
'Whispering consolatory/Soft foreign things'.

The mood of these longings for home shifted from landscape to the
family and its circle during the Second World War. As Roy Fuller said
in his 'War Letters':

> The letters are shockingly real,
> Like the personal belongings
> Of someone recently dead.
>
> The letters are permanent,
> And written with our hands,
> Which crease into their lines

And breathe, but are not so
Living as these letters.
Our hands are seas apart;

A pair might cease to live
While the indestructible letter,
Turned lies, flew to the other.

The letters express a love
We cannot realize:
Like a poignant glove

Surviving a well-known hand,
They can outlast our bodies
And our love transcend.

It was Roy Fuller who observed his comrades scribbling in a YMCA writing room, their heads bent over letters. They are old friends about to be drafted in all directions. Not only have they been scattered from their various homes, but now they will be separated from each other. So they write about

Nostalgia, labour, death. They will explore
Minutely particular deserts, seas and reefs,
Invest a thousand backcloths with their moods,
And all will carry, like a cancer, grief.

The homesick letters of Louis Rose to his wife, Celia, give up all attempt to hide distress. The Roses and their children, Alan and Sally, lived in Bedford, a very close middle-class family whose separation created a far worse anxiety and despair than Rose himself believed possible. Homesickness for him was like typhus for the uninoculated; it very nearly finished him off. He called it 'going crackers'. He was a REME craftsman, hardworking, courageous and emotional in an un-English way. His letters catch the drag of the months and years which are without Celia. Eventually he has a nervous breakdown, so sick is he for her. He recovers, fights bravely, is mentioned in dispatches and gets home safely during the autumn of 1945.

En route to North Africa 1942

Dear Celia,

Sorry you weren't home when I phoned. Anyway, dear, I am on board, somewhere in England, ready to sail. John, Ted and I are together in our berths, so everything is OK.

I don't suppose you will get this letter for a few days, but I am sure you are going to keep your chin up. Everything seems pretty comfortable and the chaps are all jolly and cheerful.

It was a funny feeling when we left Barracks. We marched with a band – it all seemed so unreal and I still think I am dreaming. You and the kiddies will be in my thoughts every minute while I am away, so I won't feel so lonely . . .

All my love,

Lou

At Sea

Dear Celia,

I am on deck now, writing this letter, and it is sweltering hot. We shall have to get used to that. I am very fit and well and eating very well indeed. I get up at 5.30 a.m., have a cold shower and am on deck until breakfast time. Do Alan and Sally ask after me? I seem to see them everywhere here, running about, and it all still seems like a dream. Anyway, I have got to make the best of it. I could write pages and pages to you, but they ask us to make it as short as possible, and you knowing what a conscientious soldier I am will understand. Keep your chin up, you are always with me.

Lou

Up the Blue 16 November 1942

Dear Celia,

It is some time since I have written a letter in a green envelope to you, but recuperating after my little breakdown has given me this chance. You know that I do not often break up like that, but I just flopped out and did some sobbing. I think that it must have been pent-up physical and mental reaction. Anyway, I feel a lot better with that off my chest. Well, dear, I have not been able to tell you a lot about my personal experiences but I think I did tell you about our landing off the boat here, and that awful march to the first transit camp. How the boys were dropping one by one by the roadside, how Johnny went out like a light and I saw him safely on an ambulance. That was how we first got parted. I believe that day will always remain in my memory. I can safely say that my first fortnight here has been my most eventful time up to yet. My first posting from the base 'up the Blue', we went by road, 400 miles or more. As we were pelting up, everybody else was chasing back. That was when Rommel started his big push. I really thought my time was up when we were dive-bombed on a goods train one night. I was underneath the train all the time. Well, darling, after getting through that, I was never in doubt about coming through this lot safe and sound. It is six months since I left England and you, and it seems an eternity. It gets harder and harder to endure, but I won't give up. I hope that before the next six months are over I shall be home with you and Alan and Sally, and make up for my lost time with you. I love you more than ever,

Lou

16 December 1942

Dear Celia,

I am writing this from the YMCA in Cairo. I am waiting for our truck to pick me up. We left base about six and got here at eight o'clock. I came to the YMCA first and had a good tuck in, eggs, tomatoes and bacon. After that I called at the bank and collected your gift, for which I thank all concerned very much. I then had a good walk round and did some shopping, some for myself and some for the boys back at the camp. The more I see of the city, the more I dislike it. It is so busy and teeming with all sorts of people. The main thing I dislike are the hawkers, beggars, etc., they pester you to death, and the shoe-shine boys can nag worse than any wife! A favourite trick of theirs is to splash blacking over your boots and then follow you about until you have them polished. If you refuse, they will sometimes make a mess on your clothes.

When we move I don't expect we shall travel back this way. Personally, I think we shall travel through Palestine, Syria, to the Caucasus – who knows, I am only surmising. Well, darling, I have been abroad over six months and have stood it pretty well, but I am missing you more than ever, and it is getting harder and harder to stand, and the thought of the two grand kiddies I have waiting for me back there is sending me crackers. One great thing which helps me along is your regular mail to me.

Lou

12 June 1943

My darling,

I thought it was about time that I wrote you another letter describing my later experiences. You may remember that after the Western Desert victory we were allowed to write our experiences up to the last phase. We were quite excited when we knew we were going to leave Egypt. I thought that we were going aboard a destroyer, but instead we went aboard a Liberty Ship. We made ourselves as comfortable as possible on the hatches – by the way, the boys were spread out amongst various boats. The hatches we slept on covered holds stored with TNT, bombs, etc., so you can imagine that we did not feel too comfortable. Next day we set sail with an escort of destroyers and felt more at ease. Life was pretty good on board. We had various piquets to do and we did quite well with our rations, and also had some good singsongs. The weather was grand and, sailing along the Blue Med., it seemed good to be alive. By the way, the boat we were in had one of the *Arizona*'s guns mounted – this was the Yankee ship which got sunk or damaged at Pearl Harbor. So we sailed merrily along for three days and without any excitement, nearing our objective on the fourth night, when we were told to expect some excitement, and by Golly we did!

As soon as dusk set in we had a dive torpedo bomber attack. What a thrilling barrage our convoy and escort put up. Although I must say that, however brave a man is, at a time like that you get a funny feeling, and all kinds of thoughts flash through your brain. You and the kiddies, Mother and everybody, they kept flashing through my brain. I don't know how many aircraft attacked, but I do know we took heavy toll of them. No one was more relieved than I was when dawn broke and we knew that it was all over. Then land came in sight, mountains, valleys and trees. Eventually, we sailed into harbour, the jewel of Musso's African Empire. We slept well out of town that night and the dew was like heavy rain. After a week or so there, we left for the airport, and I was a little nervous over my first air trip. They were big Yankee planes. I took somebody's advice and laid flat down on the floor and felt fine all the way, but lots of the boys had a rough time. Anyway, we landed safely after about six hours' flying and I was happy to put my foot on terra firma again. We were picked up in trucks and although it was raining, the sight of green fields, mountains, valleys and streams was a grand sight for sore eyes. Well dear, I hope you enjoy this little tale. I shall go crazy if I don't get home to you soon.

Lou

9 May 1945

My darling,

It is VE day here. You probably all went crazy there, but I can assure you no crazier than us here. Last night we had a free do in the canteen and I was completely sozzled, and finished up in the Sergeants' Mess with my Sergeant Major. The boys got up to some rare antics last night and my friend the Sergeant Major lost his beautiful military moustache. The boys mutilated it terribly. They then got hold of another HQMS who was sozzled, put him in a barrel and rolled him up and down the workshops. Well, darling, sozzled though I was, you and the cherubs were still in my thoughts.

   Lou

There is a sixteenth-century poem which sums up the desperation of men far from wife or lover and having a rough time. No one knows who wrote it.

> Western wind, when wilt thou blow,
> The small rain down can rain?
> Christ, if my love were in my arms
> And I in my bed again!

The novelist Henry de Vere Stacpoole said, 'In homesickness you must keep moving – it is the only disease which does not require rest.' But no amount of movement in lands which they would normally only have encountered in romantic fiction had the least curative effect for the homesick of the Second World War.

Siblings

How did he answer the irrevocable command
When infinity spoke with a soundless voice?
Did he dare to question Reality,
Did he dare to outstare Death?
Or did he turn his head away
To watch the sinews in his hand
Obey the last orders of his brain?

Captain Stephen Rickard, 'Requiem for a Brother'

The letters and journals of a single family could encompass the full experience of war, its novelty, its bloodying of the home fields, its commonplaces and its horrors. Those written by Donald and Christopher Elliott and their sister, Jean, are an example of the simple fugue-like way in which, by centring what was happening on their parents' house in Suffolk, a family could unconsciously tell the whole story. Donald, murdered by the Japanese during one of their notorious jungle marches, and Christopher, the schoolboy bicycling to air-crashes, are youthful adventurers coming to grief. Jean, the ATS girl in her early twenties, writes to ease anxiety and preserve the norm in the face of all that threatens it. She is chatty but not trivial, and has to reassure without seeming to do so. She writes hundreds of letters to 'Hope Villa' from Wales, Lark Hill and eventually from the Far East, and they are saying, 'Don't fear.' She is practical and stalwart, and aims to give pleasure. Donald writes more for himself. Killed at twenty-two, he is intoxicated by planes. Christopher writes to avenge

Donald's death, to lift his brother out of a statistic and the official 'regret'. He is tenacious and his finding of Donald's grave by way of letters to Malayan peasants as well as to the Air Ministry is the grounding of his future career as a journalist and one of those remarkable 'unofficial' historians which all wars breed.

Donald went straight from school to RAF Halton as a boy apprentice in September 1938. In 1940 he was working as an engine fitter on Dowding's special fighter intelligence flight. On his nineteenth birthday, 21 May 1941, he set sail for Singapore and was soon caught up in the Japanese advance. On 8 March 1942 he and hundreds of British airmen surrendered to the enemy on Tasikmalaya airfield in Java and from then until his death on 17 March 1945 there were no more letters, only cryptic official messages penned by a Japanese scribe. Officers could read and write, the Japanese believed, but not NCOs. Donald was a corporal. While in England, his letters are aeroplane mad. The Battle of Britain whirls around him and he patches up the machines which are being flown round the clock. The writing is simple, pleased and insouciant. He is a teenager living a tale. Already the names of the aircraft have taken on some of the epic associations with which they will be regarded decades hence. Future heroes such as Douglas Bader soar past. Later, Donald's brother, Christopher, edited these impressions.

The Summer of 1940

Plenty of different machines land here now. Wounded airmen are being flown here from their stations in Ansons. Three different lots came in on Friday, and were met by ambulances . . . A week ago an aircraft wanted to land here [RAF Halton] about 1 a.m. It dropped flares but they signalled it off and wouldn't let it. It flew across to Northolt and blew up as it landed. It was a Wellington which had been 'over' and was damaged . . . A fighter Blenheim landed here the other morning to leave its gunner after being in action. It was battlescarred, especially round the gunner's turret. That's why they left him here.

[RAF Coltishall] Every little job you do, however small, is done perfectly. Yes, of course, I have worked on some of the machines that have shot down Nazis. I expect I have been on all of them; there's not many of us for the engines of the whole squadron. We start at eight in the mornings now, and every night it's been either eight or nine before we have packed up.

[The opening day of the Battle of Britain, 10 July 1940] The German's first burst of gun fire went straight through the revolving airscrew and into his bullet proof windscreen — it's a piece of glass, an inch thick. It was like looking at snow to look through it. It's been fitted since the war started. If it hadn't the pilot would have got it in the head. As it was, he said that he had said his prayers when the windscreen splintered. I have got a piece of it.

[The Hurricane from Douglas Bader's No. 242 (F) Squadron] Jerry came again yesterday dinner time, only our fighters were ready for him. Presently, one of our Hurricanes came back full out, dived down low over the 'drome and shot up into the air again, doing a complete roll. That's the sign they give if they have scored a victory.

[RAF Kenley] There's hardly anything left standing except a few barrack rooms and the cook house. Even direct hits on dug-outs, gun posts and petrol tankers, and private houses round the camp. In the last two days [1–2 September] we have lost six or seven Spitfires. We get nothing but air raid warnings here. All round the Station are speakers to give instructions to pilots and ground crews. We hear the heights and directions of the enemy aircraft given to all the defences. We have to work out in the open now to do all the maintenance work as there are no hangars. Still, it's lovely weather . . .

[RAF Gravesend] It's like being on a battlefield here. It rains shrapnel night and day, so we have to wear tin hats outside. Nine German bombers came over here on Wednesday afternoon, and they couldn't break formation. I counted and photographed 250 shell bursts in the sky in about three minutes. I lost my machine again last night. It crashed north of the Thames.

[RAF Hawkinge] I have got two machines to work on now — or rather I did have. The second one crashed taking off but not with the pilot in it. One of the boys, an 18-year-old rigger who was at Halton when I was, decided he would like to fly. I had just gone up to the office to sign for an inspection I had done when this boy got in, put on the parachute and helmet, and strapped himself in. Then away he went across the 'drome between 60 and 70 m.p.h. Then came the crash — the machine didn't catch fire — only it is a complete wreck. One wing was almost fifty yards away. He got away with a cut hand. That left me without a machine for a day or two. Now I have got a brand-new one. I am sitting in it writing this as I have finished my inspection, and am waiting for the order to come through to start up.

[Werner Schlather's Messerschmitt] He dived along our line of machines with his guns going. Five of our boys got hit, but the pilot of the Messerschmitt 109 won't ever fly again. The ground guns got him and he crashed about three miles away. I went out on the fire tender. It was a thrilling ride along country lanes at about 40 m.p.h., with the ambulance in front. When we got there all that was left was part of a wing, the tail and a few odd bits. The rest was in the ground, about 12 feet down, still blazing.

The Winter of 1941

[From Malaya, Christmas Eve 1941] I would give anything to live that last year over again, from the time I passed out from Halton up to the time we sailed. That was real life and, although it's only a memory now, I am always thinking about the things I saw, and all that happened during that time.

Donald Elliott died during the Sandakan–Ranau POW death march, 155 miles through the jungle to a torture camp. His brother Christopher's quest for his grave somewhere in remote Ranau was a triumph of schoolboy ingenuity. As with countless servicemen apparently lost for ever in the cruelty and vegetation of Malaya, the official notification of Donald's death was a brief closing of the book. There was nothing more to be done or said. A war crimes commission would, later, investigate the behaviour of the Japanese towards their prisoners. This would not do for Christopher. A stream of letters from a persistent schoolboy in Beccles to the Air Ministry and to villagers living along the route of the death march – had the sawmills at Sandakan and Jesselton noticed unusual carvings on some of the trees? Donald liked leaving his mark on tree-trunks and old barns in Suffolk – located the grave in just a few months. It was a grave for five; it contained Donald's aircraftman's cap with his name inside. This quest was to lay the foundations of Christopher Elliott's career as one of those obsessed unofficial chroniclers of the war, the minutiae of whose knowledge of certain aspects of the conflict, in his case those of the RAF, is a specialist history in itself. Both world wars were to produce men who, because they were too young or too unwell to fight, joined up or joined in in the only way they knew, which was to pace the experiences of the front. This required great technical, emotional and social skills, also single-mindedness. Donald Elliott's teenage romance with the RAF was that of a lad in a storybook. It admitted wounds and death but not the ghastly ill-treatment which was to shovel him under the soil at twenty-two. His brother's reaction is an instance of how the squalor of the war affected children who saw scenes in and around local aerodromes, during bombing raids and along the coast which they linked with the atrocities in what were called 'the picture papers' and in the cinema. Adolescents looked long and wonderingly at what grown-ups assumed they would flinch from. Horrors at home and horrors abroad merged to fill the naturally morbid imaginations of children to overflowing. Christopher Elliott biked eagerly to air-crashes around Beccles, as did many boys, visiting some of them over and over again, snaffling souvenirs and keeping accounts.

A Dornier 217 bomber near Beccles had its tail shot off by AA
fire. Only one man, believed to be the lower rear gunner,
managed to get out in time. As the severed cabin approached a
field near Winston Hall Farm at Gillingham, two other members
of the crew were flung out, but their parachutes, just developing,
appeared to catch the blast wave as the full bomb load detonated
as the plane hit the ground. The Dornier, which immediately
burst into flames, fell near a bullock shed and a couple of stacks.
I remember hearing from my shelter bed the sound of running
feet, voices and a whistle being blown.

The weather at the time of this crash was very depressing and,
following several visits to the scene, I noted that the mile-long
cart track was so deep in mud that it came over my school
wellingtons and clogged the chain of my pedal cycle. As the rain
continued to fall, and the wind persisted, I sat for a while in the
broken end of the Dornier's pencil-thin fuselage, for no guards
seemed to be on duty. It was rather like sitting at the receiving
end of a huge ear trumpet, for the cold November wind played
softly down the hollow fuselage.

It was against this background of desolation, and a gloomy
sky full of ragged evening clouds, that one of the Belgian guards,
who had been sheltering in a barn close by, came up to me and
caused me to find no words. For he had in his hand a surprise. It
was a brown human eye. So I left the scene and the lane of the
brown eye for ever.

Christopher's and Donald's sister, Jean, had begun the war as secre-
tary to a Home Guard major before joining the ATS. Her letters are
non-introspective, level-headed, interesting and sane, and could be
described as the letters most welcomed and most posted during the
war. The world would not fall to bits as long as they were scribbled
and sent.

29 May 1943

Dear Mum and Dad,

A whole week since our last day off. Time goes awfully quickly here because we're always so busy, I suppose. But today, are we busy? No, Ma'am!

You'd love it here. We're lazing around on the most heavenly hills in Wales just above the little town of Llangollen. Hills, hills and more hills as far as the eye can see, looking down into the valley of the Dee. We're ambushed at the moment by a flock of Welsh sheep. They're fluffy and have long tails – not like our Suffolk sheep a bit. The little ones look just like toy sheep lying amongst the buttercups and daisies. In fact everything roundabout gives the impression that a wonderful album of photographs has suddenly become reality. I never saw such beautiful trees in my life before, and they go on climbing to the tops of the hills, which are not as I imagined, bare and rugged. A shepherd has just come by calling weird noises to his dog – they're rounding up the flock.

We left the Camp this morning at about 9 o'clock, complete with Army haversack rations. About two miles along the road we managed to get a lift in a car – a Birmingham businessman. He took us about six miles towards Llangollen and from there we had to hike about four miles more. We did eventually reach it and dived into lemonade shops to quench our thirst and rest our feet. Gosh, my feet! We then climbed towards a hill with a ruined castle on top of it, dropped down, took off tunics, shoes and stockings, and started on the lunch. Luckily we were hungry! Awful sandwiches of cheese and lettuce, jam, potted meat and beef, choc. cake and a sort of sausage pâté. I believe it was last Monday that we had sausages for breakfast. Still, we were lucky to have rations packed for us, really.

Pam and Daphne have gone off now – they're determined to reach the castle at the top of the hill, but Betty and I decided to rest our gammy feet while we had the chance. Betty's asleep, I believe. We worked late last night – on Practical from 8.15 to 10.15, and I didn't wake up until $\frac{1}{4}$ to 7 this morning –

it's lovely to get up at one's leisure. I was too late for breakfast so Pam brought me back tea and bread from the cookhouse.

It has just struck 3 p.m. – the bells sound so lovely coming up from the valley. We're going down to a café for tea at about 4.30. Nice thought, but it's so heavenly to be up here without shoes and stockings and feel the sun and breeze on our legs.

Our work is getting more and more fascinating every day. Wish I could tell you about it, but I mustn't. However, I can surely say that we are not going on Heavy Artillery, but to what they call 'Z' sites. I believe they are rocket gun batteries like Auntie Margory has at Streatham. The majority of these sites are manned by Home Guard, I think, because they're not used during the day. We do maintenance on them. Most of the girls' faces fell three feet when Sergeant told us about the Home Guard manning our batteries, but of course Pam and I gave the jolly old Home Guard good support! [The writer's father was a member of the Beccles Home Guard.]

Did I tell you that I paid another visit to the Dentist on Thursday? We had to hike two miles each way into Oswestry. As though the Dentist isn't bad enough without a route march on top of it! But the comic part of it all was that we all fell for our respective Dental Officers and now watch the Dentist List with as much eagerness as we do the Parcel List – almost. Actually I only had two stopped and I felt practically nothing of it. Half-way through it my Dentist said he wasn't a dentist really but was now on the fourth week of a correspondence course on the subject! You can tell how bad it was because Pam and I wrote letters and ate large buns in the Waiting Room afterwards.

Sergeant was telling me yesterday that Mary Churchill trained at our Camp. She was a L/Cpl after 6 weeks and is now a Plotting Officer on an Ack Ack site. The NCOs who knew her liked her very much indeed – they say she's an awfully nice girl and very clever. Of course, a Plotting Officer has to work on the information we send through!

Well, paper's running short. We've just realized that we've not

the vaguest idea how we intend returning to Camp tonight, but
as we have until 11.59 p.m. we're not going to bother. There'll
probably be a bus or something . . .

Bye-bye for this time

Jean

During 1938, the year in which Donald Elliott became an RAF
apprentice, another Suffolk boy was cycling around writing a book
which would turn out to be his love-letter to the county. It was called
Suffolk Scene. He was Julian Tennyson, the great-grandson of the
poet. Like Donald, he would never return from the Far East, being
killed in Burma by a piece of shell 'about the size of a little-finger
nail'. His book was a regional wartime bestseller. Such partisan
county guides, the hiking craze, the growth of the Ramblers and
Youth Hostelling movements and a flood of novels, poems, music and
films inspired by the British countryside gave the people serving
abroad an intense and well-informed sense of their roots. Patriotism
was finely localized. Tennyson describes Donald Elliott's native place
– those views so soon to be obliterated for both of them:

> Almost more than the Waveney itself I like the country that
> surrounds it. It is the wildest and most desolate of all the Suffolk
> country, a stretch of high land dipping down into tiny valleys, of
> insubordinate hedges and narrow, aimless lanes. Here the
> signposts point as they please, here you may walk for hours and
> meet nothing more civilized than a couple of horny labourers and
> a few derelict farms – and at the end of the day you are quite
> likely to find yourself back at your starting point. The wildest
> and most confusing walk you can possibly take is over that
> stretch covering the groups of villages known as the South
> Elmhalls or South Elmhams and the Ilketshalls; here, believe it or
> not, within a radius of a few miles are villages called St Cross or
> Sancroft St George, St James, St Margaret, All Saints-cum-St
> Nicholas, St Michael. St Peter, St John, St Andrew and St

Margaret again. Some are South Elmhams, others are Ilketshalls, and I don't suppose that half the inhabitants know which are which . . . Give me East Suffolk for beauty and wildness.

In the Bag

> Never a day, never a day passes
> But I remember them, their stoneblind faces
> Beaten by arclights, their eyes turned inward
> Seeking an answer and their passage homeward.
>
> Sidney Keyes, 'Europe's Prisoners'

'Naylor, J. S., Captain 2634/25/15, in Oflag VA, Germany, wrote this article.' The Reverend J. S. Naylor was a Methodist chaplain who was captured at Tobruk in June 1942; he was a POW chaplain until the end of the war.

In Bedford Gaol John Bunyan wrote *The Pilgrim's Progress*. Cervantes, in a Moroccan gaol, started a tunnel and very nearly got away. Finally he was ransomed. Galileo studied astronomical problems in prison. Benvenuto Cellini shot a line to the other inmates of his prison about his past experiences. Hitler, A., wrote *Mein Kampf*. Samson, forced to entertain the Detaining Power, brought the house down. Bonaparte, on St Helena, refused to take exercise, grew fat, and nattered about his uniforms. Sir Walter Raleigh, imprisoned in the Tower, wrote *A History of the World*. St Paul, in prison at Philippi, sang hymns with Silas at midnight and, in prison at Rome, wrote to Timothy, 'The cloke that I left at Troas with Carpus, when thou comest,

bring with thee, and the books, but especially the parchments.'
Monte Cristo in the Château d'If began a tunnel, estimating that
it would take five years, and then escaped by disguising himself
as the corpse of l'Abbé Faria. Cœur de Lion, whose prison
whereabouts were discovered by singing prohibited duets with
Blondel, was ransomed. Mary, Queen of Scots, imprisoned in an
island castle in Loch Leven, by a bit of sleight of hand, and a
table-napkin, laid hands on her prison key. William Tyndale,
translator of the Bible, in prison in Vilvorde Castle, wrote to the
governor for 'warmer clothing against the winter, for a lamp in
the evening (for it is wearisome to sit alone in the dark), for a
Hebrew Bible, grammar and dictionary' but was later burned to
death. Winston Churchill, captured by the Boers whilst a war
correspondent for *The Times* during the South African war,
climbed through the window of the schoolroom where he was
detained and escaped, swimming the Aarpie River in the process.
Jonah, having been imprisoned for three days, probably in error,
was released in particularly nauseating circumstances. Wilhelm
I, in exile in Doorn, spent his time cutting trees down, then
cutting them up. Mr Toad, imprisoned for dangerous driving,
put on his washerwoman's clothes and walked straight out.

Getting captured provoked all kinds of reaction, from rage to guilt,
from relief to fear. For Brook, a youthful infantryman just arrived in
the desert after months of specialist training, the reaction was one of
incredulity. Years of Italian and German prison camps stretched ahead
of him, and these he would scrupulously describe right down to their
cubic floor-space, though not one which was in any intimate way
inhabited by himself. His prison diaries, composed in a tiny, perfect
script, tell all yet give nothing away. The minutiae skilfully avoids the
slightest intimacy and self-analysis. It is as though the diarist is saying,
'You've got me, yet you can never get me.' He lists and cross-references
every letter he receives via the Red Cross, giving the dates when they
were posted and when they arrived, annotating their contents as

though he were a librarian. Similarly, he writes résumés of the plots and characters of all the books he reads, making critical judgements. Every meal and change of clothes goes down, and in all this painstaking detail there is a hint of a man keeping himself intact, and as he was before capture. He avoids the self like poison, using neatness to keep it at bay. The tension and concealment are extraordinarily eloquent of how some prisoners of war coped with privation, and of the selectivity of what could and could not be mentioned. Never his body or religion or dreams or politics or emotion, only a meticulous exterior. Yet few writers have caught the moment of capture so exactly.

Mechili, April 1941. We had known all the time that the enemy was on our tail but when and where he would pop up and show himself, no one had the least idea. If the officers had any ideas on this subject they had kept them very much to themselves. In fact, I am certain they had been kept just as much in the dark as we were. It had been a hectic eight days indeed. Travelling at times far into the night only to be on the road again early next morning. Whenever we halted, we knew not for what period; whether there was time to have a fry-up of tinned bacon and perhaps a cup of tea, or whether once again it must be that bully beef and biscuits which we got to know so well. Our road had taken us across the desert mostly, over rocks when the trucks had given a performance which would do justice to any rodeo display, across flat uninteresting plains and through soft sand like snow, in places axle deep. It was this latter which I think caused us the chief anxiety. To get stuck in the soft sand meant delay whilst sand channels were brought into use under the offending wheel, and then all shoulders to the truck and heave!

. . . We were tired, dog tired. Mentally and physically it was not surprising therefore that we sensed this feeling of relief on being taken into the custody of the Germans. Perhaps we should now be able to have the post which we all longed for, whatever else was due to us.

Intermingled with this relief, however, was an element of surprise. Captured? Prisoners of war? Was it possible that this could happen to us, a Rear HQ of an Armoured Division? Whilst we had known that the enemy had been on our tail for the past two or three days it never occurred to us that we would be caught. Not even on that fateful morning when the convoy had been mustered together for a final dash through to Tobruk did we realize that our effort would be thwarted. It was all so unexpected and somehow the last mishap which a soldier expects to befall him.

And finally we all had a feeling of disgust that we had allowed ourselves to be captured. Why hadn't we foreseen all this the day before and made a dash for it, each and every truck for itself? Whatever fate had so befallen us, surely it was better than having to suffer this humiliation of loss and defeat. Our period on active service had been so short. We had done nothing yet. Exactly a month ago to the day, March 8th, we had left Tahag in Egypt, a newly and well-trained unit with brand-new equipment which was to replace the famous 1st Armoured Division and carry on the good work they had started. We were nearly all Territorials who had been with the unit since the outbreak of war. For fourteen months we had been steadily training in England. In November we embarked at Liverpool for the Near East, and after six weeks of final preparation in Egypt we were all keen and ready to do the big things that were expected of us. But something had gone wrong somewhere, we all had our own opinions on that, and in this record of my life as a prisoner of war I do not propose to probe . . . The milk had been spilt and we now had to make the best of it.

Sergeant Nell of the Green Howards was captured at Marsa Matrûh on 28 June 1942. He had joined the Green Howards ten years before when in his teens and had served in India and on the North-West Frontier. To him had fallen the responsibility of surrendering and for months afterwards it weighs on his mind. Gradually, this pressure gives place to an even greater one, the realization that he is desperately in love with a girl called Evelyn whom he had hardly met before being whisked away to battle. As the Italian and German prison camps succeed each other and the war begins to look as if it will last for ever, Sergeant Nell goes crazy over Eve. Will she wait for him? Why should she wait for him? He is getting very old (twenty-nine), so why should she desire him? His longings and exasperations flood through his journal without inhibition. He writes extremely well and with touching openness, also with an engaging absurdity here and there. He at last got back home to England on 26 April 1945 – and married Eve just over a week later.

Notes from a Prison Diary, 1942–4

This is probably the last entry I shall make this year, the 29th year of my life. A lot of things have happened to me this year, 1942. I *nearly* got a commission; I *got* concussion; I have been in hospital; I have seen a fair share of action; I have sprayed a horde of Germans with a Tommy-gun. With only a dozen men left I walked over to the enemy and capitulated as though I were a general surrendering a city. I am a prisoner of war in Italy wanting the ultimate victory of the Allies and my subsequent repatriation to England and a home. A very big year in my life, probably the biggest year I shall ever have, but it has only one more day to live, and then 1943. Roll on 1943 with the victory we are expecting! Roll on England!

To while away the last two hours of the old year Gerry and I tried to estimate the cost of setting up a house. He thinks it would take about £200. My own estimate is £150. Gerry, of course, is reckoning on paying about £30 for records for his radiogram. I am not that keen on music. Anyway, I hope to start my home-making this year. Evelyn and I are going to get a lot of fun out of it. I hope she knows something about it – I don't. Perhaps our mothers will help us ... The house I could afford would be a very modern affair indeed. A small kitchen, a dining-room, a sitting-room, two big bedrooms and one small one. I would like to have carpets in all the rooms but I am afraid that I shall be able to afford only one, for the sitting-room. The other rooms will have only linoleum. Perhaps I had better not have any ideas. Evelyn will most surely have her own way. I would rather not put forward any ideas than have them overridden by a woman.

Talking of old times, I wonder what my lads think of me? What did they think of me while I was their sergeant? I shall never know. I made many mistakes in my dealing with them but I can conscientiously say that I always did my best, right up to the ultimate capture. I had to summon all of my courage for that show. The Germans were blasting everything and everyone before them. The party, coming our way, along the woods in which we were most inadequately dug in, had a mobile artillery-gun and some light automatics. The gun passed within a few feet of us. We should have been blasted to Hell had they seen us. Then the party of infantry with their light machines passed within a few feet of us. They stopped thirty or forty yards from us. Our predicament was most disconcerting. We weren't in a position to fight. We were between the fires, the gun on one side and the machine-guns on the other. What ought we to do? I asked myself. I asked Terry Bray, my 2nd in command. His view was that we were finished. It was up to me to make some sort of decision. I decided to surrender but before doing so I went round my men to find out did they disagree with my decision and had they any better supposition? One man, Frank Robinson, wanted to fight. I pointed out to him that we should all be killed without advancing our war effort in the least if we tried to fight. He cried, actually sobbed, and pleaded with me to fight it out. But fighting was out of the question, so I very carefully crawled out of the trench, stood up and, trying to look much braver than I felt, walked over to the Germans. It was only a short distance but it seemed an awful long way to me. One of them saw me. He shouted, 'Come on, Tommy! Come on, Tommy!' I shouted, 'All right, lads, come out!' They came out, some with their hands up. It was all over. We were prisoners. I felt a little ashamed, but everyone told me that it wasn't my fault and that there was no other way out.

Heard some blokes talking about food tonight. Bread, butter and jam, and also bread, butter and cheese, fried in batter were discussed. The fellows who were talking seemed to consider them as delicacies. Must try them when I get home – if I go home. There is nothing to do. Very little physically. Nothing at all mentally. We are rapidly being ruined. Every one of us is miserable and there will be no happiness for us until we go back to England. I have been very despondent for the last couple of weeks. Perhaps it is because I have had no letters from Evelyn for such a long time. I wonder, are we still engaged? It would shake me considerably were she to abandon me. Somehow I can't get it out of my head that I am almost middle-aged. I keep on telling myself that at 29 one is still a young man and ought to be for another ten years. It must be this POW life, I think.

Our sheets were changed today. The new sheets will be as lousy as the old ones in a day or two. This morning I finished the book *The Lake* by George Moore. A very good book, I think . . . I ought, I think, to let Evelyn know of my intention of staying in the Army in the event of there being no prospect in the Civil line. I wonder what her attitude would be. I shall mention it in my next letter to her. This afternoon, talk with Le Dyer about soldiering in India. He intends to make a career of it. Well, the pension at the end of it makes it worth considering. He says that the pension of a private for 21 years is 25/- per week.

I received a letter from Pam today. She has had her letters to me when I was captured restored to her. One of them had been opened and someone had written on it, 'I'm surprised at you!' Poor Pam. She thinks she's in love with me. I wonder! Yet what can I do about it? I wish she would meet some nice fellow who would fall in love with *her*.

*

A couple of days ago I gave Johnny Riles some money to buy Communist books for the Camp Communist Party. My benevolence apparently entitles me to borrow such books from them . . . The war seems to have slipped into neutral again. We are all waiting for the Allies to invade Italy – but will they? We all thought that the collapse of Fascism would mean the collapse of Italy but it didn't. The people want peace. Why can't they have it? What is their government holding out for? I wish the invasion would start. A bloke has just told me that an Armistice has been signed between the Allies and Italy. I wish it were. 21 hrs. It *wasn't* a rumour!!! Yesterday morning this camp was a Hell of depression but today everyone is jubilant. We are all wondering how long it will be before we are again in England. Eve's birthday is on the 31st October. I wonder if I can make it in time. Received a letter from her. I shall never be able to repay her for her loyalty to me. She has stuck to me nearly three years and for two years she hasn't seen me.

The war in Italy is progressing slowly but surely in our favour. The 8th Army is coming up the east coast, that is, on the same side as us. They may be with us in a few days. It gives me a very pleasant feeling to think that my own battalion is with them. Some more men deserted last night. When is it going to stop? It is much safer in camp, and anyway their efforts won't be appreciated. The situation is tense. Literally hundreds deserted yesterday. Although I have used the word 'deserted' it doesn't really amount to that. Fellows are doing what they think is best . . . But the 8th Army doesn't seem to be coming our way. They seem to be going all out to meet up with the Americans' 5th Army, which is still in difficulties around Palermo. We aren't in any danger here so long as the Germans don't come down the east coast. The latter is the eventuality which I am waiting for. If, or when, they do come, it is my own and Gerry's intention to leave camp and do our best to join the 8th Army. I am now going to pack my haversack with the articles I don't want to lose. When I have to move, if I do so in British service kit I don't see that the Germans can have anything against me if they catch me.

Later. All hopes of escape have evaporated. A few minutes ago while we were on roll-call parade, German soldiers mounted duty in the sentry-boxes. We are prisoners again! I am rather upset but it is no good crying over spilt milk. Yet I am very sorry for Evelyn's sake. She has waited so long for me and just when it looked as though her waiting was at an end, I find myself in the bag again. Roll on the 8th Army! Roll on the 5th Army! And roll on the Russians!

20 September 1943. There is still tension in the camp. No one seems to know what is going to happen. Yesterday the Germans brought us thousands of Red Cross parcels from the camps which have been evacuated. Their explanation is that they can't take them for themselves on principle, and that they won't let the Italians get them . . . We clutch at straws. Not one word of our secret news bulletins is missed. We are unimportant and consequently unfortunate.

31 October. Eve's birthday – and what a day for me! I have had all my hair taken off, had a hot shower, was dried in hot air, had certain intimate parts of me painted with iodine by a Russian, been inoculated, vaccinated, have had my clothes disinfected by cyanide gas, have been registered as a German POW and have been finger-printed and photographed, and am now waiting to be X-rayed to see if I have TB. I wish I had never joined the blasted Army – but on second thoughts I don't. I should never have met Eve if I hadn't been in the Army. Letter-cards were issued today. I am going to send mine to Eve . . . I feel happy and healthy but my mirror tells me that my youth has left me. When is this blasted war going to end?

I have written to Margaret *and* Pam. I daren't write to only one of them because they are so unreasonably jealous.

Christmas Day. Looking ahead, I see no release – just a tunnel of time broken by roll-calls. When will I break out of the darkness into the light? I was showing an old photo to a friend. He saw the little photo of Eve among my collection. How proud and happy I was when he admired it. I dare not look at it myself. It always aggravates my already intense longing for her.

New Year's Day 1944. They can't win. Hitler is losing lives for nothing. We heard yesterday that the Russians have launched an offensive of 300,000 men. The Russian steam-roller. May it roll everything before it. An educational scheme is afoot. At first I enrolled for English, Electricity and Psychology, but have since changed to the London Matriculation Course. I wonder, can I do it? How much longer is the war going to last? I could put up with fighting but this endless turning over of days in a POW camp, waiting – waiting – waiting. When is it going to end?

5 February. I went to the theatre this evening and saw the play *Boy Meets Girl*. When a man is dressed as a woman he looks astoundingly like the authentic article. None of us have been on speaking terms with a woman for some time; perhaps that has something to do with it. It is almost two years since I even spoke to a woman. Letters!!! Three of them, two from Eve and one from Father. At long last I have got letters from my darling Eve. Oh, Evie, my sweet.

20 February. My thirtieth birthday. But I kept it a secret. I am worried about Gerry. He has fallen to pieces because he has failed (in his own estimation) as a writer. Since last June he has been working on a novel and now he finds that he can't carry on. He is distressed and eating next to nothing. Eve wonders if I have changed much. I wonder how much she has changed and in what ways? I take for granted that she will be much prettier. I wonder if she can cook yet? Oh, Evie, my darling, if you knew this terrible longing I have for you. A little boy may cry for what he wants. Poor Eve, she doesn't know it, but for some time I am going to be her baby. What a delightful mother I am going to have. Eve, my darling – or shall I say 'Mummy'?

Later. I think the Germans are worrying about the war. They have issued three blankets to every Russian prisoner and have given them coal. It is rather late in the day to be humane. Thousands of Russians have died of TB as a result of malnutrition by the Germans. They actually hope that their treatment of hapless POWs will be forgotten. British and French prisoners are treated well but the other nationalities get no more consideration than animals. As I lay listening to the drone of hundreds of planes and the explosion of their bombs, I thought of the children and old people, terrified and being maimed and killed and rendered homeless. And then I thought of Eve.

26 April. At the bath-house today I saw some Russians who had just bathed. They were naked, waiting for their bodies to dry in the air (they have no towels). What a ghastly sight they were, nothing but skin and bone. Their skin was stretched tightly over their ribs, their stomachs were distended like bladders, there was no flesh where their buttocks should have been. It would be inconceivable that human beings could treat their fellow man as the Germans are treating the Russians were we not here to see it. And I was in the same condition once. May-day is a National holiday to celebrate their National Socialist Party's coming into power. It will be their last celebration.

  . . . I am thirty years of age and going bald, what will Eve think when she sees me? There is nothing but a spiritual link between us and the war would seem to be slowly but surely breaking it. And I am sure my heart will break with it . . . The Camp – that propaganda paper for POWs – has shown us the type of temporary house to be supplied to people in Britain after the war. It is made of steel and has four rooms. Not very big but it will do until proper houses are provided. I wonder if Eve and I shall get one? Oh, how I long for the day when we can live together!

21 June. A man has just been shot and killed. He was reaching through the fence to pick some wild strawberries when a German soldier drew his pistol and shot him . . . Writing! Mine is getting worse. We write, they say, as we live. I am nervous so I must write nervously . . . If I weren't a prisoner I could be with my Eve. It makes me wild when I think of it. Eve is very sweet in her last letter. She asks me to marry her as soon as I get home. Gosh! I never knew that the time would come when a girl would ask *me* to marry her! Letters are so few and far between. They are next important to food – they *are* spiritual food for us prisoners. I want Evie all day . . . I have agreed with her regarding our not having children until we have our own home. Our children must not be left to chance as I was. My childhood was a mild form of Hell. Roll on peace and the scaffold for the Nazis.

13 October. My comrades here, although longing to have their women again, are rather shy of them. They think that their absence has made them too lustful and that their women will despise and dislike them for it. I am not at all afraid. My love for Eve will govern my action. I want her, but not so much that I will not be able to control myself. And I don't suppose that she will want to withhold herself from me. She must want me otherwise she wouldn't have waited. In the years to come, when I sit in front of a nice warm fire, my Eve by my side, reading this, I suppose I shall derive some pleasure from it, but at the time of writing it isn't much fun at all. Life in retrospect is always the best.

Keeping a Strict Account of What Happened

~&~

> We worked our way over old farmlands, and crossed the Old German Line, attacked and passed by the British a year before, in that typically wasteful experiment or audacity, the Aubers Ridge battle. The old trench lay silent and formidable, a broad gully, like a rough sunk land rather than a firing-trench. It was strewn with remains and pitiful evidences ... I saw old uniforms, and a great many bones. One uniform identified a German officer; the skeleton seemed less coherent than most, and an unexploded shell lay on the edge of the fragments. What an age since 1914!
>
> Edmund Blunden, *Undertones of War*

Sergeant Pexton was one of the 30,000 British and French troops who failed to make it to Dunkirk on 29 May 1940. By then he was enduring a nightmarish rerun of First World War geography as the Germans marched him off to near-starvation and slavery. He was thirty-four and thus was filled with memories of a Flanders-dominated boyhood. And here he was, unbelievably being chivvied along the old death roads of the Aisne through forests of bright Portland stone grave-markers, all as neat as a pin. Can he really be trudging into Le Cateau and Cambrai where so many 'fell' in 1914 and in 1918? The summer rain pours down on him and on the cemeteries. Now *he* is gnawing a single biscuit at Cambrai and beating off the rats at Doullens. Now his 'lot' have been massacred — 'My God, how few of us stood up.'

Now he, like those August 1914 prisoners, might have four years' disappearance from home stretching ahead of him.

Pexton's diary lasts as long as its usefulness as a measure of his hopefulness lasts. When hope dies, he packs it in. His terse, factual style is impressive. Though writing purely for himself, he lacks egotism. His diary is a kind of 'lest *I* forget'. The narration is hard and specific, full of times and dates and place-names. He is telling himself where he was and where he is, and when. There is a tragic sense of *déjà vu*, from the march along the roads of the Western Front to the farm-labouring on the German–Polish border. It is the wartime and peacetime fate he would, at his age, have heard a lot about. Is he recording in his strong, abrupt, intelligent hand the moment when Hitler has won? He hears that Hitler has taken all Europe. Blitzkrieg! The fast triumph. However, there is a dogged edge to what he puts down, which, with hindsight, can be seen to threaten these quick gains. On the German farm he becomes the serf of any century. He might have been the prisoner of Napoleon or Frederick the Great. But the way they treat him won't crush him; it will make him dangerous. He is an ox-like man who, though hard-driven, will be, bullets apart, indestructible. His sufferings are those of a lost animal.

12 *May* 1940. My 34th birthday. Heard this morning that Germany had invaded Belgium. Had to take up positions. Refugees pouring through by the hundreds. They look awful and are running for their lives.

13 *May*. Ordered to move tonight, and don't know where. Got into lorries at 8 p.m. Headed south.

14 *May*. Arrived here at canal at 3 a.m. Stood to at 4 a.m. and got dug in. Very cold but all quiet. 9.30 a.m., bombers came over and dropped a few in the village to our rear. Spoke to two French soldiers at midday and find we are just north of Cambrai. We're holding the Old Albert Canal. All quiet . . .

15 May. Stood to at 3.30 a.m. Very quiet up to 4.15. German spotting plane came over pretty low. 6.30 a.m. First taste of bombers. 68 of them all trying to create hell upon earth together. What a day – just about blew us all out the ground. Got shelled all day too. Getting very warm round here now. Don't mind the bombs so much as the planes' machine-guns. They're wicked.

16 May. Stood to again at dawn. Quiet. Told they had come through Luxemburg with four armoured divisions, but that they could only last till Sunday with petrol. '*Must* hold them at all costs.' Still more shelling. Cambrai must be in a mess by now. Got some more bombs today.

17 May. Dawn again. Lovely morning. Can't believe that war is anywhere near. Refugees still pouring out of Cambrai. I am only fifty yards from the main Cambrai–Arras road. Big steel bridge not far from my dug-out. Heard from Coy Commander today that Engineers will blow it up if he gets too near.

18 May. Stood to again. Pretty cold this morning. Spotter came over again at 4.30 a.m. Started getting a bit deeper into Mother Earth ready for his mates to come. They came all right. One hundred and seventeen bombers and fighters. Quite sticky while it lasted. The village that was in our rear just isn't now. Fighters began to machine-gun from the main road. What a mess. Be glad when night comes.

19 May. 2.45 a.m. Hell of a bang. They have blown the bridge up. He must be advancing again. Shells coming all over the place. Just in front of our position. Hope when he lifts he goes well over our heads. Lots of dud shells coming. Went to see the bridge at 9.30 a.m. Lots of dead there – must have gone up with it. Took a chance in between shells and dived in café. Got a bottle of Rum and two bottles of Vin Rouge. Didn't stay long. Good job, as café went west five minutes later. Direct hit. Shells are giving us some stick now, 12 noon. Afraid we shall have to retire soon. Can't hold tanks with rifles or bren-guns. 4 p.m. We HAVE to hold on till 8 p.m. and then retire. Roll on 8 p.m. It's been hell all day. Air battles have been worth looking at though. Got out at 8 p.m. and marched 6 kilometres and got some lorries. Arrived at small village at 3 a.m.

20 May. Slept till 8 a.m. Went out of barn to see what was happening and if possible scrounge some grub. Found that some grub was going on in one of the lorries but had to wait for the next party. Don't know where they are going. Refugees still coming through from somewhere. Saw two men running down the road. Refugees said they were Parachutists. Captain Martin and myself called on them to halt but they didn't. Not immediately. Dropped them. Both dead when we got to them. 10 a.m. Fun began. Germans came from nowhere. Properly surprised us. Got down to it in the open and fought for all we knew how. Getting wiped out this time all right. Got back out of the farm buildings, and he's sending everything he has at us. 11 a.m. Still holding out and there's a bit of a lull. Kid on my right will keep sticking his head up above the clover. He's sure to get his soon, I'm thinking. Can't really remember much about the next hour. Remember the order 'Cease fire' and that the time was 12 o'clock. Stood up and put my hands up. My God, how few of us stood up. German officer came and spoke in English. Told to pick up the wounded and carry them to the road. There aren't many that need carrying. We have to leave our dead. Took us off the road into another field. I expected my last moments had come and lit a fag. Everyone expected to be shot there and then. Patched up our wounded as best we could and were taken back about two miles. Stayed the night in a Roman Catholic church. Learned that this village is called Ficheaux. Note: out of appr. 1,400 men only 425 spent the night in this church.

21 May. Roused out of it at 6 a.m. and put on road. I'm just beginning to realize that I'm a prisoner. We have had nothing to eat since Sunday and today is Tuesday. My water-bottle is empty now. Hope they give us something to eat soon. Got nothing to eat today.

22 *May*. Marched today to a village called Leincourt. They 'promised' us some food but still we got none. My tummy is getting used to nothing now. We are just living on water.

23 *May*. Left Leincourt at 7 a.m. and marched to Frevent, the very village that we left to try and stop him. I'd had a few decent meals, and beer as well, in this place. Hell, but I could do with a meal now. Left here at 8 p.m. for Doullens and warned that if anyone tried to escape they would shoot the officers they had in the car with them. No one tried to escape. Got to Doullens at 3 a.m. Flaxmill. Rats galore.

24 *May*. What a night. Rats running all over the place. Left Doullens for Albert. Sent off with one packet of English biscuits and half a tin of bully. Did 21 miles today, and very hot. They keep us away from all water and it is hell. Got to Albert at 8 p.m., just about all in, and went to aircraft works. Slept on the landing-ground. He'd made a mess of things here. Airplanes smashed up and the works badly smashed as well. I realize I'm a prisoner now all right. Just about fed up with everything. Wouldn't take much for me to make a break for it. It would be a quick way out anyway so long as he shot straight. Suppose I must not think that way and just carry on. It can't last for ever.

25 *May*. Had a very cold night at Albert and was glad to be on the road again. They gave us two packets of German biscuits and they taste awful. Black and bitter. Still they help to fill a terribly big hole. Lovely day but far too hot for marching, and in our condition too. Men are dropping out every mile now. Feet are in a terrible condition. I don't know how some of them march at all. Just the British spirit I expect. We're never beaten. Passed Delville Wood Cemetery today. Very big, and later passed Caterpillar Valley as well. Not as big but just as tidy. Cemeteries

are all over this part of the country. Must have been some bother here in the last war all right. They look nice but I hope I don't end up in one. Arrived at the field and find this place is called Flers. Had a big thunderstorm just before arriving and got nice and wet. Everything wet to sleep on so I expect another lovely night.

26 May. The worst night yet. Left here for Cambrai and they gave us ONE biscuit on marching out. What a march. Will never understand how I did it, but here I am in the French barracks at last. There must be 30,000 of us on the road now. French mostly slept on the square although it was pouring with rain. We are that hungry we can't feel the wet. Germans say the war will be over in one month. I wonder.

27 May. Terrible night. Left for Le Cateaux. Long march and went right through, and got to a place called Cattilou. Got no eats all day. Sent letter home from here but don't think that it will get there. Still, I must chance anything that comes along.

28 May. Left for Avesne at 3.30 p.m. Raining heavy. They gave us a bit of black bread and a piece of cheese. Long and quick march. Gave us each a bale of angora wool to sleep on in the mill. Nothing to eat.

29 May. Left here at 10 a.m. and crossed into Belgium at a place called Sivry. Got one slice of bread and margarine before marching out. Have got an awful cold in the head. Head is buzzing like a top. No wonder, living this cowboy life. Very hot today for marching. Halted at place called Philippeville.

30 May. Very cold night. Left at 9.30 a.m. and marched to place called Marienbourg. Arrived at 5.30. Got soup, meat and bread. Heard we go by train to Cologne in the morning. Shall have to wait and see.

31 May. Many happy returns of the day, Ena. Suppose my good luck will begin today, on your birthday. Have had nothing but bad luck since my own – unless being alive is lucky. Left here at 9 a.m. and marched 20K to this village. Got ladle full of soup on arrival. Very weak. May get some later. Don't suppose we shall get any more food until tomorrow. Hope Ena has had news that I am a prisoner; would be a good birthday present for her. Place called Doische. No food.

1 June. Left Doische at 9 a.m. and marched to what looks like the railhead. Hope it is. I'm about fed up with tramping around France and Belgium. My boots are very bad. Got small ladle full of 'coffee' to march out with. Nothing else. I'm as hungry as hell. If I didn't need what boots I have left to march in I'd eat them. Boys are trying to boil dandelions and nettles to make soup. Hope it works. Stayed the night here. Dandy went down all right but bitter. Sick afterwards. Place called Beauraing.

2 June. Stayed all day. Ate grass.

3 June. Left Beauraing at 9 a.m. and got a little soup and a small piece of black bread. Arrived at St Pierre about 3 p.m. Very hot. Not a long march but getting very weak in the legs. Had a drop of barley soup. No bread.

4 June. Looks like staying here at St Pierre all day. Stayed the night.

5 June. Left St Pierre at 5.30 a.m. Longest march yet. Got nothing on marching out to place called Bertrix. Marched about 43K. Lost three mates during the march.

6 June. Left Bertrix at 3 p.m. by Rail after the first really good dixie of soup. Arrived Luxemburg at 9.30 p.m. Only stayed half an hour and then went to a place called Trier. Climbed the big hill into Concentration Camp. We're just in Germany now, 3 a.m.

7 June. Left Trier at 10 p.m. after having some bread and jam. Passed through Germany via Hamburg and Posen to this place in Poland called Torun. I believe we have come to the end of the long trail at last. Just three weeks of it and I am all in. Shall be glad to stay anywhere for a bit. We spent 46 hours on the train from Trier.

9 June. Yes, this is our home camp. Getting treated a lot better now. Better and more food today.

10 June. Letting us rest for a day or two to get some of our strength back before going to work.

11 June. Got our numbers today. 8806 is my number. This camp is called Stalag XXA (17). We shall go to work soon.

12 June. Handed in our money today. 50 francs and 10d. in English is all I had. Got a receipt for it but don't suppose this will matter much. Heard today that Italy had declared war on Turkey and that Russia was helping Turkey. Wish it was all over and done with and I was on my way home again.

14 June. Told today that on Monday we could write home. This will be the first time. Hope it's true. Could do with a smoke but I reckon I'll have to wait a bit yet. Still hungry. Was told today that the Germans were in Paris but don't know how true it is.

15 June. Had a busy day. Went for a bath. First decent wash for five weeks. We are being issued with a blanket today. May sleep better tonight – Saturday night of all nights. Nearly heart-broken to think I should be having a pint and a game of darts. Never mind. It will have to end some day, I suppose.

16 June. Wrote home! Could have written a book of wants but space didn't allow. Hope it won't take too long for an answer. I'm not getting my strength back on this food. Can't get nearly enough to eat. Smokes are out of the question. Tried smoking the leaves off the trees but it didn't work. What an awful experience. Roll on peace and let's get home.

17 June. Monday and just a month a prisoner. Seems more like a year to me. Can't think how I've survived this length of time. Marching, fighting and hunger is a hell of a lot to face. I'm sure I couldn't do it again. Got some roasted spuds tonight on a little fire I made on the sly. Glad I wasn't caught.

18 June. Got caught boiling spuds after 'dinner'. Don't know what is going to happen.

19 June. Nothing happened about the spuds, thank God. Put my name down as a shoe repairer. Might get decent job for the winter.

21 June. No sign of work for Sergeants. We're not allowed to work yet. Men are getting work and extra food with it. Heard today that Hull had been bombed. Petrol dump had been set on fire. Hope everyone at home is OK.

18 July. Getting very monotonous now, more so when you're as hungry as hell. Wish we could get some sort of news through.

19 July. Heard today that Hitler had broadcast some peace terms and that Churchill had told him what to do with them. Don't know how true it is as the camp is always so full of rumours that you can't believe anything you hear. Hope they do patch some sort of terms up as everyone here wants it, and to get home. Still, I'm not being the soldier I thought I was, wanting peace terms.

23 July. Got a basinful of macaroni from German cook. Had been a prisoner in England during the last war. Very decent chap. Thinks war will soon be over now. France has given in. Hope he is right. He was as fed up as me with it.

24 July. Told that English mail would be issued on Friday. Hope
I hear from home. Never thought I should miss a letter like this.
Or a parcel.

> There's a constant and careful collecting
> Of strongest brown paper and twine,
> There's a special pen-nib for directing,
> Free-flowing and not over-fine.
> There's a far-sighted skill in the packing,
> For the problem's increasingly great,
> Not to leave out a thing that he's lacking,
> And still keep an eye on the weight.
>
> There's a soreness of feminine fingers,
> For the knots must be terribly tight,
> There's a look that half nervously lingers,
> For fear the address is not right.
> There's a trust that the waves will be tender,
> That no submarine lurks near the coast,
> And a wish in the soul of the sender,
> That she might go too, parcel post.
>
> All soldiers whose comforts are meagre,
> When the corporal sings out your name,
> When your hands are schoolboyishly eager
> To seize and examine your claim,
> Do you guess, as the paper you're tearing,
> And the gifts in your pockets you shove,
> That each parcel from Blighty is bearing
>   An ocean of love?

28 July. No mail yet. Got deloused today to move to farm
tomorrow. No idea where but I think it will be in Germany.

31 July. Rotten camp this. Under canvas and very wet.

2 August. Heard today that the German army pay had a 25% cut.

Could do with a nice fish and chips supper – or a hunk of bread, if it comes to that.

6 *August*. Red letter day. Left for farm at a place called Neuteich. Got bread and lard for supper from the farmer.

7 *August*. Went tying and stooking barley until dinner. Threshing all afternoon until 8 p.m. Never felt so tired in all my life. Am as weak as water. Bed at 9.30 and locked in by guard.

8 *August*. Threshing. Then it rained, so knocked off and worked inside until 7 o'clock. In bed by 8.30. More food now but very plain. Not much meat either. Just *waiting* for a letter from home. It wouldn't be so bad then.

9 *August*. Rained again today. Mixing meal all morning. Can't do much in this weather. Farmer sent us back to billet for half a day providing we work half day Sunday if it is fine. Don't give anything away, these Gerries.

12 *August*. Threshing today. Feet very bad. It's these terrible wooden Dutch clogs we have to wear. No socks, just toe-rags. The balls of my feet always seem red-hot. Roll on.

13 *August*. Just work. Had to go through village to field and got spat at and called names by a fellow. Don't know what he said but had a good guess. German pig.

16 *August*. Went 10K to work today with Poles. Girls as well. I love to hear them sing while they work, although what they find to sing about beats me. They're as badly off as us. Bed means straw, no blanket. Just lay down in what you work in, except taking these awful clogs off. We haven't a towel or soap, and only clothes to stand up in, shirt and thin drawers. All lousy. Even our uniform is full of them. Can't keep them down no how.

17 August. Saturday again. Wonderful. We got some soap from the boss, a small cake that I'm sure is pure sand. Been cutting beans with a sickle. Rotten job, but then I think these people like to make a job as rotten as they can for us.

18 August. Had a funny dream about getting discharged in Halifax on December 5th. Hope it comes true.

19 August. Beans again. One of the Pole girls has decided that I'm the only one to work with. She ties up behind me. Will insist I learn to speak Polish. If I'm here about ten years I might be able to say something in Polish. What a language! *Still* no news from home. Wonder if they think I'm dead.

20 August. Just the same as usual. I don't think I shall keep this diary up as it looks to me as if I shall not need it.

18 September. I pity the last war's prisoners having four years of it [last entry].

My Kingdom for a Book

People say that life is the thing, but I prefer reading.

Logan Pearsall Smith, *Afterthoughts*

Gunner James Witte was a lanky blond, worldly, resilient, good-natured, tolerant and a survivor. In the maddest of human situations, with the rest of society stood on its head, there will always be a Gunner Witte lost in a book, or making a pretty penny, or frankly enjoying whatever is on offer. A bit of a dandy, he seizes on the moment and has a very interesting time. Blatantly self-interested, he has yet great charm, most of all when he is being ignoble. He was captured in the Western Desert in April 1941 and spent the whole of the rest of the war in a series of Italian and German prison camps, about which his candour outran anything resembling the caution of most POW commentators. His wartime writings begin with a jolly description of himself as a flash young recruit on the town.

It was a happy band of warriors which crowded into the leave trucks for our first leave since we were called up. We TA men wore our cavalry uniforms, and spurs jingled as we clumped down the station platform with riding whips under our arms. Some of us had gone one stage further in our efforts to pose as dashing Royal Horse Artillery men. There was a tailor in the village where we were billeted who had altered our uniforms.

First of all he 'boxed' the collars on our jackets, which meant that he did away with the points so that the jacket fitted snugly round the neck. Then he 'winged' and 'piped' our riding-breeches, so that they became tight round the legs, blossoming out into 'butterfly wings' at the thighs. The only trouble was that it was almost impossible to get into them, and equally hard to get out. But we didn't care about that. In my enthusiasm, I had even removed the rowels from my spurs and inserted silver threepenny-pieces instead, because they made a better jingling sound.

The TA men completely outshone our Militia colleagues who were drafted to us in 1939. They wore the shapeless battledress and comical side-hats of the early war years. Their blouses buttoned right up to the neck and tall, thin soldiers were able to tuck their chins inside the gap. They looked like sacks of potatoes tied in the middle.

I lived in a small Essex town near Southend. It had a popula-tion of about 2,000. In January 1940 there were no troops stationed in the area, so I had almost a clear field except for a few local soldiers home on leave. But they didn't wear spurs, save one, and he outshone me. I knew him slightly before the war when he had joined the Regular Army about 1938. I clanked into the Castle on the first night of my leave and there he was by the bar, surrounded by civilians buying him pints of wallop. He had removed his British Warm and stood resplendent in 'Blues', the Number One dress of a famous cavalry regiment. His uniform fitted him like a glove. A two-inch yellow stripe ran down his tight trousers and he wore highly polished boots with swan-neck spurs. He was slightly drunk. He turned to me and said in a broad Cockney voice,

'Wotcher, mate. What's your mob?'

'TA mob.'

'No such thing, mate. It's wartime. We're all the same.'

He and I arrived at Liverpool Street Station about ten o'clock the following morning. To be like me, he had put on his khaki uniform, which was practically identical with mine, except that his puttee tapes were yellow and mine were a bright green. We clumped across Bishopsgate, conscious of the admiring glances of office girls nipping into Lyon's for their morning coffee. He kept saying, 'Did you see that one?' I don't know to this day how many pubs there are between Liverpool Street and Ludgate Circus, but we sampled the beer in most of them and didn't pay for much of it either. Later, we stood in the street wondering what to do until they opened again. I was standing with my boots at the 'ten-to-two' position. I wanted to move but found that I couldn't, and fell over with my feet outstretched. I wondered what had happened. He got me up with the help of a friendly policeman. I began to get worried and thought I was paralysed or something.

'It's your spurs, mate, they're locked together.'

The policeman told us we should go to the Windmill.

'You'll like that,' he said.

One of the greatest enemies in POW life is boredom, especially when the stomach is reasonably well filled and you've had a smoke. The best antidote to boredom that I know of is a book, any book. I bought a Sexton Blake off a chap for five English fags and went away well content. After I had finished reading how the great detective tracked the master criminal I went round the barrack-room calling out, 'Any books to change?' like the knife-grinder must have done to advertise his wares in nineteenth century England. I soon got an offer; this time it was a lurid gangster yarn well laced with amatory adventures in down-town hotels. But what I really wanted was a hard-back with some meat in it. There was a studious-looking soldier lying down on his pit with a large tome propped up on his chest, which must have taken some lugging around. I got chatting to him and asked whether he would care to swap it for my well-thumbed James Hadley Chase, plus ten English fags. To my surprise he jumped at the chance and I became the owner of William Prescott's *History of the Conquest of Mexico, and of Peru.* A great work, but the only trouble was the thought of having to hump it around when we moved. But I said to myself that I would think about that when the time came, and got down to some serious reading.

When we did have to leave Sabratha and go back in the little train to Tripoli *en route* for Italy, I was more than two-thirds of the way through my great book and the exploits of the *Conquistadores*. I never ceased to wonder how men clad in full armour ever managed to get through fever-stricken jungles, let alone wage war against the Incas and Aztecs.

In Italy there was a small library in an empty hut. This library was to grow quite large as the months went by. On issuing day one of the matelots appeared with about fifty books, which he laid on the floor, whilst the queue remained outside. He then opened the door and we all surged in, grabbing the nearest book. It didn't matter what it was about as long as you got one. When you had read it, you returned it to the matelot, who dished it out again. Next time you tried for another. Having finished Prescott, I decided to give him to the library. Next opening time I dived in and got somebody's *History of France*: a chap behind me got Prescott and bore him away in triumph. Soon I was immersed in the doings of Charlemagne. It was from Prescott and an obscure *History of France* that I gained a taste for history.

One event almost shattered us. We had to have our hair off. I don't think that there is anything so demoralizing as losing your hair. It transforms the handsomest of men into caricatures of old-time convicts – people convicted for offences like fraud – but for those not particularly endowed with good looks, it made them look like real villains. To crown it all, we were obliged to have our pictures taken for record purposes, and with large numbers across our chests. Once your hair is shaven it takes almost nine months to get it back to normal.

We slaved in a German factory. One day, four lads, inseparables from the South Wales Borderers, left their work and marched solemnly to a wide-open space where the conveyor which carried locomotives in and out of the factory operated, and took up imaginary billiard cues. They then began going through the motions of playing snooker, putting the balls in the frame, going off, potting the colours, snookering each other and marking the scores. Every so often one of them would chalk his imaginary cue, whilst another would walk round the imaginary table looking for the best way to play a difficult shot. This performance really got the Germans wondering – and all the other nationalities too. It was the French who first cottoned on, for they began to enter into the spirit of the game by loudly applauding an imaginary pink being potted. Soon there was a great army of people around the imaginary table, with heads going backwards and forwards. Machines were left unattended and welding equipment was hurriedly switched off as more and more people came over to watch the mad Englanders. Soon, the hierarchy itself was involved, and then the works manager. Then the Taffs realized that enough was enough; they put their imaginary cues back in the imaginary rack and walked away to their respective jobs, followed by the bulk of the factory workforce.

It was the camp theatre which was the great draw at the prison in Sulmona, Italy. Its production company put on a great many shows from *The Belle of New York* to the *The Second Mrs Tanqueray*. The girls really looked like girls. Dutiful swains used to wait outside the theatre for them to appear after the show. They couldn't take them to dinner, so they took them instead to quiet places in the compound. The trouble was, though, that there was very little privacy for a love affair of this nature. The boy friends used to get very jealous if you so much as glanced at their girl friends. There was a corporal in the Military Police who was violently in love with one of the actresses called Gerry. Both were missing during a roll call and were found snuggled down together under a blanket in a corner of another compound. This amused the Italians, who put them into solitary together for a week. Another gorgeous piece was Frankie, who had a touch of the tarbrush about her. When she took a bath, half the camp used to come and watch. Frankie, though, kept herself to herself and fended off all advances, for she was only a she on the stage. Homosexuality, however, was by no means the prerogative of good-looking 'girls' and husky corporals of the Military Police. Liaisons sprang up between all sorts of people, tall and short, fat and thin, the good, the bad and the ugly. They took many forms, from parcel-sharing, holding hands, heavy petting and the actual thing. Love was given impetus by the Italian climate. During the winter months, when Italian rations were poor and the issue of Red Cross parcels irregular, love took a back seat. But when summer came, so Cupid came into his own again.

I had many misgivings about mucking in with Hill because he was such a gannet. Our first issue was Canadian, the parcel containing corned beef, Spam, tinned milk called Klim (milk spelt backwards), biscuits, coffee, tea, chocolate, raisins, cheese, and prunes, which inevitably were eaten last. At first Hill and I mucked in, eating the Spam one day and the corned beef the next, and so on. But after about the third issue, Hill wanted to eat the corned beef the same day as the Spam, and in fact eat the lot, and then wait around until the next parcel-day. He had joined the ranks of the parcel bashers. We tried dividing everything out, but then I caught him cheating on the Klim, and so I opted out and looked for another partner. In the end all the parcel bashers got together, leaving the steadier kind to form fresh partnerships.

I joined the foursome which worked well until the Italians surrendered. My three companions, from Yeomanry regiments, were good-natured, easy-going, and fond of lying on their beds reading. Each day we took it in turn to brew up. We divided out eatables between the four of us, making everything last until the next issue, and we made superb cakes from biscuits, raisins and prunes, which the cook baked on payment of a few cigarettes. Soon a pattern emerged in our barrack-room of those who would eat their parcels in one go, and then not wash or shave until the next parcel issue, and those who made them last. When the parcel-day arrived, the parcel bashers would be up with the lark, all washed, shaved and with clean shirts, ready to Eat. The contents of the English parcels varied, so merchants sprang up in the barrack-rooms to trade in commodities for a small cigarette percentage. Anyone wanting to exchange a meat loaf for a tin of Spam went to a merchant, and you went to them if you wanted to buy a Yorkshire pudding, for instance. Each merchant had a list of current prices attached to the barrack-room door which the buyers consulted. Like London's Leather Lane, prices were much of a muchness. When the private cigarette parcels began to arrive, you could live like a king. I was fortunate enough to receive several at a time from relatives, friends and the firm where I worked. This enabled me to set up in business as an entrepreneur with business headquarters at my bed-space. The only drawback in being a tycoon was the fact that I had always to be at the premises. I grew richer and richer. I became a camp Croesus. Soon I could afford to pay people to look after my wealth whilst I strolled around the compound passing the time of day with other business associates.

The Italians said that if we cared to make our own football pitch they would supply the goalposts, corner flags and footballs. Each barrack-room took it in turn to supply a working-party to level the ground. I exempted myself from this toil by paying the room-corporal a few cigarettes each time Hut Number 4 was on. I just couldn't afford to leave my wealth unguarded. The room-corporal, myself and one or two more in the magic circle would spend the day, instead, playing Bridge and Monopoly. Or, best of all, reading.

Alan and David

> Young men walking the open streets
> Of death's republic, remember your lovers.
>
> Sidney Keyes, 'Remember Your Lovers'

Most prisoners of war came to recognize a double entrapment, the emotional as well as the physical. For some at this time it seemed easier to contemplate a break-out through barbed wire than the breakdown of the wall of reserve with which they had been trained to hide so many things. A little memoir entitled *The Cage* is among the writings to examine the double entrapment in some depth. It is the work of two friends who may or may not be the confused lovers whose first-person confessions gradually come to dominate an unusually vivid and intimate book. They were two officers in their twenties who were caught at Tobruk in June 1942 and sent by air to Italy, where 'We first got the feeling of *not being allowed* out

> Not for just an hour,
> Not for just a day,
> Not for just a week,
> But always.

As a matter of fact, the imprisonment of Dan Billany and David Dowie was to last only fifteen months before, with Italy's surrender in September 1943, they were released, only to be killed presumably trying to escape further capture by the Germans, for they were never heard of again. But their joint manuscript was returned to Billany's parents by the Italian farmer to whom it had been entrusted, and was published in 1949. It is partly about falling in love, very profoundly, with somebody who is incapable of returning anything other than pity and irritation. The two kinds of victims use their prison-book as confessional in an attempt to understand themselves. The would-be lover is working class, with Communist parents, a 27-year-old virgin who was a schoolteacher before being called up. The beloved is a 23-year-old ex-public schoolboy, good at ballgames and bridge. Billany and Dowie, who may be these awkward friends, set out their dilemma in a series of remarkable dialogues or conversation pieces in which all the inhibitions and clichés about male behaviour are aired, making the reader realize how vastly things have changed since.

The Cage also reveals the time-bomb which the men and women in the forces are already beginning to roll towards Churchill and the Conservative element at home, for as in prison camps everywhere, there is everlasting talk and debate about what the British intended to do after the war. They intended, of course, to have a singularly British-style revolution, no less. When viewed from the varying perspectives of a battlefield, a prison or a distant land, the mean pre-war scene of millions of slums, unemployment, minimal education, diet and doctoring, and social inequality generally appeared less an injustice than plain idiocy. As Sir John Verney, a young officer stationed on the Palestinian coast, wrote:

In the early spring of 1943, the Beveridge Report arrived out in the Middle East, a morale-boosting assurance that hostilities might end some day and that a benign Government was already taking steps to see that those who eventually reached home would find a less disgraceful state of affairs than they had left. I was camped at the time with a jolly band of pirates beside the ruined Crusader castle of Athlit. The GOC Middle East, or someone of that kind, personally forwarded the Report to us, with a request that it should be carefully explained to all ranks.

We were legitimized pirates, about fifty strong and from most English walks of life, with the odd Greek, Pole and Dane thrown in. The Upper Classes were represented by a Socialist young peer, a truant Conservative MP and a morose Oxford don; the Lower by a poacher, a painter, and various butchers, bakers and candle-stick makers. But most of us were too young to have had much experience of pre-war employment – or, for that matter, unemployment ... Still, in fairness to Lord Beveridge, something had to be done about his Report. The Socialist young peer, the truant MP and the morose don all refused to be bothered, so the document was handed on to an Army clergyman who held a watching brief over our spiritual welfare. He was asked to read it through and give us a talk one wet afternoon ... To me, as to the rest, the Beveridge Report was too far removed from present realities and pleasures to have more than a vague academic interest. But it did start my thoughts wandering in a direction that, for the past three and a half years, I had not dared to let them take – the idea of still being alive in the post-war world.

Soon Sir John would be in prison, which for him – though not for everybody – was like being at university.

After the war kind friends occasionally asked me if my experiences as a prisoner had been *Hell*. I could but reply, with a tolerable degree of truth, that on the contrary I had seldom enjoyed anything so much. For one thing, and for the first time in four long years, I was free to read as much as possible and try and learn to draw and write. For another, an Italian POW camp at that particular moment, August 1943, seemed to offer a pleasant temporary respite from the war itself ... You could take up pretty well anything, from chartered accountancy to aero-dynam-ics, from bridge to baseball. There were language classes, lectures, plays, debating societies, concerts, an excellent library; or, if you preferred, there was the opportunity for incessant conversation. To which was added continual sunshine, sufficient minestrone and pasta, and a daily half pint of vino ... There were about fifteen hundred British and five hundred US officers, under the command of a senior British officer. The Americans had joined the camp recently, but most of the British had been prisoners at least a year, some for three years. A few were near the edge of despair, a few had passed over the edge, but the great majority had long since learnt to accept the succession of empty identical days . . .

'I am much struck by the *kindness* of everyone' I noted in my diary. Soldiers on active service may not keep a diary. Unlike so many generals I had stuck to the rules, thus denying myself this simple form of consolation, and now I plunged happily into one.

In their successive prisons at Capua, Fontanellato and Rezzanello, Dan Billany and David Dowie fought off what was happening to them, played cards, read Aleck Bourne's *Health of the Future* and the Beveridge Report, and attended debates on 'Reconstruction in Post-War Europe'. They too were at a spartan university, but emotionally at the edge and uncheerful.

Alan Falls in Love with David

Spring came and was over very quickly. A flaunting of leaves, and a passionate singing of birds, a sudden great blaze of life while we lay in prison and watched it go by without us. Another spring will not come again. This one went past like a May-day procession in which we were not taking part. The first day I was here I remember looking out of the lavatory window and seeing the bare branches of the trees along the road to the cemetery. You could see the fields, gardens, and houses beyond them, netted in the branches, the laundry on the line on washing days, the bright colours the girls wore snipping mint in the gardens, the village life. Then, in less than a fortnight the branches were covered in leaves, and the view was closed with a rich green curtain. I saw it all happen with a few glances out of the window. The others, though they lean out of the window hours every day, did not notice that the world had put a new dress on. They don't see the world, because they are part of it. I see it because I am outside the process. Left over out of life.

Now the leaves are full and heavy and summery, though it is only June. Crickets scramble in hundreds among the stones in the compound. And the nightingales sing all day and all night. The air all over the plain of Lombardy must be ringing with voices of nightingales.

I have been very unhappy. I feel as if I had been ill for a long time, and am now neither convalescent nor getting worse, but exhausted. In this time of tiredness I see only one thing I want.

Tiredness teaches me.

Sleep.

More than sleep for the body. Physical sleep is a respite for blood and muscles, so that the body can carry its pain a day further along the road of life. But it does not help the soul. The soul may be stunned into silence by physical tiredness, but it does not rest and renew its strength in the night. It needs its own conditions for its own unique sleep. I need more than physical sleep in a bed where I am alone. My spirit is trembling from its long effort. I dread waking in the night, to be alone in the dark with my loneliness. Life has been wrong for me all the time. With great difficulty I have imitated outwardly the actions of successful people, and always thought that they probably felt the same inside as I do. But they do not. They are getting results all the time which satisfy them. I have got nothing out of my life. I have been acting for nothing. It is all my own fault.

It is no use pretending that I am going the same way as the others. However I imitate them, I am on a different road, and I am alone on it, and I am afraid it bypasses life and leads directly to death.

I need the sleep of the spirit, which only comes in someone else's love. To give up preparing my reactions. To be taken for what I am. To sleep in his arms. It will never happen. Never.

. . . Looking down into the hall from the balcony I can see the table, the four heads, the cards, and a glass of *vino* by each hand. Quietness, steadiness, mutual understanding. Cigarette-smoke floating. Interest and humour on their faces, looking at their cards and at each other. The lamp-light on his gold-brown hair. Heedless.

David Cannot Fall in Love with Alan

And the waste that is Alan. Alan who hasn't the strength to fight. Admit it. So I must carry him. I must let the light in. Open the gates and let Alan in. But I daren't because I don't trust him. Afraid of his needs ... Can't work, can't read. Can't lie on my bed and just think because Alan is there on the next bed, silent. Walk listlessly through the building and wish to get away, be alone, but it's impossible to be alone in a prison camp. Friends look sympathetic and try to cheer but they know the mood; they say little and wait for it to pass. Prison blues. Lean from the end window. A lovely day, a lazy day, a hot sun speckling the tree-lined dusty road to the cemetery. A gramophone next door; the same record, the same crooned sickly sentiment and twenty officers sunk in nostalgia because they remember Frances Day and *The Fleet's in Port Again*, and they remember home and they wonder how long.

And on Sunday, all the little girls from the village and all the smart, silk-stockinged evacuees from Parma make bright patches of colour on the dusty road. Flowers in hand to visit the cemetery; wind-blown skirts; forty yards and two rows of barbed wire and every window that side of the building frames two heads, and each head two overworked eyes. Leching. Pleasant torture. Content to know that these are women, the other half, the complement. Let half-forgotten memories flood in. There, that girl might be Jill; she walks like that, pleased with herself, enjoying life. Women have a civilizing effect on me. But they have no effect on Alan. [It's] because he doesn't know ... There's a shell around him ...

We were sitting at a table on the balcony, writing our letters home; again we were back to our old indifferent relationship after that stupid business four nights before [David's defences had been lowered after a party], but it was not quite what it had been. At that earlier scene, when I had taken his hand, I had given him something of me, and temporary irritations could only eclipse that, not annihilate it. As I had felt his misery flow into me, so some qualities of me had entered him. It appeared to me that though we might hate each other for a long time, even beneath the hate there was a link we both acknowledged. He might call it love. I knew it was not that, in the usual sense at any rate. It was not even that we made each other happy. The best way I could express it would be to say that, however far apart our lives might lie in the future, we should never be able to forget each other entirely; at odd moments, in certain situations, I knew he would always come to my mind, and I to his.

Since taking his hand, I don't think I had once been whole-heartedly furious with him. At his worst I always felt a touch of sorrow that he had to be like that – though often this unavoidable sympathy also irritated me with the sense that I could not get Alan outside myself, could not externalize him completely, so that when I hated him there was a faint tone of guilt in it – which made me try to hate him worse.

He was altered, though I suppose only superficially. He seemed to have given up hope. Since making such a fool of himself I daresay he had thought it over and concluded he could do no more. He seemed emotionally tired; he could not work up to the old intensity any more. Between his own folly and my indifference he felt that he had failed completely in all that his life demanded.

There was a time, writing at the same table, when he would have finished first and sat watching me with adoration till I looked up and scowled at him. But he did not do that now. When he had finished, he lit a cigarette and lounged over to the balcony rail, where he leaned, looking down into the hall. He was lost in his own thoughts, which apparently no longer tore him to pieces, for his face as he looked down was, for once, quite calm, even gentle. He had forgotten to be expressionless. His eyes were reflective. It seemed tragic to me that as soon as I spoke to him, the humanity would vanish from his eyes, he would turn to me a false, strained mask of good-humour and flattery. Why must it be? Couldn't he trust me to like him for what he was? How could I be his friend, when his soul bolted like a scared rabbit into its burrow whenever I approached?

I wondered how often he had leaned on the same balcony rail to watch me playing bridge in the evenings; I thought probably that was what he was seeing now – the bright-lit hall, the quiet, interested players, and himself outside. But as I watched him, and his quiet expression deepened, I realized that he had forgotten me altogether – forgotten me and the prison and all the things round him, and was far away in some reverie which cancelled everything but itself.

At last for a few moments he was out of pain. The reflective sadness of his face had also humour and tenderness in it. A barren personality that should have been so rich and warm. I thought of all the agonies and torments of soul he had suffered on my account, driven by some unfathomable weakness always to seek my affection, never for one moment relaxing his terrific effort; needing me as a reassurance for life itself; driven by the emptiness of his life to find fulfilment in me. Why had he made his life so empty? What horrible thing had crossed the path of his life, what had broken him? He should have been so much, and he was nothing. An overmastering fear had separated him all these years from the warmth of intimate life, and now at last the dam of his emotions had broken down and engulfed him hopelessly, so hopelessly that I could not help him. How could I, when he demanded so much?

His own demands betrayed him. I was willing to give a lot, but always he seemed to be asking for just a little more. His eyes were always on the margin of my generosity, craving for whatever was just beyond. It was so bewildering and exasperating because surely he could see that affection is all a matter of trust, and if he whole-heartedly enjoyed as much love as I could freely give him, then in time I would gain reassurance, and give him more. But no, the little he did *not* get invariably preoccupied him more than the much he did. That, of course, must have been why I thought him greedy at Capua. He must have had the same attitude about food. That was one thing he had shaken off, at any rate. And if he wanted to be happy with me, and ultimately with the world, he must drop his love-greediness. What did he

want? To be taken in my arms, to be kissed, to be trusted with
the warmth of my own life? To sleep in my arms, as he
sometimes said? Well, he could not have those things, not
primarily because they might be unnatural, but just because he
wanted them and could not be happy with the genuine affection
I gave him short of those things. It seems obvious to me that
there's no harm in affection and in intimate contacts, but they
must arise out of real tenderness, must come to their true place
when the emotions they represent have developed to the point
where they demand expression. Alan couldn't wait for that. He
was afraid it would not happen. He might well be right, perhaps
I never could care for him enough to embrace him spontaneously
– but that was no reason at all for trying to force demonstration
before I had enough feeling to demonstrate. It did not work –
from his own viewpoint he was wrong. He was throwing my
affections back in my face. Couldn't he see that I was human, as
he was, and that his greediness continually checked my trust in
him by revealing him as basically selfish? We are not strong all
the way through; all those months of wrangling, yet if he had
been different I could have put my weight on his affection for
me, and it would have helped me. The thing he wanted, that I
should trust him and lean on him, would have been worthwhile
for me too, to depend on his infinite devotion. But no. He
himself would not let me. He was his own enemy and mine as
well. He denied himself the support of my life, and denied me
the support of his.

He returned to the present and came back to his chair, but
failed to put on again his mask; it was almost like seeing him
naked. No practised expressions, nor neurotic tenseness. 'Lots of
love in it?' he said, referring to the letter I had just written.

To Show Thy Pity upon All Prisoners and Captives

'The horror of that moment,' the King went on, 'I shall never, *never* forget!'

'You will, though,' the Queen said, 'if you don't make a memorandum of it.'

Lewis Carroll, *Through the Looking-Glass,*
and What Alice Found There

Prison camps became centres of creative writing. Miss Dryburgh, a missionary captured after the fall of Singapore and interned in Sumatra, became the unexpectedly accomplished editor of the *Camp Chronicle*, a magazine which contained travel and social features, a weekly news bulletin, a crossword puzzle, a needlework section and notices of events. It was hand-written on any scrap of paper, fixed together and passed around. She saw how essential it was to bring some kind of normalcy to a devastating situation, because, as she said,

> February 15th is labelled our black-letter day, for on it we lost our freedom and became prisoners of the Japs. After two months of blitz we escaped from Singapore. Though very near death at sea we were luckier than many refugees, and eventually disembarked at Muntok, Bangka Island. Muntok is a pretty little town with attractive buildings, lovely trees and flowers, but the impression it made on me was of horror, apprehension, discomfort and sorrow.

Crammed in the camp with a crowd of frightened women and girls,

Miss Dryburgh began to write. She wrote a hymn which they all sang each Sunday. It began:

> Father, in captivity,
> We would lift our prayer to thee,
> Keep us ever in thy love,
> Grant that daily we may prove
> Those who place their trust in thee,
> More than conquerors may be.

This hymn spread to other women's camps all over the Far East.

But she also wrote tough indictments of the ghastly standards and attitudes of Japan's prison camp system, such as the following. Lewis Carroll's logic is brought to bear on the evil and madness of it all.

Alice in Internment Land

'Is this a barracks?' said Alice, looking around a dusty square enclosed by wooden sheds with thatched roofs. 'I see no soldiers. But surely those are the women and children I have seen before on The Hill. Can they still be interned?'

'Yes, alas,' said a voice at her feet. Alice noticed a black cat. 'Midnight, at your service,' said he, looking important. 'I can give you any information you want.'

'Why are these people not free yet?' asked Alice.

Midnight looked a little crestfallen. 'That I cannot tell you,' he said, 'for we get no outside news here.'

'How distressing,' said Alice. 'Please tell me how they fare here. What are these buildings?'

'This is the main entrance, where we are standing,' said Midnight. 'On your right is the hospital, on your left a dormitory for the hospital sisters and Roman Catholic nuns. Right opposite, at the other end, are the kitchens. The two blocks on the right of the square are occupied by the British, the two on the left by the

Dutch. The shed in the centre is meant for the children and acts as school, playground and church.'

'It certainly isn't a palais-de-luxe,' said Alice. 'I expect they all feel distinctly aggrieved.'

'No more than I am,' broke in a fretful voice.

Alice saw a long thin figure in red and yellow, with a pipe dangling round his neck. 'The Pied Piper, surely!' she said in great surprise. 'What are you doing here?'

'It's what I'm not doing here that annoys me,' said the Pied Piper, glaring at Midnight. 'Word was brought that this camp was overrun with rats of an outsize variety. The tale went that one was so busy eating the stuffing of a mattress which was being repaired, that he was sewn up inside, and only discovered by his squeaks when sat upon, and yet I was not invited to deal with the scourge.' The Piper cast a baleful glance at Midnight, who nonchalantly licked his lips. 'A curse upon you!' shouted the Piper. 'May you meet with a bad end', and he vanished.

'Rats are not the only trouble here,' said a new voice.

Alice saw a worried-looking little man carrying a very large notebook.

'I am the Compiler of Camp Complaints,' said he.

'Let me hear some of them,' said Alice.

'With pleasure,' said the Compiler. 'Sit down – that is if you can find anything to sit on. Our few odd chairs are falling to bits.' He opened his book. 'A is for Ants that we find on our shelves, B is for Bathroom and Bugs in our beds.'

'I can understand a complaint about Bugs, but why one for Bathroom?' said Alice.

'Come and see for yourself,' said the Compiler.

He led Alice to the central section.

'This is the bathroom for two hundred people,' he said.

Alice looked around incredulously and noticed some roughly constructed compartments. 'These are the latrines, I suppose. Only seven.'

'Only seven,' repeated the Compiler. 'Look inside.'

Alice saw a deep drain with a slightly raised cement foothold on each side of it. Nothing more. 'No wonder they complain,' she said. 'How are they cleaned?'

'Each day a bathroom squad flushes them with pails of water, sending the contents to the septic tank just outside. This has to be emptied each day by a noble band of hygiene specialists affectionately known as the BAD Brigade.'

'I should think it was a very good brigade,' said Alice.

'Oh yes. The BAD Brigade consists of British, Australian and Dutch women who go round together hunting for germs. The bathers bring their own water to the bathroom and bathe in public. They complain that they are dirty before they leave the bathroom, for the floor is full of holes filled with water which has been muddied by the feet of those coming in. My list goes right through the alphabet,' said the Compiler, turning over his pages. 'In fact, there is no end to complaints. The Dutch complain about the British and the British about the Dutch. There are complaints about the shop, the rations, the bed spaces, about working and about slacking. Some people find a kind of joy in complaining and would be wretched without a grumble.'

'I think I will have a look at the dining-room,' said Alice. She wiped away a tear as she gazed at the pathetic assortment of enamel mugs, broken plates, coconut shells, old tins and glass bottles that formed the equipment of the diners. Changing the subject, she asked Midnight what the internees did to amuse themselves.

'They read all the books they can get. A librarian changes the books in the woodshed twice a week. The centre shed acts as a rendezvous, gossip corner, school and church. And also as a public hall where Announcements are made by the Authorities. On occasion it is a concert hall.'

'Oh, what kind of concerts do they have?' asked Alice.

'They have songs by a choir that practises in the kitchen, solos, and a special choir which calls itself a Vocal Orchestra. It aspires to classical music and hums it in four parts. The result gives quite the effect of an orchestra. Once a Variety Show with songs and dances in costume was produced. The Japanese visitors were so pleased that they gave the performers bits of soap and tins of British army rations. However, concerts have been impossible of late because of the black-out. Still, there are mild forms of amusement, cards, auction sales of clothes, gossip about the guards, who have nicknames. Oh, I forgot to mention, the writing of recipes is very popular. That reminds me, you had better see Mrs Feed-Em. There she is, outside the kitchen. Go and talk to her.'

'How are you, Mrs Feed-Em?' asked Alice.

'Oh, not so well as I was when I came here,' she said.

'How is that?'

'Come into the kitchen and I will tell you some of my troubles,' said Mrs Feed-Em.

Alice looked at a ramshackle shed with a long brick fireplace at one side where four large fires were burning. Roman Catholic sisters in their long robes were stirring huge cauldrons of rice.

'This is the Dutch Communal Kitchen,' said Mrs Feed-Em. 'The British did individual cooking at first. The kitchen was a regular inferno in those days because of the smoke from so many fireplaces, and full of noise. When the military authorities took over they made the British cook communally. Come and see the kitchen.'

They passed into a shed which was more decrepit than the first, where four cauldrons were supported by precarious-looking piles of bricks and stones, an iron ring or a home-made iron grid.

'Are those safe?' asked Alice apprehensively.

'Not very,' said Mrs Feed-Em. 'That is one of the reasons for my worries. The women have to make them with anything they can find. No wonder there is a collapse sometimes. Once, the wall fell out as the cook tried to steady herself whilst lifting a cauldron. Have a look at the rest of the establishment. This is the woodshed where a squad deals with the carrying, sawing and chopping of the logs sent into the camp. Hard work, as you can imagine. Axes are scarce, one for at least 137 people, so ours often loses its head. It seems to fly off at the slightest provocation. Here is the British vegetable shed.' They approached an open shed with rough tables and benches. 'The vegetable-cutters have their set days too; my department is quite well organized,' continued Mrs Feed-Em, and the glimmer of a smile lit up her worn features. 'From 3.30 a.m., when the fire-lighters start the day's work, until 6 p.m., when the fires are all put out, everything goes by clockwork.'

'Now that I have seen the cooking arrangements, I would like to know more about the food,' said Alice. 'Have you thought out any exciting recipes?'

A look of gloom descended on Mrs Feed-Em's face. 'I am more than satisfied if I can give them the barest necessities nowadays,' she said. 'Here is the British storehouse. Look inside.'

Alice obeyed, and saw another tumbledown shed where some empty kerosene tins rested on a bench and some rice sacks lay on the ground. 'Where are the stores?' she asked in surprise.

'This is a low time, but something will come in,' said Mrs Feed-Em. 'We have three sources of supply. Come and see them.' She pointed to three automatic machines between the storehouses and to a little door in the corner of the camp. The first was labelled Rations, the second Shop, and the third BM. 'We press the button each day,' she said, 'not knowing what will come out. Rice, of course, is a dead cert. Usually a supply for five days, unpolished or white, arrives. Often the bags are not full, though we are credited with the whole amount. Vegetables come daily but they are often faded, and never are there sufficient for all.'

'Does meat come every day?' inquired Alice.

Mrs Feed-Em had to sit down from shock.

'Meat!' she exclaimed. 'I should think not. Pork once a month is our average.'

'Well, the rations sound very meagre,' said Alice. 'I don't wonder underfeeding is among the complaints. Does the Shop not help matters?'

'Considerably,' said Mrs Feed-Em. 'Once it came on Sundays

and the contents of the bullock-cart were checked and shared out in the shed. Now the goods come by the back entrance we never know when they will arrive. There is great excitement when the gate creaks and many eyes watch expectantly for it to open. Sometimes the Shop brings fruit, eggs, curry biscuits, coffee, beans, and even sweets. These are sold at very high prices, but are bought eagerly by all who can afford them.'

'What about the BM machine?' asked Alice.

Mrs Feed-Em looked round blankly. 'What are you talking about?'

'Well, I saw a third machine labelled BM,' said Alice.

'Are you sure?'

'Absolutely,' said Alice, looking at the spot where the machine had been. 'Why,' she faltered, 'where is it now? Has it disappeared?'

Mrs Feed-Em smiled. 'Move back a step,' she said.

As Alice obeyed, the machine came into view again.

'We have to camouflage it,' explained Mrs Feed-Em, 'as it is not supposed to be here at all. Press the button and see what happens.'

Alice somewhat fearfully obeyed. To her surprise, a black figure appeared, grinning and carrying a parcel.

'You are too early,' the black figure said. 'This button should be pressed only by night when I can't be seen, for I am not supposed to exist. Black Market, you know,' he whispered. 'I had better vanish, I think', and with these words he disappeared.

'There are various ways of sending messages to the BM,' explained Mrs Feed-Em. 'Sometimes the guards oblige. It has even been said that orders for sugar and other things have been sung to a hymn tune about the time for devotions. In the darkness baskets are deposited at agreed spots, then at dawn the selling begins. At sky-high prices, of course.'

'But what about the poorer people?' asked Alice.

'Many have sold their jewellery and clothes. Some, of course, have only been able to sniff and covet. These poor people have the very slight satisfaction of feeling virtuous when Authority occasionally bursts in and threatens dire punishment for all concerned in such nefarious traffic.'

'I am sure you must be tired of hearing about food,' said a new voice.

Alice turned and saw a scholastic person at her side. 'Are you a professor?' she asked respectfully.

'Correct,' replied the gentleman. 'I am Professor Toromento, LMT.'

'That degree is quite unknown to me,' said Alice.

'I daresay,' said the Professor. 'It means Licentiate of Mental Torture. I specialize in experimenting on the emotions.'

'In what way?' asked Alice, shocked.

'Various ways,' he swaggered. 'I have tried the effect of a Mental Vacuum on the internees. Formerly, news used to leak through from the hospital, but I have put a stop to all that and I now rigidly exclude all news from the outside world.'

'How cruel,' sighed Alice.

'Maybe,' answered Professor Toromento. 'Come and see my apparatus.'

Wonderingly, Alice followed him to where a kind of seesaw was erected, only one plank being visible. It was joined to a barrel-shaped machine labelled Mental Vacuum on one side and Secrecy on the other.

'What a strange machine,' said Alice. 'How does it work?'

'Well,' said the Professor patronizingly, 'as we are past-masters in the Secret Service, it is the easiest thing for us to create a Mental Vacuum. However, nature abhors a vacuum so we fill ours with Rumours. We know when the barrel is full when we see the internees gather in groups, talking and smiling, and the spirit of the campers rising mysteriously.'

As he spoke, he turned a handle, and the plank rose.

'I am beginning to understand,' said Alice.

'When there is a great wave of optimism it is time for me to act,' said the Professor. 'Watch.' He inserted some object into the barrel and the plank began to descend.

'What happened?' asked Alice.

'I sent an old newspaper into the camp, with news of our early successes during the war. Just enough to change the balance, as you see. Watch again.'

The plank began to rise once more. When it was quite high, the Professor passed a torpedo-like object through a slit in the barrel. Down came the plank with a terrific bang. 'A bolt from the blue,' he said, 'a sudden order to get ready to change camp, or a Rumour that things may worsen in a few months. Ha ha! I do so enjoy seeing the change from gaiety to gloom. Now they are afraid to believe anything they hear. As "Be Prepared" is our motto, we arrange Alerts at all hours of the day or night, so that nobody knows if they are real or faked. Now I shall explain another of my experiments, one known as Delayed Action. I announce that something will happen shortly, and then postpone the event at will. I love to see the internees hastily packing their goods, ready to move at a moment's notice, and then, after a fortnight or so, relapse into uncertainty!'

'How wearing on the nerves,' said Alice.

'Why should they have nerves?' asked the Professor. 'When they are listless, I use my opposite method of Precipitation. Without warning, I give orders for sudden action. It is funny to see the commotion, like an anthill being disturbed!' And he laughed heartily. 'Oh, and by the way, there is another little form of torture I use. I have allowed no communication with friends and relatives overseas except one postcard.'

'In *two years*!' gasped Alice.

'Of course,' chuckled the Professor. 'These insignificant women can mean nothing to their kinsfolk. But we make a concession to the women with husbands in neighbouring camps. We always let them know if their husbands have died.'

'Oh you stupid, ignorant monster of cruelty!' burst out Alice indignantly. Then she saw a look of apprehension, almost of fear, come into the Professor's eyes. Looking round, she saw the shadowy figure of a Red Cross nurse approaching. The nurse raised an accusing finger.

'What have you done with the hundreds of letters and parcels sent so lovingly and trustingly to those pining under your guardianship?' she demanded.

'There is a parcel on its way now,' said the Professor nervously. 'It will be distributed at once!'

'When was it sent?'

'Only eighteen months ago. What is that to complain of in a war of several years' duration?'

The Professor hastily departed. So did the nurse, leaving Alice alone and to ponder on what she had seen and heard. Her reverie was interrupted by a cheerful voice asking, 'Would you care to see my Conjuring Show?'

'I certainly need brightening up,' said Alice.

A stout figure in a tight uniform appeared from nowhere. 'I am the Wizard of WIC and can effect the most marvellous transformations with a wave of my hand,' he said.

'What is WIC?' asked Alice.

'Why, Women's Internment Camp, of course. Shall I repeat some of my performances for you? Shut your eyes. Now open them.'

Alice saw the compound covered with yellow dust, and with a few clumps of grass here and there. The Wizard waved his hand. Down came a shower of rain and Alice saw a quagmire of squelchy mud. It gradually took the form of regular rows of sweet potatoes and tapioca plants divided into plots by narrow yellow paths.

'What an improvement!' said Alice. 'How and why was it made?'

'We thought that the women weren't working hard enough,' said the Wizard, 'so we threatened that, as food would be short, they must plant their own vegetables. We used our own famous methods to tantalize them, of course. We encouraged them to dig plots, and supplied them with a great variety of seeds. And then, just when the first shoots were appearing, we scrapped this scheme. Pressed labour was used to dig up the whole compound. The women had to dig and manure (from the Septic Tank) and water the plants each day.'

'With water carried in from the hydrant, while they had to use dirty water for personal use, I suppose?' said Alice severely.

The Wizard looked annoyed. 'Who has been telling tales?' he demanded. 'It was just unfortunate that our gardening scheme synchronized with the worst drought known for many years. But we succeeded,' he added brightly. 'Look at those luxuriant plants – quite a credit!'

'Yes, but look at those miserable little yellow ones,' said Alice. But the Wizard was looking elsewhere.

'Now for another change,' he said. He waved his arm and the compound became dirty as before.

'Why this change?' asked Alice.

'Orders came to move camp and so *we* ordered the plants to be pulled up.'

'Were there any roots?' asked Alice.

'A few small ones,' said the Wizard. 'But there were plenty of leaves to eat. They provided food for two whole days – or was it three?'

'*Three days*' food after weeks of strenuous toil!' exclaimed Alice.

'Oh, discipline is good for the character,' said the Wizard. 'What right have these women to complain about using their hands? Our women take it as a matter of course.'

'Well, I don't think much of that transformation,' said Alice. 'It's as bad as those by which you have changed buxom women into walking skeletons and well-dressed ladies into Cinderellas . . . ' But she found herself talking into space; the Wizard had gone. 'Now I wonder if there is anything else to see in this sad place?' she mused.

'Yes.'

Looking round, Alice observed a worn woman carrying an empty disinfectant bottle in one hand and a grey bandage in the other.

'I am Hygeia,' said the woman, 'and I'm in a sad condition, as you can see. Come and sit with me outside the hospital, for I feel too weak to stand, and hear my tale.'

'From what I have heard and seen,' said Alice, 'I should think you have a desperate task trying to combat unhygienic conditions.'

Hygeia held up her empty bottle. 'With unlimited supplies it would have been difficult enough, but I now have nothing to help me except a few drops of disinfectant, a small number of pills and some bandages washed over and over again. Look at this one', and she showed Alice her discoloured bandage. 'Even old rags have been hard to get. Would you like a peep inside our clinic, though there isn't much to see.'

Alice saw a tiny room with a table holding a meagre assortment of ointments and powders.

'This is all we have,' said Hygeia, 'in spite of frequent appeals.'

'How lucky that you have doctors and nurses among your internees,' said Alice encouragingly.

'Yes, but workmen, however accomplished, cannot do much without tools or instruments,' moaned Hygeia sadly. 'Look in the hospital next door. Can you see any bedpans, bedrests or air pillows? Are there any invalid requirements such as hot water-bottles or thermometers? Even towels are scarce. Occasionally a small consignment of lint and sticking plaster is brought in, but it is used up immediately.' She put her head in her hands and sobbed. 'Oh, how I long for buckets of Keating's Powder and buckets of Chloride of Lime, for soap and hot water! I can assure you, it is utter misery to take ill in the middle of the night, for there is neither light nor water nor anything.'

'I suppose the diet, or lack of it, is responsible for many ills?' said Alice.

'It is the main cause,' sighed Hygeia. 'The entire camp is badly debilitated and unable to resist germs. Nerves are strained by uncertainty and ignorance of world happenings outside the camp. Our foes are numerous. There — see what menaces us continually.'

Alice saw a miserable-looking person holding a cigarette-tin passing by.

'Diarrhoea,' said Hygeia.

'Why has she a tin?' asked Alice.

'No toilet-paper or rags available, so water is used. There go Dysentery and Typhoid – whom I cannot fight without Medicine and proper food.'

'And this yellow-faced creature?' asked Alice.

'Malaria, of course. The swamp round the camp breeds mosquitoes and we cannot escape their attentions. Here comes Beri-beri suffering from our unbalanced diet.'

Alice saw a figure with puffy eyes and feet limping along. 'A pitiable sight indeed,' she said. Toothache and Eyestrain followed, while Heartstrain, due to the lifting of weights too heavy for a woman, dragged herself along. Last in the grim procession came a cloaked figure whose name Alice did not need to ask.

'So Death has visited the camp?' she whispered.

'Nine times already,' murmured Hygeia. 'And even the dead are deprived of their due. The only mortuary is an open shed. Coffins are often late in arriving and the hearse is an unswept lorry. No respect is shown by the guards.'

'A tale of woe, indeed,' said Alice. 'What will the world say when all these tragedies are brought to light? All that makes life lovely and worthy has been snatched from these women.'

Troopship

'You're alone on this sea,' a voice said, and I said under my breath, 'you're alone on this sea.'

I went away a moment, when those others weren't looking, I went right past her poop, I stood where her log was, saw that serpent's line spin out and wondered where, wondered how deep, she was. Saw that water thresh, I heard the sounds of her screws. Then I looked out, far out, beyond where that white log-line could end, and then I felt something, didn't know why it came, didn't know what it was, just went on looking, and suddenly I knew. Oh the vastness I saw.

James Hanley, 'Sailor's Song'

The extracts below are taken from notes kept by R. N. Currey during the voyage of the US *Trooper* from Gourock, Scotland, to Cape Town, South Africa, 16 June–21 July 1943. Ralph Currey was thirty-five, born in South Africa but educated in England, at Wadham College, Oxford. His wife was the novelist and playwright Stella Martin Currey and they had two small sons. He was now a gunner officer and was soon to be recognized as one of the best poets of the war. During the slow and fraught journey on the crowded troopship he managed to work at translating French poetry. Eventually, in India, he and Ronald Gibson, a journalist who had worked on *The Times of India* and who was now serving in the Royal Indian Army Service Corps, recognized the value of the poems being written by their fellow soldiers and other personnel, all of them forced into some kind of literary expression by the impact of the vast dominion. Their anthology, *Poems from India*, appeared in 1945, only two years before British India vanished. They found that these contributors, few of whom would have thought of themselves as professional writers, and all of whom had been brought up on the glories of imperial India, simply shed these Empire views once they had landed and wrote on what they themselves saw and experienced during their posting to this most disturbing of all Britain's possessions. There was much forces writing in India. Currey observed:

> It seems that despite the limitations of living in camps and cantonments, many of those serving out here are interested in India for what it is, and not merely as a more or less reluctant provider of commercial resources, facilities for *shikar*, cheap labour, and the mysterious 'glamour' that is so much more obvious from a high and spacious bungalow than from a *basha* or tent.

He too is on a journey which will transform his life. 'During the First War our civilian soldiers ranged over Europe and the Near East, feeling for the most part nostalgia for home and disgust with the countries they had by overrunning helped to spoil . . . By the Second War we were, as a nation, if not better informed about the peoples of other countries, at least more aware.' Lines by the Welsh poet Alun Lewis seemed to Currey to epitomize the loneliness of every soldier on his first arrival on the subcontinent, with all its 'size and strangeness' and the 'indefinite years of exile ahead'.

> I sit within the tent, within the darkness
> Of India, and the wind disturbs my lamp.

It is ironic that on his way to war he should round the Cape, that classically dangerous tip of his homeland. In comparison with the hundreds of men crammed aboard the US *Trooper*, few of whom had travelled further than to their local seaside resort in Britain, Currey 'had seen the world', as they said at the time. He writes against this innocence of not having gone far which shows ever more plainly on the faces of his comrades. He writes for himself, not for Stella or for a prospective book. He writes as an Hellenic poet who found himself being carried across dangerous waters on a warship might have written, alertly and making light of the miseries. When, earlier, he did complain, it was with good reason:

> This is a damned inhuman sort of war.
> I have been fighting in a dressing-gown
> Most of the night; I cannot see the guns,
> The sweating gun-detachments or the planes;
>
> I sweat down here before a symbol thrown
> Upon a screen, sift facts, initiate
> Swift calculations and swift orders; wait
> For the precise split-second to order fire . . .

16 June 1943. Said goodbye to Stella at Woolwich station, positively the last appearance for some time. As usual, long wait on parade. March off to men's parade. Long wait there. March down to station with some attempts at whistling and singing, an odd sight, a column of officers marching by, but nobody took much notice. Into train fairly soon, then a long wait while people bought beer from small boys who climbed down off a railway bridge like monkeys, carrying quart bottles. Long slow journey through suburbs, back windows filled with waving girls, women and children. They often seemed to wave to you individually: pleasantly affecting.

17 June. Long interesting journey, waking for a glimpse of Durham Cathedral, which I have never seen before, and for tea at Waverley Station. A journey I would have enjoyed in peace time, in spite of sleeping on the train sitting up, though the afternoon was exacting. Detrained at Greenock at 2 o'clock and did not get aboard until 7.30, all that time standing by one's kit on the deck of the tender. Found we were going on to an

American ship, so the voyage would be dry! Also some unwelcome rumours of our destination. We got on finally, and were allotted cabins by a gentlemanly ship's adjutant who knew Marcus B. Tod at Oriel, thus a disciple of the most polite don at Oxford, and rather too eager to accommodate officers to their liking – hence, perhaps, our long wait. A good cabin with a lavatory and shower and one distant porthole for six. These were myself, Barker from my regiment, Horner who was in the West Indies as a schoolmaster, Brunfitt who was at Margate and Portreath with me, Todd and T. R. Thompson. Had dinner at nine, chicken, fruit and cake, and coffee with cream. Hear we are to have only two meals a day, but this was an excellent one.

18 June. Breakfast shows just how much rationing has affected us in Britain. Coffee, cream with porridge, the hardly remembered shipboard procession of fish, bacon and egg, toast and marmalade. One man asked for the marmalade and the steward put a heaped tablespoonful on each of our plates. I wish I could send some of this home. There is no real shortage there, but crumbs off my present rich man's table would give them treats. Dinner tonight was so good that you couldn't avoid going through most of it. One's system insisted on it, but not without misgivings. Nothing to do all day but walk round crowded decks in the rain. The men are horribly crowded everywhere. I hope their food is correspondingly as good as ours. No place to sit except in cabin. Three on my camp bed, one on end of camp bed in porthole alley, one in chair, and others standing or lying. Perhaps things will be better organized when we get going. Have written Stella a letter which can only reach her after some time, and which will mystify her by telling her so little. But it is best to write, I am sure. This is a wonderful port, and it was lovely to see it in yesterday's sunshine. Join the army and see the world! A world like the schoolboy's skeleton, with the outside taken off and the inside taken out. But that's not fair!

Wind rises tonight, with rain blowing over the decks. Sheltering at intervals. Skirling of bagpipes comes in gusts over the water, and we see in a launch that is dancing wildly someone just recognizable as a piper. He should be playing, 'Over the Sea to Skye', but the bursts of music form no pattern.

Rumours abound. We know how big – or how small – our ship is and have an idea about the number of men it is carrying. Beyond that we guess and listen to guesses. We are going to Alexandria, to Syria, to India round the Cape, even to Texas for oil. We are going in a large convoy, in a small convoy. A ship we can see is full of ATS, WAAFs – full of Circassian slave girls. We will see them at Gibraltar and New York, Murmansk and Shangri-la!

No news from the outside world. Still cut off and still not moving. The waiter told us that this ship carried some German and Italian officers from, or to, New York. The Germans were still convinced that Hitler was going to win, but were dumbfounded by the number of ships in Gourock harbour. 'What are all these ships?' Couldn't believe their eyes. Today's activities between our two widely separated meals consisted of hunting for luggage in the dark hold and buying cigarettes, etc., and one or two meetings re duties and boat drill. Buying cigarettes quite a pilgrimage. Have to buy for a whole cabin and can only buy in bulk. So a trip into the bowels of the ship and a long queue, with a disappointing result. The tobacco gone before we got there. So I have no tobacco and may not have any for the long time that it takes to get to Shangri-la. Quite a lot of milk chocolate. I *wish* I could send some to James and Andrew. The striking thing about today? Two ideas. B says the thing that strikes him is that everyone has now settled down. We talk rumours but accept what is coming to us without question. My feeling is that it is an odd day because we are quite cut off but have not started, being suspended, as it were, just off the ground.

Later, 11.45 p.m. There are more obvious reasons to remember today. At 9.45 p.m. we sailed! The anchors were drawn up with

a fearful noise while I was searching for luggage in the forward
hold. Came on deck to get glimpse of ships and misty waterside
towns. Saw the pilot dropped and move off waving, a small
rugged figure. A few minutes previously we had passed the
submarine net. Once outside the harbour we carry life-jackets at
all times, and must sleep in our clothes for the first three nights.
'Canvas shoes may be worn.' It's a hell of a long way out on to
the decks; some of the men are terribly far down. We are being
allotted duties, i.e. sleeping down there with them from today.
Final reason for remembering today – put second pip up and
hardly noticed it.

20 June (*Sunday*). In some respects a *dies non*. I was queasy
most of the day. I intended to go down to dinner but failed at
the last minute. Sailing along in a convoy gives a pleasant feeling
of tempered security. You do feel you have a chance of being
picked up. My chief fear is not being able to get out on to one of
the decks through jamming of doors by the crowds trying to get
through them. One of the lads in this cabin is the brother of
Ruthven Todd whose verses I have been aware of for some time.
I find Horner and Thompson went to Monkton Combe.
Thompson was at Cambridge with Terence Tiller and John
Manifold. Thing that stands out in my mind for the day is
Thompson reading out a review from Todd's copy of *Poetry*.
'My God, they let each other have it, these minor poets! Listen
to this: "He does discriminate between the flavour of one small
poet and another, Kenneth Allott, Ruthven Todd, Geoffrey
Grigson, Dylan Thomas and Day Lewis ... " I've never seen
such bollockings as they give each other!'

I think of Waley's translation of General Sulike's poem to his
wife: 'I suddenly remember the distance I must travel ... With
all your might enjoy the Spring flowers, but do not forget the
time of our love and pride. Know that if I live I will come back
again ...' (*c.* 100 BC).

21 June. The American padre on this ship works hard, Chaplain

Parker. He is a sort of welfare and entertainment officer. Reading the news: 'This is the news, but it is not Stuart Hibbert reading it.' He *always* starts the daily prayer with the words, 'Remember now thy Creator in the days of thy youth ... ' Community singing last night. Chaplain Parker led us in a 'Transport Song' of his own composition:

> We'll get you guys across
> You'll get two meals a day and that is all
> You'll get them standing if you eat them at all
> You'll get no water to wash your neck
> You'll be sea-sick and you'll smell like heck
> We'll get you guys across.

His use of the word 'across' fits with the ship having been used previously to carry American troops, even more tightly packed than we were, on the five-day crossing from the US to Britain.

Was on duty for the first time today in the bowels of the ship. I have to take my stretcher to the top of a wide staircase leading down to a deck-section containing tiers of bunks, and spend the night there, armed with a revolver in order to be able to discourage troops from rushing up the stairs in confusion if we are torpedoed. The men throw their letters on my bed for me to censor. A misty evening with some dropping of depth-charges and some racing round the fringes by destroyers. I was below on duty when two went off. They sounded like big-ends pushing through sumps in the engine-room. Up on deck, when some were dropped earlier, our steward said, 'A coupla trash-cans going over the side!'

22 *June*. Had to go down to the hold again and found I wasn't as far recovered as I thought. Everyone ill today in some way or another. Had an extra duty on account of there being two 'dead men' in our lot. Read half of *A Sentimental Journey*. Thin after *Tristram Shandy*. On late duty spoke to a Rhodesian pilot who knows South Africa, and also to a Free State Afrikaans-speaking

Air Force Captain. The place must have changed unrecognizably, and will be a power to reckon with after the war. The Afrikaner was very bitter about Tobruk. Some excitement after dinner when a destroyer made a wide sweep and some depth-charges were dropped simultaneously on the other side. Did some more censoring of letters, often pathetic, sometimes puerile. Sometimes amazingly brave. 'To think that I am doing what I would have to pay over a hundred pounds for in peace time!' A thing I forgot to put down yesterday was an all-in wrestling match in one of the well-decks. They were, I was told, just 'two chinas' amusing themselves. Whenever they broke from a clinch they chopped at each other with the backs of their hands, taking off pieces of skin. They were strutting round in their wounded splendour for hours afterwards.

The fore-deck now is rather like Blackpool without women, tea or newspapers. Men play housey-housey, or Bingo, and scatter paper scorers. There is talk now of classes in Urdu, the Indians on board assuming a new importance.

Have been on a raft-launching party, so it seems that chances of escaping in a lifeboat are slender. Our steward has been 'bumped' three times, twice in the last war, and once in this. He was in a lifeboat in the North Sea for half an hour, in a lifeboat in the Med, and adrift in the Pacific for three days.

25 June. An extraordinary event this afternoon, or so it seemed to us. Half the convoy and its escort left us without fuss, apparently making for the Straits of Gibraltar. I have heard farewell speeches on less solemn occasions. Had an 'abandon ship' alarm late in the evening. Went to my post in the bows, talking late with an OCTU friend while watching first the orange sunset and then the lace effects of the bow-wave, and of phosphorescent gleams in the hurrying water. Hot enough for me to try sleeping on deck tomorrow?

26 June. An army concert which I attended after coming off duty. Rows of us sitting on life-jackets. Very good cushions. The interesting thing about this concert is its absolute conformity to type. A tenor who sang 'Trees', a sergeant who told sergeantish jokes, a major who recited 'The Green Eye of the Little Yellow God'. We sang 'Land of Hope and Glory'. Chatted with A who was stationed in Malaya, and who has visited Bali. Says their sandstone temples are constantly recarved. Married recently and baby due in a month's time. Rumours continue to fly around. Our next port of call will be Freetown, where we will change to another boat. Why? The only thing I like about our apparent destination is the route we seem to be taking to get to it!

27 *June*. Had the doubtful pleasure last night of sleeping on D deck with the troops. Amazing how their bunks are fitted in. Metal frames with canvas stretched between; two singles side by side in tiers of four, 2 feet 6 inches between each. Perhaps 3 feet 6 inches between top bunk and ceiling. Sets of eight, sixteen and thirty-two as space allows. Men on top bunk use projections on which to put odd items of kit, but kit-bag and small-kit clutter the floor-space between the tiers of beds. A tendency to smoking which had to be curbed. Passed one of the Canary Islands at breakfast time. Saw a sailing boat. Tried my hand at translating Baudelaire's 'Journey to Cytherea'. Paper-back anthology, but no French dictionary. Passing the Canaries in cloud and thinking about what is to come, the poem has meant something individual to me:

> Free as a bird, I feel my winged heart run
> And soar above the rigging joyously;
> This sailing ship, beneath a cloudless sky,
> Rolls like a glittering angel drunk with sun.

28 *June*. Today, after parade, saw some flying fish from the well-deck not much above the surface of the sea. Was astonished afresh at their delicate marine colouring. Also noticed that they have tail-plane fins as well as wings, albeit set rather far up the fuselage. They seem to fly about fifteen to twenty feet only

before diving out of sight. Looking for them is rather like looking for a shooting star.

Some difficulty this morning over men who wanted to get to the lavatories just before parade; these were closed for an hour to restore head of water for flushing, but a most stupid time. I had to send the most pressed cases to the sick bay to perform there. As the naval MO said to me, 'Nature has a way of building up its own pressure at this time.'

I've been watching the phosphorescence, the bow-wave cream-ing over and being reproduced in miniature by lesser waves all along the side of the ship, repeatedly spreading out into shawl-like patterns of open-work lace. The night is dark and there is no moon. The ship is subject to rigid blackout, there is not a cigarette or torch, yet the water on the edge of the ship is as luminous as if the lower ports were open and stretches out behind in a broad white shaft of light. This is background for the phosphorescent effects. On it are thrown handfuls of stars, luminous gleams that come and go, pools of light that flash on and flash off. This ugly old tub moves through the water turning up unbelievable beauty in the same way as boys, with dirty necks and pockets full of gobstoppers, sing like angels.

29 June. Finished off and sealed a number of letters, hoping they will go from Freetown when we arrive there; apparently we cannot go ashore. This ship seems to have hundreds of decks. Above A deck there is an intermediate deck, then the boat-deck (officers'), and a higher deck still. The bridge is one above this. The decks go down to E, eight altogether without the bridge, and I do duty on D deck. Getting infinitely hotter. Rather overpoweringly so, and I had TAB and Tet-tox today. Today we began the study of Urdu, sitting on life-jackets under a companion-way, near some cages of homing pigeons. I connect problems of Urdu grammar with their rank smell.

The sunset was astonishing this evening. Men crowded the rails and filled the deck, staring at it in silence. I've never seen anything like it, even those in Jamaica seen from Barbican. The complete circle of sea with the convoy making small purposeful marks across it, an expanse of almost glass-smooth sea. As the light grew less strong it took on first a grey, and then a green-grey, then a succession of red shades, brick-red, heliotrope, maroon, each one covering the water as far as the eye could go. Meanwhile the whole circle of the sky took part. The sun went down in a tremendous patch of magnificent red, tapering off to orange and yellow, and then to a prune colour in a broad band along the horizon. Above this lavishing of colour were tier on tier of clouds, looking as stable as mountains, and above these came the dome of the sky, a pale duck-egg blue with little cotton-wool tufts on it, and a single brilliant planet.

Then the heat. The ventilation system broke down when I was on duty on D deck and the heat was appalling. I took a number of men up to the deck to sleep, a hopeless job trying to help them in complete darkness full of standing and recumbent bodies. Then had to return to the Black Hole of Calcutta. Made what inquiries we could. The dynamo had broken down. It was ghastly down there. Heat, airlessness and sweating human bodies. I don't sweat easily but was soaked. Heard next morning that one man had gone off his head and tried to knife somebody. This among the crew. Air came on about midnight, then failed in the early hours. I woke at 5.30 feeling terrible. A sticky paste all over me. Heavy and stupid. Had a shower and went on deck. Dodged men hosing the deck until 9.30. Breakfast postponed half an hour.

1 July. A day of expecting to see land. Urdu class in morning. Saw first signs of land about five; came into Freetown harbour at 6.45. I was at dinner and on duty immediately afterwards, but had one glimpse in the half-darkness. A grand thing to see land again. And no blackout! My best moment of the day was when a small French boat passed. Two matelots in striped jerseys and red-button berets. Very black natives in very red fezzes. Something lifted right out of the pages of *Babar the Baby Elephant*! Anti-mosquito precautions. Ports shut and mosquito ointment.

2 July. Spent a long time last night looking at the lights of Freetown. The excitement felt by everyone was shown most clearly by the men sitting side by side on their lit-up deck singing, very well indeed, all the old nostalgics.

Up first thing this morning to have a look at the land. Two tiny canoes suddenly appeared alongside. The men seemed to bale out by pushing one foot forward. The bigger of the two canoes was painted with the name J. P. Black and was immediately christened 'Blackout' by the troops. The canoe men dived for 'Glasgow tanners', refusing to take any notice of pennies. One, catching a lighted fag-end, put it in his mouth and puffed out smoke. 'All right!' he said. A penny wrapped in silver paper won the remark, 'Bastard half-crown!'

Amusing scene after dinner. Lights all round the harbour. Cigarettes shining out of the dark. A warm scented night. The men's singing was interrupted by a kilted officer playing the pipes on the boat-deck. A contest between the singing and the pipes, the pipes winning. Loud cheers and boos from the foredeck interrupted by a transatlantic voice through a porthole: 'Say, what are you doing? I got to be on watch at 4 a.m.'

The ventilators on D deck broke down again, the effect in port seeming even worse than when we were at sea. Spent some hours making my way up, through various channels, to the ship's adjutant, and was sent on by him to the ship's captain on the bridge. He surprised me by being a German, Captain Krugenberger. I asked permission to have the portholes opened on D deck while we were in harbour, and he gave permission, insisting on certain safeguards, for alternate portholes to be opened, explaining that he never knew when they might have to make a sudden move.

3 July. Have been reading a life of Cobbett today. Most interesting. Conversations with H and a South African naval officer who has been shell-shocked. His father fought against us in the Boer War. A member of Smuts' commando when it went down into Cape Province. Name Walker. Very pleasant to stand outside talking until late. H's great-uncle was an RSM in the Crimean War. H had his sash at home. The great-uncle wept when there was no action. He died in the regiment and had a military funeral. After the funeral the colonel said, 'Dismiss now. Go back to your quarters without getting drunk.'

4 July. We had hoped to have letters here, but they now seem unlikely until we have reached our destination. Asked about a half-sunk ship on our way into the harbour. Told by a former Merchant Cruiser officer that it was sunk in 1940, along with three others – all hit simultaneously.

5 July. No news bulletins since July 1st. Started to sail this morning but halted by a signal from the Depot ship. I was astonished to see through a glass that the Depot ship was the *Edinburgh Castle*, which must have been of some age when I travelled on it as a child in 1910.

Translated most of Villon's 'Regrets de la belle heaulmière'.

> I heard the woman who used to be
> The lovely helmet-maker sigh
> For her lost youth.

Long talk with the RAF chaplain who knew Peter Howard in the Oxford Group. Peter Howard is his prophet on earth. I'm afraid I need more conviction. Every kind of story to explain our non-starting.

6 July. Left Freetown before breakfast when it was possible to get a clearer view of the land. The name Sierra Leone gives an accurate idea of the general look of the place. A destroyer stopped this morning to deal with a lifeboat floating in the sea. Not possible to see if there were any survivors in it. Saw some porpoises while on boat-drill in the well-deck from very close. First a mother and daughter – or father and son – performing a smooth roll out of the water and under it again. A lovely sight. They were as fat and sleek as English carthorses going to a show. One expected ribbons to be woven into their tails. Though they moved fast, they came out with a solid motion rather than with the quicksilver movement of salmon. I wish my own two boys had been there to see them.

> Over the bow-wave, smoothly sliding,
> Two plump porpoises ambled away,
> Sleek shire-horses, mother and daughter,
> Groomed tails plaited with ribands gay;
> Away from the well-deck, packed with pitiless
> Human predicament, shabby and grey,
> Over the bow-wave, smoothly sliding,
> On that bright morning I rode away.

It was announced later that twenty-seven survivors from a boat had been picked up. One of three. Also some news bulletins for the first time since July 1st. German advance in Russia and unconfirmed landing in Italy.

7 July. Slept on D deck. An alarming increase of cases of dysentery. Have had to surrender my camp bed to hospital. Rumour that an RAMC major has thrown in his hand because ship's authorities won't co-operate – they give no food or drink to sick men. He threatens to report them when we land. No meat for dinner. Is this a precedent?

9 July. Time marches on. Most people are bored to death, but I am fortunate in having the translations. Decent weather, although very near the line. Translated de Vigny's 'Le Cor'.

> How sad it sounds at night, in the deep woods
> Singing of hunted stags in their last grief.

Class in Urdu. These up to the present start about three quarters of an hour before breakfast. We collect on B deck aft, just forward of the rear gun, which is roped in. A corner where men sitting as close as on Brighton beach scramble to their feet and make off. We settle ourselves on our lifebelts on the drier spots, preferably with something to lean against. The place I had first smelt undefinably insanitary, and proved to be just round the corner from the pigeon cotes. Ahmed, our excellent teacher, goes through a rule at a time, with some twenty officers repeating after him. There is a ceaseless stream of men down the gangway, a disturbing element, to say the least, and as we do not take up all the corner, air-force men climb into the few feet to one side of us and sit there reading, or staring interestedly at this bunch of officers repeating unnameable combinations of sound. Sometimes a parade is held in this corner, men standing in three ranks, and more or less on each other's feet, while a corporal issues instructions. Our lesson is surprisingly interesting, but one's bottom goes to sleep.

10 July. Invasion of Sicily. The main interest today. Have only seen the headlines after American news about the Solomons, Fortresses, etc. Some excitement during boat-drill. Fog-horns, guns manned, ships changing relative positions, destroyers circling and dropping depth-charges. Talk with Belgian airman about French poetry while on duty in the bowels. Airmen playing cards at our feet as well as piled up in tiers all round us. I had asked him the meaning of a word in a poem I was translating. Reading it, he said, 'This is very good!' and declaimed line after line. Real enthusiasm.

Fragment of overheard conversation: 'Had a date with a pusher called Susie for Tuesday. Found I was going on leave on Saturday, so flogged the date to a Chinaman for two bob. She didn't turn up, so the Chinaman wanted his money back.'

11 July. Odd view of two religious services as I walked round the boat-deck. On one well-deck a short plump Presbyterian officer in a kilt hammering out his points: 'He haad compaassion on him! He haad compaassion on him!' On the other, the American padre, collar open and one hand in his pocket: 'Yes, and she was mighty purty to look at!'

Translated Gautier's 'Chinoiserie'. Very dissatisfied. Needs to be hard and enclosed in brittle rhymes, and we haven't got the necessary English ones . . . She whom I love lives in a far domain . . . In a high tower of delicate porcelain.

Our odd progress, mostly NW, for the last day or two – to avoid U-boats, the pundits say – leads to some other ships joining us. Trying out my hose-tops and puttees. Seems something unworthy of record, but when in an atmosphere of sleep and boredom I took these pieces of uniform out, Br, who had worn puttees on Gibraltar, made an occasion of it – 'Just so, and this bit to be cut off.' Mine the puttees, myself the unwilling patient, and T, suffering from some illness in the upper bunk, leans over to give the full weight of his advice. Later in the evening he brought me a poem to criticize.

13 July. Enough to make me superstitious. It appears to have been decided that, owing to lost days, and consequent food and water shortages, we will call at Cape Town instead of Durban. The end of more than one daydream. I had hoped that the Government might be doing for me what I have not yet been able to do for myself, show me Durban again. We have now been twenty-four days at sea. Apparently, we crossed the Equator last night. Weather very cloudy, overcast and quite cold.

Have just finished Neil Bell's *So Perish the Roses*, a delightful life of Charles and Mary Lamb. Most touching account of her outbursts of insanity. A word about the blowers which ventilate this cabin. Since the weather has been less hot they have been doubly powerful. But you need the air they bring. The cabin soon becomes impossible without them, though the noise is deafening. Someone compared it, not unfairly, with the noise on a tube train. You have to shout across the cabin.

14 July. Curiously cold weather for this region. Water smooth as glass and dirty. Near mouth of the Congo? Low mist but not bad on deck. Had a long and interesting chat with Surgeon-

Commander L, who tells me that he was at Uni. when I was at Wadham. He pointed out that it was the Quatorze Juillet and prophesied a landing in France to celebrate it. A French ship in the convoy 'hung out its washing' this morning to do so. He described his first crossing of the Line in the Navy. He had recently inoculated the crew and it had proved rather a strong brew. When they reached the Equator everyone was gunning for him, and he was tried by Neptune's Court on a list of charges which included 'Pumping rat-poison into the crew'. Sentenced to the maximum penalty: three duckings upside-down in each tank and a dose of purgative pills. I got some tobacco at Navy prices. Fantastic. Two pounds for five shillings. Distributed it round the cabin. Chaps flabbergasted when asked only sevenpence-halfpenny for a quarter pound.

Have noticed recently the very different effect of an overcast sky in Equatorial regions to that in England. Here, with a much stronger light behind the clouds, the effect is at once more luminous and milky, like opal. Sometimes the whole sea and sky is this colour, especially in the morning and evening. Opal. There are fiery lights shining through. I can still remember the opal effect in England. I once wrote a poem to Stella starting: 'I found a new world on an opal morning . . . '

Washing. Salt water only. I wash shirts through in water I have washed myself in, a cupful to rinse after. Result better than expected. Two strange creatures carry on a laundry, permitted to do this by the men of importance on the same basis as Jewish usury in the Middle Ages. They scrounge water, soap and a place to wash in, and also irons, and lay down the law to their less mighty customers. Must be making a good sum of money. We have some Marines with us and they know how to wash in salt water. The rest of us don't. They look much smarter than anyone else.

16 July. A new restlessness in the air. Definite orders for prepara-tions for reaching port. Scrambling visits to the baggage-hold and I can foresee some days of further scrambles. Another morning of opalescent sea and sky. Pearls and opals are the jewels of the tropics. Memories of Conrad and his correct use of 'opalescent'.

17 July. I have thought a lot about Coleridge in this weather, and this morning even believed that I had seen an albatross, but I am told an albatross is white and this bird had a white body and very long black wings. A Norwegian told me that these birds were called 'shoemakers' in his language. Definitely cooler, with banks of fog. Ships' paravanes look like spouting whales. Amazing sight at night. Banks of fog slipping over the ship so low that the full moon shines brightly through it where it has thinned. The effect on the sea is as water running over stones. Lifeboats glistening in the moonlight through the fog.

18 July. Stella's birthday and unable to do anything about it.
   Finished a version of Théophile Gautier's 'Symphonie en blanc majeur' with the lines,

> O, who can bring a hint of rose
> To that indomitable white?

   Chief event of today is an attempt to get down to the baggage-hold with some hundreds of other officers also trying. One entry only through a trap in a bulkhead and down a ladder. Increasing wind all day, a wind you can't stand up against. The moonlit expanse of sea didn't look level at all, but like a glistening desert of ridges and hills, with the suggestion of an immense crater depression not far away. Slept in the bowels last night and felt the effect of it tonight. Fell into a stupid sleep after dinner.

19 July. A fairly rough sea. Strong wind and some squeamishness. Post closed today. Wonder if there will be any mail when we arrive at Cape Town. Attempts to write stillborn. Depth-charges. Marvellous to watch destroyers in rough sea. Some manoeuvring among ships, partly to put out the paravanes. Very cunning how these work.

20 July. Smoother as the day went on. A great blessing to me. Mounting excitement as we approach – or believe we do. Venus very bright, and I have now identified the Southern Cross. I had thought of the fifth star as more central and had forgotten the system of working the pointers.

21 July. Sighted land soon after breakfast and came into sight of Lion's Head, Devil's Peak and Signal Hill, all covered with cloud, at about 10.30, and soon afterwards into marvellous full frontal view of Table Mountain, the top hidden in cloud. A very fine sight. Circled the Bay over and over, testing the paravanes, then came in. Saw the South African flag for the first time to notice it. Very un-British, as of course it is meant to be. Tied up in Duncan Dock at 3 p.m. prompt, the time scheduled. All flags at half-mast for Sir Patrick Duncan's death [Governor-General of South Africa, who had died in office on 17 July 1943]. The words 'Nie rook nie' [No Smoking] painted across one of the corrugated-iron buildings. The sight of African natives slapping their bare feet along the dock satisfyingly familiar. Very exciting to see South Africa again. Cannot go ashore tonight. When can we?

Twenty years later Lt R. N. Currey's son James, while working against apartheid with Patrick Duncan, the son of the Governor-General, had to jump from a ship in Duncan Dock to avoid the South African Police.

   As Ralph Currey's journey carried him to active service in India and to an appreciation of the writings of servicemen and servicewomen, his wife, Stella, sent him these letters.

Mount Harry Road, Sevenoaks, Kent.
6 June 1943

Darling Ralph,

I wonder where you are this evening? It seems six months instead of only a day since that horrible moment in the rain at Woolwich Station. When I got home last evening Jean had begun bathing James and Andrew, and your mother persuaded me to have a meal while she got them into bed. Then Jean and Ian very kindly took me out to The Vine. I did appreciate it. Since Ian has been invalided out he is so exhausted when he gets back from London in the evening. I went to bed early and only woke up a couple of times. No sirens and no carrying the children downstairs. I have decided to go back to Daventry next Tuesday. Then I must try and get down to some writing again. How I hate the thought of there being no possibility of being interrupted by you! I wonder when you will get this? The children guess and guess. The train from London Bridge was very crowded last night. An amusing interlude about feet. A man was sitting in a corner and objecting to the way another man was placing his feet. 'I'd like to point out, before you tread on my feet again that my feet were here before your feet.' 'There are six of us standing in this carriage. We can't hang ourselves from the rack, you know!' said the other. 'You'd like me to twist my feet under the seat, I suppose, so you'd be completely free?'

Two manuscripts, from the *Listener* and the *Observer*, arrived today. I will send them elsewhere when we get back to Daventry. I must try to work hard at writing in order to achieve something – and also to make time pass! James was talking about a camping holiday after the war. 'Andrew and I will have a tent, and you and Daddy can have a nice cosy sleep in the caravan.' Oh, for such a sleep.

Stella

Kingsthorpe, Badby Road, Daventry.
23 June 1943

Darling Ralph,

We are at Daventry again. I find it very depressing to return, something about seeing your shirts and things waiting neatly back from the laundry. But there it is. I'm not used to it yet. It's going to take a long time to get used to it – if ever. It's time we were back. I felt your mother had had about enough. She looks worn out these days. She was before we went, so it isn't just us. James said tonight, 'I don't feel quite settled at Daventry yet.' He did enjoy it at Sevenoaks, and both kids were extraordinarily good. I was very pleased with them. Today we had a very pleasant quiet journey. Your father came down to the station and saw us on to the train. James was very braced at the grand view we had of St Paul's. The view is good coming into Charing Cross now that the bombs have removed so much of the grubby foreground. I had promised to take them across London in the Underground, and they loved that. And the electric train *was* red, as ordered ... I miss you very much and am very glad I have some work to do in addition to looking after the children.

   Stella

Daventry
26 June 1943

Darling Ralph,

We have just received your first letter. So good to have, though you are allowed to tell us so tantalizingly little. I am so relieved that wherever you are you are happy and comfortable, and that you have good people with you. We are sending you a telegram this afternoon and hope that you will get it before too long. We talk and think of you constantly. Poor old Shandy. I hope you are not right about distemper taking a long time to get over. James is going to add a word or two to this.

THANK YOU FOR THE LETR AND I HOPE YOU WUL HAV SUM
ORANGES
LOVE JAMES XXX

PS Andrew has drawn a train on the back. Not a bad one either!
Stella

Daventry
29 June 1943
My darling,
Another word with you. There's nothing further *from* you, of
course. It's beautifully warm here and there is a good breeze
from the East. The children are sitting on the rug you left and
singing an absurd song in which the refrain 'Spatter, Spatter,
SPAT!' seems to be the chief ingredient. Both kids have just got
up and are dancing with pleasure because a sparrow is in
Shandy's dinner bowl, having a glorious wallow among old bits
of toast. James is very bucked because he made thirteen runs this
morning. He sat down when he came in from school and gave
me a full account – the first of many such, I fear! No letters to
do with writing this week. I haven't been doing enough to get
missives from Curtis Brown. No news about your works. However, I have had a letter from your mother this week, and the
family has had a joint letter from Brother Hal. He has been out
to dinner with some of the local Arab potentates, and had a
colossal meal of the sort T. E. Lawrence describes. It lasted
about two hours. Your mother was delighted to get a letter from
you. She says that one small portion of it had been censored. No
part of mine was. She says it must have been some quite
innocent remark you made beginning 'Dad, you would have
been surprised ...' She says Joan, writing from Ipswich,
described a dream she had searching for you in room after room
in Barbican ... I wonder if you have been doing any writing on
the ship?
Love from
Stella

Daventry
2 July 1943

My darling,

The children and I are in our permanent abiding place, the garden. James is sitting on the top of a ladder, fishing, Andrew walking about with no shoes on, fishing as well. It's a brilliantly sunny day. I expect you'd think it was mercifully cool. Five high altitude planes have just gone over, glistening like minute fish. Aunt Jane came yesterday, full of beans. She has made arrangements for us to stay the first fortnight in August at Strode farm and the second fortnight in the empty flat in the Vicarage, so we will be away the whole month. It will give everybody a change and give the kids a good start for the winter. James and Andrew are entranced with the idea of going to the sea. Clevedon being so near Bristol means we shall be able to see Grace much more than usual. Lovely. I shall try to fit in as much writing as I can, and after viewing my bank statement this morning I feel some such effort is necessary. I have got about £35 credit, which is rather less than I thought I had, as I hadn't subtracted the £14 4s. every month as I should have done. I have about £14 to come from Curtis Brown, and that's about all I can count on at present. RA wrote today from Colchester with the rent for the house. I'll write you another of these letters straight away . . . I miss you terribly.

　　Stella

Daventry
6 July 1943

Darling,

I wonder what you are doing at this minute. I am sitting on James's bed, endeavouring to prize Andrew out of his afternoon lethargy. This morning he came very early into my room, and within a few minutes succeeded in scratching me severely on the nose with his toenail. Afterwards I said, 'Aren't you sorry to have scratched Mummy?' and he said, 'I didn't, my toenail did it.' I said, 'But doesn't your mind tell your toe what to do?' 'Yes,' he said, 'my mind told my toe not to do it, but it did.'

Two days ago I said to Andrew, 'Who is coming home today?' (Meaning Kate.) He smiled seraphically, 'Daddy!' he said. I sent off one of the copies of the *Dublin Magazine* to you yesterday, with your story in it.

Your row of parsley is splendid and we will be eating your peas from now on. The cucumbers under the frame are quite good. I wonder where you are. Goodbye till tomorrow or the next day. I hope you are well and the old battleground is not giving any trouble.

Stella

Daventry
11 July 1943

My darling,

Yesterday the invasion of Sicily started. We are all waiting now to see how things are going. Do you remember that morning when you were on leave and that Canadian convoy thundered down Badby Road? At the time we all muttered about Canadians being the spearhead of an attack, and now it appears that the Canadians who left this country 'some time ago' may have been in on this job. The men who went through here were so obviously well equipped in every way, that I suppose it is quite likely that they went to Sicily. You, James and Andrew were waving at them, and now those men are probably in Sicily, and you are Lord knows where!

Yesterday a very strange convoy got stuck outside in the rain. We decided it might be animals or pigeons. If it hadn't been for the routine army paint it would have had the slightly rakish air of a circus. Andrew, Shandy and I went for a walk after the convoy left. The weather at the moment seems to be good for the crops and detrimental to the tempers of adults. It is a joy to go walking in the rain and see how magnificent the wheat-fields

are. Great fat ears waving at you over hedges. The land looks fit
to burst with plenty. This week we've had lots of cherries, not
without rather high expense, but it's worth it for the moment. Is
there anything prettier than Andrew eating cherries, a bunch of
them clasped in his fat hands! Quiet for quite a long time, he
asks, 'Can I have another cherry? Just one more, and that's the
end.' He says he is going to put a kiss for you in this letter. I kiss
you too.

    Stella

                                               Daventry
                                      13 July 1943

My darling,

    I am upstairs in the bedroom at the top of the house where
Andrew and James are sleeping while Aunt Frances and Uncle
Douglas are here. The boys have got the floor laid out in a
fearful and wonderful way, a farm, a zoo, a railway and a car
park. They love being up here in the attic. As you know, we
don't have many sirens here, but if we do it's a long way down.
Mother always makes a party of it when we're all together
downstairs at night. It's difficult to get to sleep afterwards.

    It's been quite exciting talking to Uncle Douglas about his
rehabilitation of the captured Italian ship at Freetown. On his
way out he had to sleep in the Pilgrims to Mecca Hospital as he,
and the second mate he had taken out to help him, had to give
up their cabin to the Commodore of the convoy. When they got
to the ship, which was supposed to be well-found and well
stocked with everything, they discovered it had been stripped by
natives who had carried everything away in their canoes. Not a
spanner, a screw-driver or a length of piping. He got the ship
refitted, and found a crew for it. Then he managed to take it to
Rio de Janeiro and bring it back from there with a valuable
cargo. Wasn't that amazing! He had to go up to London immediately to report this, and received many congratulations. He
was told, 'Now you want a month's holiday.' So now that is
what he is having.

Today we hear that the Allies are in the outskirts of Ragusa. We keep being told that much worse things are going to happen and that the fighting in Sicily hasn't begun. I kiss you goodbye.

Stella

Daventry
16 July 1943

My darling R,

I thought about you particularly this morning at breakfast when I heard from Curtis Brown that John Long, a subsidiary of Hutchinson's, have taken my novel *Following Charles*. When anything like this happens I so much want you to be here, for it would be so much more fun to talk with you about it than with anybody else. At any rate, this is what Mrs Curtis Brown wrote: 'I am very glad to tell you that John Long are definitely prepared to take *Following Charles*. They would pay the same royalties as Cassell did for *Marry we Must* . . . with an advance of £40. They seem extremely keen on the book and think they have sufficient paper to bring it out fairly soon.' Darling, I am wondering now when we shall hear about *This Other Planet* [R. N. Currey's poems written, as he said, 'as an artillery officer of exile in a world of mechanistic killing' and published in 1945.] They are so slow. I do so long to hear something good. I feel we will somehow. Uncle Douglas and Aunt F were at breakfast with us when the Curtis Brown letter arrived. Aunt Frances, after reading it, asked if she could show it to Douglas, saying, 'I don't expect he's seen anything like this before.' He read it through, and then came round the table to me, and gave me a mighty shake of the hand. 'Many congratulations, Stella!' he said. In anybody else this would be funny, but you couldn't make fun of his solemnity. He is such a likeable, sincere person. I really have enjoyed hearing about the captured ship and feel I have been reading an exciting seafaring book. Darling, I will write again tomorrow. You might let me know where you *really* are!!!

Stella

Daventry
18 July 1943

My Sweetheart,

I have already written you a longish letter today by ordinary mail, but I send this as well because it is my birthday. Tomorrow night I am going to see *Thunder Rock* as a small birthday treat. It's a film about a man in a lighthouse on one of the great Canadian lakes who is visited by the ghosts of people who were drowned there seventy years before. Anyway, it has been well reviewed, and I wish I was seeing it with you. Interval for telling James that he must not say he will kill Andrew! To proceed, the boys are now tumbling and racing together, making an awful noise. I am wondering if the proofs of my novel will come while I am at Clevedon. I hope they won't but they may do. Andrew has just come up to ask if walruses love us. I have had to reply in the negative, and he says, 'Why don't they?' and looks ready to burst into tears.

Stella

Daventry
20 July 1943

My darling,

Somebody told me they had already heard from their son, who had left England roughly at the same time as you, so apparently you are not in North Africa, or I would have heard as well. Uncle Douglas seemed to think that most of the traffic to India would still be going round the Cape. If so, you might have a chance to look in at Cape Town and your beloved Durban.

I keep thinking how lucky the children are to have such grandparents here. Mother plays quite a lot with them, and loves Shandy. As for Daddy, when James is at school on a rainy day, Andrew often ends up with Shandy in the knee-hole of his grandfather's desk in the study, while an *Uncle* story drifts down from above. [Stella's father, the Reverend J. P. Martin, was then writing his classic *Uncle* stories for children. They were published in 1965.] On Saturdays Daddy often makes a point of bathing the boys, saying to me, 'Scrubbing them gives my hands a good soak for Sunday!' This evening the two kids put on a circus for the benefit of Kate and myself. They dipped blue and green pastels in water and covered their faces with colour. This made them incredibly soft and blossomy. They dressed up in old coats and hats and did turns.

James reads to Andrew in the mornings now. He reads with tremendous expression ... Now I am going to put Shandy to bed and will go myself. Would that you were coming with me!
Stella

Daventry
26 September 1943
Darling ... John and Mabs are here. John looks very well in his uniform, with three stripes up. He is now at Morpeth, near Newcastle, on one of those bomb-disposal sites of about twenty miles radius, so that everybody has to cycle everywhere. [Stella's brother John Martin was later awarded the British Empire Medal, Military Division, for bomb disposal].

I have decided, now that Andrew is a little older, that I ought to do some voluntary work. I am going to help for one day a week at the British Restaurant. I began on Friday by serving 290 portions of cabbage. It is really hard work from eleven to two-thirty. Certainly I think that the shilling dinner they get is awfully good value. People can send in and get large tureens filled and take them home. I've also agreed to do some packing of munition parts from the Ordnance Depot at Weedon. Your father is sitting on the floor at present with the boys, playing with their Indian soldiers and bricks. I do hope the prickly heat is better.
Love
Stella

It's Being So Cheerful As Keeps Me Going

TOMMY HANDLEY: Lumme, what's this apparition coming along?

MONA LOTT: It's all right, sir – it's only me – they've made me 'Miss Waterworks of 1943' . . . I drive around to each reservoir and say my little piece . . .

O water, sparkling water,
A boon to both the sexes;
You slake the thirst of Stafford Cripps
And wash the schoolboys' neckses.

TOMMY HANDLEY: Who wrote that? T. S. Eliot?

MONA LOTT: No, sir. Mr Drip the Sanitary Engineer.

Ted Kavanagh, *ITMA*

From a hospital in Bath Mrs Cheeseman writes to her brother Gunner Fred Hawkridge, serving in the Middle East. Joan Cheeseman has a broken leg. She is what they used to call 'a scream' and has an unrelenting cheerfulness. Such cheerfulness, though ghastly, was a much admired feature of the Home Front. Behind her determination to amuse her brother lies a realist with a considerable literary ability with which to sketch the temporary muddle in which she finds herself. The letters were sent during the spring of 1945.

Dear Fred,

Had my leg re-set on Monday. Came round crying and announced I was 'so happy'. They asked me if I'd like some water so I said I'd *like* a double whisky. We had a super sort of tart for supper last night. Marvellous sort of almond paste and things. A nurse passed the end of my bed with a piece in her hand murmuring in hollow tones to no one in particular, 'Lovely for the bowels. A real stuffer-up.' Everyone thinks I am 24 or 25. Good God, good God! Oh my hat! But I think I'm going to die. No I'm not; we're going to have a cup of tea.

. . . Actually, the lorry driver lost his head. It was a lorry towing another. The lorry behind had a driver too. Jack [her husband] is basing the hopes of compensation on the fact that no arrangement had been made against the possibility of the rear one over-running the forward one. I think my letters to you have been rather dreary and queer, and yes it is the fear of being thought a fool, or perhaps of being thought *afraid* that keeps me from making a fuss. I can remember a big doctor saying, 'How's your bottom?' and me saying, 'Fine thanks, how's yours?' I felt awful the first time I saw the newspapers with the accident in them, and hearing people say, 'How wonderful!' and all that. No, they were not Yankee lorries, so you can ease the boys' [Fred's comrades] minds about *that*. If they had been I'd be playing a harp by now, as they move much too fast. Bung ho! I'm OK.

. . . For Gawd's sake look after your legs. Irene, a young girl (she's 33 but only looks the same age as me), was playing skittles, threw the ball, twisted her muscles, and they broke her leg. And the others in the ward here 'just fell down' and broke their legs. Old Girl has a vicar come to see her. He's the Parable type. Talks as though he's reading. Amazing. He told her that she needed a rest and that this was the way (a broken leg) God found to give it to her. I've been unable to write before in answer to your air-letters as I've not been able to get any air-letters. I shrieked with mirth re. Vera and the jeep. Some Yanks picked her up, she said. At times jeeps could almost be used as taxis – at a price!

. . . This time last year I was in the throes of childbirth and wondering why that sort of thing has to happen, and asking, 'Muvver was it werf it.' In the next ward there's a Cockney lad with a shattered thigh. I thought he was about 40 but he's only 26 and he's made the most marvellous things. He's awfully nice. Help anybody – and 'do' anybody too. I've been here nearly six weeks, oh dear. I'm *very* pleased that you're off the beer, or almost off, for the sake of your paunch.

. . . With feeble fingers a Broken Woman takes up her pen to write a few lines. I have five clergymen to my score. Now this may sound rather a strange thing to say, rather as though I've spent my time, gun in hand, round church lintels stalking unwary men of God. But five clergymen have visited me – no, five clergymen *and* our Church Worker. They flock from far and near. There is Woggly (the curate), the Rector, the RC priest (say that quickly), the Vicar of Box ('Only witness') and a ghastly local affair who visited me today. He swept up in his gown and said, 'Mrs Cheeseman?' and held out a soft, very feeble paw. It rested limply in my hand for a moment and then he quickly withdrew it. 'I've heard about you.' 'What a blessing,' I said. I have yet to meet someone who hasn't either seen my accident or who knows someone who has. Mrs Light's husband was the policeman called to the scene and Irene knows the ambulanceman who took me away, and Dorinda's mother was on the bus which was held up until the road was clear. Gosh, Ice Cream?? They're just bringing round Ice Cream. Ice Cream. Ice Cream. Cheerio.

The Cockerel and the Woman Opposite are discussing Lexicon – you know, the spelling game. They're waxing quite eloquent about it. The Cockerel said, 'It's a nice game, I'm sure, so laughable.' Sister is in the ward. It is a pity. I'm not a great smoker but I likes me fag when I wants me fag. 'Oh my godfather' has Gone Home, if you get the significance of the capital letters. I heard her die. Beyond me I can see nothing but the end of the page. I've made a pair of black and white gloves that look really smart. To go with them I am going to make a small white lamb in felt, and sew the edges with black. This is to wear with my grey costume. They tell me Vera was met in London by Margo in – the only place – Piccadilly. She was not hawking her wares, as you might suppose, but just taking a stroll! She's going around with a Dutch soldier. I'm writing with the wireless on. By gosh, It's plenty jive!

. . . I would have been very thrilled indeed to receive 'cheering notes' from the boys. I've always wanted to have a more personal touch with them. What simple souls men are. Had Jack been the type to object, do you think I'd have been fool enough to show him their letters? I presume that Marjorie has hurried off a letter to you telling of her engagement to Woggly, the Reverend Alan Brown. Help. But he's got a heart of gold, I'm sure, if nothing else.

. . . Aren't the prison camp stories horrible – and the Photos. But I do think they ought to be shown and also to give the full details of everything the Nazis have done. Fancy women SS men! Such horrible faces. They ought to be handed over to women themselves. Actually, women are worse than men when they get going, I'm sure of that.

I read in a Woman's Paper that we must Expect Our Men Back Hardened. I am sure they will be. You will be pleased to hear that the skewer-like rod which pinned the fracture has gorn! But gosh, the going! The Doc buzzed up with a thing like a starting-handle and fixed it to the protruding end of the rod, or Steinemann Pin, as it is called – I shut my eyes. He twisted it round about three times and then pulled . . . I sat there like a stuffed rabbit afterwards, waiting for the Doc to go, and then burst into tears. Now, isn't this funny, after all that I drempt I was skating.

> Twinkle, twinkle, little star,
> Went for a ride in a Yankee's car.
> What she did she ain't admittin'
> But what she's knittin'
> Ain't for Britain.

Bung ho
Joan

Gunner Fred Hawkridge's letters from the Mediterranean Expeditionary Force to his family evacuated to Bath are racy but protective.
Although he is abroad for the whole of the war he remains the man of
the house. His regiment sailed for the East in January 1941. The
following is from a letter to his mother.

The sergeant says I have to tell you that he has a cold. I said,
'Do you think my people care if you have a cold?' 'I shouldn't
think so,' he said, 'but you never know.' The exploits of Freddie
the Fearless Fly, Korky the Cat and Desperate Dan still receive
our earnest attention and the adventures of Hungry Horace and
Hair Oil Hal delight the stooges [his mates] beyond measure.

It is difficult to write as I am in my hammock, swaying from
side to side as the 'liner's stern ploughs the foam'. In the
morning, of course, we 'lash up and stow' the hammocks. We
have orders not to use so much bad language – unprecedented in
the Army's history, I should think. I have heard of appeals by
the padre for a toning-down of blasphemy and obscenity but it is
a new one on me for actual *orders* to be issued to that effect.
'And a very good thing too,' you will say. But it is woefully hard
upon the sergeants, who will be expected to show an example. I
hope Bath still remains unbombed and that Marjorie will not go
back to London. Neither you, Joan or Marjorie should return
until the war is over, no matter how little London may be
attacked as the war goes on.

There are many different dialects at each Mess table and
Barbara would love to hear the West Country accents, and the
Eastern Counties' accents, the latter seem to be spoken by living
characters from any of S. L. Bensusan's short stories. It is very
nice to get the weekly airgraphs – one good invention that the
war has brought about. For our Christmas 'do' we have to put
up a very large tent, and the fellows are organizing a concert,

etc. Still, 'Oh, what's a table, richly spread, without a woman at its head?' Mail is not so copious lately, so there is little to write about. Doubtless, the North African affair is occupying the mail. Planes, I mean. They are no doubt using them for bombs instead of mail. I'm wearing my overcoat, so cannot write easily, hence poor calligraphy. Also I'm using ink Made in Germany which does not allow the pen to slide over paper. Yea, verily, the weather is somewhat colder now, and how the Wogs stick it out in their flimsy nighties I'm sure I don't know.

Fancy the poor old Duke of Kent getting bumped off. Still, why not: it's good propaganda that our Royal Family should not only be bombed, but suffer loss like the man in the street. I've sent you an ornate-looking Crucifix I purchased in Jerusalem whilst on leave. Very fine workmanship. Also a New Testament with wooden covers made from olive wood actually from the Mount of Olives.

Letters from India

> The war proved educational for nearly all classes, including
> the British.
>
> Byron Farwell, *The Armies of the Raj*

The realities of India after the high romance and Empire pride accorded it in the British education system, and in the popular view of the vast subcontinent which appeared in novels and films, came as both a shock and a stimulus to the serviceman. The shock was caused by the scale of the poverty and the void which existed between the native population and the white men and women who had ruled it for centuries, while the stimulus lay in its scenery and ancient culture. Letters, journals, stories and poems poured from the country to families and friends at home. Those from Troop-Sergeant Clive Branson of the Royal Armoured Corps were not at all typical, for he was by birth a member of the Anglo-Indian establishment, an army officer's son born in Ahmadnagar, Maharashtra, in 1907, and was sent home in the usual way to an English public school (Bedford) to be trained to take his place among the sahibs. Instead he became an artist, studying at the Slade; he exhibited at the Royal Academy by the time he was twenty-three and had shows at the Lefevre Gallery. But soon after the outbreak of civil war in Spain on 18 July 1936, Branson forsook all this youthful success to join the International Brigade of Anti-Fascists. Four years earlier he had become a Communist and like countless of his contemporaries had every reason to see the world in strictly Right and Left attitudes. Franco and his Italian and German assistants confirmed the Left's fears. Branson, both in Spain and during the Second World War, was a passionate warrior for Socialism. Although captured soon after landing in Spain and thrown into a concentration camp, he was soon back in England running an International Brigade campaign to raise over five thousand pounds to spend on medicine and food. Harry Pollitt, the Communist leader, described Branson living in Battersea and painting feverishly during the interval between the end of the Spanish Civil War and being called up to fight against Hitler in 1941 because 'it may be my last chance'.

It was. Branson continued to draw and paint until he was killed in Burma in 1944, but it was the moral and political implications of the struggle against the Right which absorbed all his energies and imagination, leaving little time for art. Whether as a social worker and educationalist in Battersea, or a prisoner, or an NCO, his mixture of natural authority and selflessness, informality and cool logic made him both loved and formidable. He died in action on the Arakan Front aged thirty-seven. A young soldier who was by his side wrote this obituary: 'He now lies buried somewhere among the green-covered hills, but he has left us a high idea of the meaning of human dignity and the immortality of life. Our new humours and reversed outlooks are monuments to his mental virility. It now remains for us to honour him and justify the risks he freely encountered.'

After hearing of her husband's death, Branson's widow allowed the Communist Party to publish his letters to her, and also part of his diary. Their account of an India so close to independence and yet so unaware of it is radical and vivid. As an Anglo-Indian, he is scathing about the snobbery and philistinism which pervades the Raj, and about imperialism generally. He reveals the ordinary British soldiers in a kind of limbo, having no place in this glorious piece of their own Empire. They take shelter from its vastness and complexities in the cinema, YMCA, NAAFI and brothel. He gets into trouble for his perpetual asking, 'Why this?' 'Why that?' as he rocks the military or Raj boat, the unforgivable sin. The artist side of him is strong and often gets the better of his politics. Landscape and human nature, the beauties of person and place intoxicate him. He writes like some short-lived saint who is torn between the wonders of the earth as it is, even with all its unfairness and stupidity, and the splendours of life as it should be — he believes, will be — come the revolution. This revolution will not be a bloodbath; rather men will grow up and come to their senses. In Spain and India he is not fighting in the revolution but for the conditions which must bring it about after the defeat of Fascism. Like so many idealists of the time, his writing lacks almost all notion of what will actually occur after the war, and especially in India.

Bombay
May 1942

So it is India! I have arrived very fit, and in good spirits. On the boat, I ended by giving many lectures on the International Brigade, and found many friends. Although I have been in India a little time there is one problem which hits you in the face — the life of the peasantry; and, in Bombay, the housing. But oh what a people this is for painting! I shall make many small notes and studies for pictures when this bloody business is over. Gad Sir — when I was in Poona in '42 . . .

I am continually struck by the extraordinary dignity of the little girls out here. I shall never forget one tiny wee tot walking by a field. She walked along bolt upright. She had a turquoise blue dress (blouse-skirt, European kind), jet black hair, dark face and, behind her, there were brilliant, luscious green stalks of young sugar springing up and curving their new yellow-emerald leaves just above her head.

These last few days I have been suffering from an upset tummy which has not improved my temper when dealing with those bloody idiots in the regular army who want to indulge in abuse of the Indians. They treat the Indians in such a way which not only makes one tremble for the future but which makes one ashamed of being one of them. Really, some of the most ignorant men here are to be pitied. They joined the regular army to get away from family trouble in Blighty. They never write home,

they try to suppress all feelings about Blighty, they vent their
own misfortunes on any hapless and helpless Indian, and they
look upon army life as a scramble for good jobs. The art of war,
the character of war, the outcome of the war outside of India
do not concern them; they dare not let themselves be concerned
for fear of burning homesickness that smoulders beneath their
simulated toughness. I had the chance of talking to a few – my
God, what *hideous* lives they lead. Eternally on the scrounge for
petty gain; eternally feeling they have been swindled by the
paymaster, by the canteen, the shopkeeper, etc., and therefore
ready always to swindle someone else; disunited by the bitterness
of life and yet united by their common fear of life and common
hatred of the individual to whom they attribute at the moment
their exile from humanity.

Gulunche
Nr Poona
20 June 1942

You have little idea how badly we need the news of the
second front – it is the difference between a body of good,
stolid-humoured Britishers and an inspired army of warriors.
This morning we went out on a scheme on foot in units
representing tanks. We covered ten or twelve miles or more over
ploughed fields. It was magnificent exercise and although I felt
pretty tired I enjoyed it no end. That sort of thing will make real
soldiers of us.

But tonight I had a terrible set-back. On parade this morning
we were asked who had seen active service. I said I had. When
we came back from the scheme I was told that I was to go on an
inspection by the Duke of Gloucester in a few days' time. This
parade is purely bullshit. It will take several days to polish
boots, brasses, etc. It will take days and nights for some eight
Indian tailors to alter, clean, press, etc. clothes for the white
sahibs to wear like bloody waxworks. The Indians, of course,
will not be on parade, the lucky fools. I have often been asked,
'Have we got a fifth column here?' Yes, we have! For nothing

could help the enemy more by undermining morale, destroying enthusiasm and making us incompetent fighters than this kind of tomfoolery. The farce develops. This morning we had an inspection. The Duke's show is in five days' time. On *the* day we get up at 5 a.m. Our clothes will be packed in boxes and taken by lorry to the scene of battle, where we will get into them. Sebastopol is falling and our CO is disappointed at the lack of polish on the topee chin straps.

Well, the Duke's show is over, at immense expenditure of precious petrol, wear and tear of vehicles, deadening bullshit. The Duke merely shook hands with unit commanders and squadron leaders – the men just didn't exist. Today a General paid us a visit. In one squadron they had many men change into PT kit, some ready to box, some to do PT, some to form two basket-ball teams, etc. They were kept sitting about doing nothing for ages until a scout saw the General's car. The scout signalled, and immediately everyone began boxing and playing basket-ball. As soon as the General disappeared the men were marched back to their tents. This is how things are going on here.

As a result of the rain the country has a lovely rich earth and green look about it; what enormous wealth could be produced if real irrigation was organized! I am feeling very tired and depressed, mainly because everything here is like a mad-house though apparently quite sane to the superior inmates.

Dhond
7 November 1942

This afternoon I went for a walk in Dhond City! A modern railway line with great steel engines runs by the straw, tin and sackcloth 'houses' of the people. A huge engine of war roars past a settlement of the poorest of the poor. Dhond is derelict, filthy and poverty-stricken – I mean where people live, not the workshops, etc. Whatever is put across the Indian people, nothing can argue against the logic of their living conditions in contrast to the motor-cars that mock their bullock carts. And, however much people at home believe in British imperialism, there are four hundred millions who *know* by bitter daily experience the reality.

The other day, out of the blue, I was interviewed by my squadron leader and adjutant re. my doing some painting, with the promise that any cost of materials would be met by the RRI. Now I know it may sound just like cussedness on my part, but I cannot get up any enthusiasm to paint life in the army. If I paint at all, I want to paint the Indians. Of course I want to paint – just as I want to live. But my conception of life is my conception of painting. I don't paint things I want to forget, and this is not a people's war so far as we are concerned – there is nothing constructive in our motive for fighting – we are the unwilling tool of progress.

I have just got back from a swim – it was lovely. It is of course piping hot – a cruel sun that makes the earth sand-dry even within a few yards of the water's edge; and the green long leaves of the young sugar cane glint like bayonets. But oh, the ghastly poverty of the Indian people! Wherever one goes it is the same thing. Little clumps, sometimes village-size, of broken stone walls, sacking, bits of tin, corrugated iron propped against a wall, and matting, called 'home' by millions of human beings. In the middle, or nearby, a temple or a church, and far away in the cities the swine who live wealthily. I am fit, working hard and quite happy under the circumstances.

Bombay

> Come with me and I will show you,
> Almost hidden in the shadow
> Of an Indian night,
> Pavements strewn with human bodies
> That with all the other shit
> The authorities forget
> Even to worry about.
> Here's one
> Still lives, though all his flesh has gone.

The vulture remains invisible
Till the meal is insensible,
But Life is not so patient as the vulture,
In India, not so poetical.

Ahmadnagar
10 July 1943

Today I went into the Mess to look at a paper and heard a
sergeant say to a friend, 'The Gerries have begun their offensive.'
There came over me once again that feeling of combined anger
and frustration that I felt over Spain and have felt ever since
Dunkirk. I suppose now we will 'stand amazed' for the third
time running at our heroic allies, present them with more golden
swords – and make dozens of speeches reminding ourselves of
Tunisia, etc., till it makes one feel as ashamed as one did in
those terrible days of Munich and Barcelona.

Men condemned for years on end
To suffer freedom to do nothing.
The white-washed sky is their cell walls
And earth the floor they walk along
To nowhere. Everything is theirs,
Trees, fields, birds, wealth, tanks, gems,
So long as they don't do, don't think, don't
Want to buy with their wages, build
With their hands and enjoy
Life that is living. They've been warned
'Who wants to take the storm up in both hands
And break this calm to smithereens
Shall go to prison.'

At table there were a lot of cynical remarks all arising from
the same feelings as I have. One sergeant from Lancashire said,
'In Blighty last month there were big manoeuvres. Landing
operations on a big scale. No joking. We took Blackpool from
the Canadians.' You have no idea how deeply angry the men are
at the fact of thousands of soldiers just sitting around.

On leave in Bombay
18 July 1943

I caught the train from Ahmadnagar, and on arrival here tried
to get a room at the YMCA – full up. So I went round to the hotel
where I have stayed before and am paying 12 rupees a day all in.

This morning I spent several hours with the comrades. We
had a long discussion. I had a meal with them, Indian fashion,
and wore sandals and no socks while I was there.

This evening I had a sad experience. It came about in this
way. I saw an advert in a shop window on a lecture on the
modern Mahratti novel organized by the PEN Club. So I went,
both to hear the lecture and, at the back of my mind, with an
idea that I might meet someone to talk with. The lecture was
excellent. Then we all came out and one of the audience – all
were Indians except myself – pushed towards me obviously to
speak to me, so I said, 'Very interesting lecture – I enjoyed it
enormously.'

'How was it you came – did you see a notice in the papers?'

'No. I saw one in a bookshop window.'

'I was just wondering. It's strange to see a soldier at a meeting.'

And the whole thing dawned on me – in their minds I was a
foreign soldier, in an army occupying their country, and therefore
must have been *sent* to the meeting. My answer didn't satisfy
him in the least – not even when I showed him I wanted to learn
about India – having read Tagore I wanted to read more.
Whatever propaganda is put over here – and however much by
an accident of history we may be on the side of democracy –
Indians who think know just what we are.

Well, I followed up the lecture by buying a little book
produced by the PEN called *Indo-Anglian Literature*. On page
43 it describes Mulk Raj Anand, who is actively connected with
the All-India Progressive Writers' Association and the author of
Coolie, *Untouchable* and *The Village*. I thought to myself, here
at last is the kind of book I want about Indians. So I go to two
of the largest bookshops. They tell me politely they have none of
his books in stock, and then one assistant blurts out, '*Coolie* is

banned.' I was livid with anger. In this bookshop you can buy
Mein Kampf and the autobiography of Bose, and everywhere
filthy literature and photographs, but novels about the Indian
people by a progressive Indian writer are banned! Words fail one
sometimes to describe the hypocrisy of the British ruling class
when they pose as champions of culture and democracy.

2 December 1943

Every experience I have had out here bears out the fact that
Indians have a tremendous respect for cultured Englishmen –
they speak with most profound gratitude of the work of the
English director of the Calcutta School of Painting who virtually
re-awoke Indian artists to Indian art. I have been promised when
I come back here I shall be taken to see a very famous Indian artist.

It is December 4th and we are again on the move. It is nearing
zero hour. One cannot say this and this are the things I am
thinking of, except perhaps a concentration on clothes – darning,
buttons, vests, socks and pants, etc. All day I have been sewing
clothes and in general preparing for the day ahead – trying to get
every detail arranged, underclothes washed and so on. I will post
this letter as soon as I can, as of course I don't know what is
going to happen next.

Always remember that one is given by fate only one lifetime in
which to live and work for humanity. There is no greater crime
in my opinion than to renounce the world, no matter for what
excuse. If anything should happen to either of us, never say, 'It is
finished.' For we have both lived for one purpose, the emancipa-
tion of the working people. If by chance one of us has to leave
this work before it is done, then let the other go on and see it
through – not in the spirit of holy sacrifice, as a monk or a nun,
but even more in the fullness of human experience. What we
miss we can only find in knowing humanity more deeply and not
in the ever narrowing circumference of private memories ...
Whatever happens you must go on *living* – there are so many
years of grand work ahead.

Today we got our orders for tomorrow,
A few brief sentences as a title page
Preludes a book. Each one wonders how
The story will turn out. What's over the edge?

22 December 1943

It is still very difficult to write. Our Colonel gave us a lecture the other day during which he said, 'I told GHQ that if you were not used I would take my hounds away altogether; but I hope to get you blooded nevertheless.' The phrases were familiar, but I could not help thinking of Fred [Friedrich Engels] who also rode to hounds and had ideas about warfare.

4 January 1944

I have just seen a little fish coloured black and yellow, like a wasp. There are also other fish with horizontal lines for camouflage. Also a number of fish constructed very like a lizard – a very long body which is curled up when they rest on the sand or on a rock. I have not been able to get close enough to see whether, under the fins, there were legs or just two stumps. It is staggering what one can see here. I have found butterflies with a similar pattern on the wing as our peacock butterfly, and the case above of the zebra-wasp-tiger-fish camouflage seems to hint at some law of coloration. I have come across a common creeper with purple flowers, the leaves of which are in pairs. The colour when old is gold-yellow, when fresh a green which goes golden when the sunlight shines through them. This creeper is the hunting-ground of a yellow-gold butterfly whose wing shape is exactly the same as that of the leaves.

16 January 1944

From now on my letters will consist of scraps of paper written at odd moments during the coming campaign. We are only a few miles from the front line, and yet see very little sign of war – an occasional distant barrage, a few aeroplanes and, yesterday, A A puffs chasing a Jap machine. As to my own feelings, very rarely I feel a tinge of fear, plus regret. In the main I worry whether I shall command my tank as a Communist ought. I only hope I shall do the job efficiently. I am keeping very fit; in spite of being many years older than most of the fellows, I can still do everything they do, except run – there I am beat.

My gunner, Monte, has just got back from a trip to the forward area. What most impressed him is that while the British and Japs shell, mortar and bomb each other, cattle continue to graze on the battlefield, and peasants with children work on the road and farmsteads. He came across five graves of British soldiers, with the only mark a beer bottle – no cross, etc. The fellows, on hearing this, said it was a fine sign of good spirits, and just as good as any other tombstone.

26 January 1944

We are now only a few hundred yards away from glory. 'There are those who would like to philosophize on the question of sacrificing space to gain time.' You will remember the reference. But even so, it is still like a mad hatter's picnic. We make our beds down, we sit around and chat, we sunbathe (not so openly as before) and we sleep. While overhead scream mortars, etc. To this, and all other incidents of war, such as AA, Jap planes, or our own barrage, the lads react with 'Ignore it' or 'Quiet!', and just carry on sleeping or reading. But I must say one thought runs through my head continually – Spain. This morning a party is going to watch some strategic bombing. I am sending two others of my crew on the principle that the more each man knows of the landscape, the better in every way. The bombers are just coming over. We climbed up on our tanks to have a grandstand view of twelve Liberators and dozens of Vengeance dive-bombers exterminating the Jap positions at Razabil cross-roads. Now that the bombers have gone there is a real barrage of small stuff. This may be the solution of the Burma problem. Now I am ever so excited to hear the reports of what was the effect. It may seem strange to you that in a sort of way I cannot help gloating over the affair. It is the reverse of Spain a hundredfold.

4 February 1944

This morning we cleaned up the tank, made ourselves more comfortable and prepared for rain, and did some washing. One fellow caught a snake about eighteen inches long, green on top and, just behind the head, a salmon pink. I have just seen what may be the smallest moth I have ever seen, white, with blue-black markings on wings, and light brown head. I must get ready for a tank commander's lecture.

Today a VIP is turning up, so we have to be in overalls, boots and berets, instead of our usual shorts and stripped to the waist. 'How long have you been in the army? Always in this regiment? How long troop sergeant? Find things all right in this country?' And in everyone's mind is one thought, how to get on with the war, instead of being asked useless questions. After the 'do' we recalled all the Generals we had been inspected by. Later we reminisced about games we'd played and seen. My driver, who had been quiet all the time, suddenly chimed in, 'The only team I ever played for was the street team. I was in reserve. We called ourselves the Primrose Juniors. Whenever the other side got rough, the reserves were called up. It always ended in a scrap.' He comes from Glasgow and is broad as he is tall, but with quite a baby face – an *excellent* lad.

Clive Branson was killed just three weeks after writing this letter to his wife during the fighting for the Ngankedank Pass. 'Life here glides by like a falling leaf,' he had told her just before moving up to the battlefields of Burma. A few months later, his letters to her were published by the British Communist Party and entitled *A British Soldier in India*.

War, the Temporary Distraction

—◦—

7 March 1944. In the army men live conscious all the time that their hearts, roots, origins lie elsewhere in some other life. They live as a planet lives revolving round its parent sun. They measure the hardships, privations, weariness here against the memory of a past that they hope to continue in the future ... Since their hearts reside elsewhere they face the present with an armoured countenance.

Keith Vaughan, *Journal*

Captain David Elliot typified a generation of young people whose revulsion of war, born of the catastrophe of 1914–18, had to be set aside when the evils of international Fascism became a threatening reality. His letters to his sister, Diana, recently married to John Collins, the future canon of St Paul's Cathedral and leader of the nuclear disarmament movement and of the anti-apartheid movement, are a good example of how so many men fought for a more equitable Britain of the future while fighting Hitler.

Elliot personified the English upper-class ideal of athlete–scholar. At Rugby he captained the School Cricket XI and at Oxford (Christ Church) the University Squash team, and was thus a half-blue. And also, both at school and Oxford – and very much when fighting with the 1st Army in Africa and Italy – he was absorbed in philosophy, poetry, novels and music. He joined up soon after war was declared and was commissioned in the Welsh Guards. At the beginning of 1943 his battalion was sent to North Africa, and in February 1944 to Italy, where it was ordered to take part in the battle for Cassino. Its object was to capture the summit of Monte Cesasole, where the Germans were in possession. On the morning of 11 February Captain Elliot was killed while leading the successful attack on this summit in terrible winter weather. He was twenty-four. His letters to his sister reveal an impatience to get the war over so that they can both get down to the urgent business of seeing that Britain alters its old ways. He writes with unconscious self-assurance and authority in the last full year of his life.

APO 450 5
19 February 1943

All that the above address signifies is a vineyard somewhere in North Africa. We disembarked in a beautiful warm sun and showed the flag by marching through the town. We received quite a good applause from the populace. I wonder if this fickle mob would have done the same had we been Germans? Probably. The country flat as a pancake but with snowcapped mountains not ten miles away. Wine and fruit are the main products. So you find a good many orchards – oranges, tangerines, lemons, grapefruit, and field upon field of vines. The local vin rosé is excellent, the vin rouge very robust and full of the grape. The Muscadel is practically the most intoxicating in the world. The natives – berbers or arabs from the mountains, bare of foot, clad mostly in old sacking – do practically no work at all on the land and live by thieving. They sell us fruit and eggs at exorbitant prices. One of the guardsmen managed to sell one two left shoes for 100 francs (10/-). We print a daily news sheet and a list of useful French phrases. Not wishing to give official sanction to illicit love, we have not included any of the language of love.

5 March 1943

I am very well and very happy. How shall I put it? There is a certitude in one's immediate life.

9 March 1943

I have a very great deal to thank you for in the way of mail –
Picture Posts, *New Statesmen*, Penguins, *Life of Talbot*,*Dialogue
of Death* † etc. and two most excellent pipes. How really clever of
you to get the shortstemmed type which do not break nearly so
easily. Your letter about Richard Hillary ‡ arrived today. I was
most interested. Don't send me *The Last Enemy*, as I devoured it
about eight months ago. I should be able to repay you in part. I
have just been on four days' leave in Tunis, arriving back today,
and I am sending you a pair of unwearable shoes, or rather
sandals, and two highly coloured scarves which you may find
wearable or merely of academic interest. I have also sent what
delights in the name of a 'chemisette'. I hope you find an
occasion on which to wear it. It really is rather French. Tunis
was almost civilized – after three and a half months of
barbarism it seemed wonderful. Without a doubt the most
striking thing was how extremely well dressed the girls were,
and with what beautiful colours. You will see a sample of them
in the scarves. The cathedral at midnight mass on Sunday was a
sight for sore eyes – nothing but exquisitely dressed women.
Irreligiously enough, I walked round the aisles and had a really
good look.

I have visited Fondouk and the holy city of Kairouan –
untouched by war. This lovely sounding name is merely a
corruption of Caravan. No doubt you have read many descriptions of the place, the fourth and last of the Moslem holy cities.
The great mosque is full of Roman pillars and very fine
woodwork – cedar of Lebanon and plane tree – preserved by the
yearly anointing of olive oil. There were two lovely pillars of
porphyry. The second mosque I visited was much revered,

---

* E. S. Talbot (1844–1934), Bishop of Winchester.
† *Four Dialogues of the Dead*, by Matthew Prior (1664–1721).
‡ Richard Hillary's autobiography, *The Last Enemy* (1942), challenged the
  current service memoirs with its painful, inverted heroism. Arthur Koestler
  believed that 'his name had become one of the symbolic names of this war'.

harbouring, so it was said, three hairs of the prophet's beard.
The holy gentleman who took us round was clad very conspicu-
ously in Army socks.

More about Tunis. There is tremendous propaganda by posters
and newspapers for General de Gaulle. The majority of people
are, I am sure, de Gaullist. The poster itself is interesting. Above
his picture are the words 'Honneur et Patrie' and below, 'Voici
le Général de Gaulle' – the implication being of course, 'here's
the general whom you've heard so much about of late, but until
then had no idea that he existed'.

13 March 1943

The nearer one is to the actual fighting, the less one knows of
the circumstances of the 'Cause' for which we are fighting. I did
not know anything about the reception given to the Beveridge
Report in the House, so if in your letters you could give me a
commentary on the political problems at home and abroad
(especially North Africa!), and perhaps cut out and send me any
newspaper articles of interest, I should then be able to take my
place as a knowledgeable citizen of the world. If also you could
send me *Picture Post* and the *New Statesman* I should be in the
seventh heaven. Could you also send me two more pipes, some
writing-paper and envelopes and a flannel. I fear I am becoming
importunate.

I have been reading *The Spirit of Man** – actually for the first
time since I arrived in North Africa. The desire to read poetry is
with me very strongly. I expect that everyone at home is pretty
disappointed with the course of this North African campaign.
That is a feeling shared by us out here. It would appear to be a
stalemate, with the Germans slightly the stronger and holding
the initiative. Three nights ago I took out my first fighting patrol
at night. We lay in wait for the Boche for nine hours, but he did
not turn up, so our long vigil was for nothing. This was I think

* *The Spirit of Man*, by Robert Bridges (1916).

one of the hardest things which I have ever done – to lie down in the dewy grass, and know that for nine hours one must keep awake and motionless.

25 March 1943

Two nights ago the moon reached its fullness and there is good reason to hope that the weather will be more fine than otherwise. We have been floundering about in mud ever since we arrived and it is difficult for anyone actually here to understand why there is no big offensive yet. I am longing to get home, but nevertheless my morale and fighting spirit are very high.

20 April 1943

Regarding the heavy bombing, a prisoner taken out here had a letter from Germany with these words, 'When you meet the Tommies – remember Berlin.' I don't suppose that I shall ever see the film of the 8th Army – I should be especially interested to compare it artistically with the German film of Victory in the West, notable for its magnificent music. I left hospital on the 12th, still feeling pretty tired, and succeeded in finding my battalion on the 16th. In hospital I read, among other things, The Spanish Farm* and The Mill on the Floss,† both of which I enjoyed immensely. I was very glad to get back to the battalion because it had been into action in my absence, and the first news I had of this was when one of the officers was brought into the same ward on a stretcher. He intimated that there were more to follow, and also gave me an incoherent account of the battle which merely excited my anxieties without allaying them. This, for me, was the most disheartening experience I have had out here. To be lying in bed and watching people come in, many of whom I knew, with wounded limbs and bodies, and not to have

* The Spanish Farm (1924), a novel about the First World War by R. H. Mottram.
† The Mill on the Floss (1860) by George Eliot.

the mental escape of activity brought home only too well the side of war which is so appalling. I am now a captain.

Now I am sitting outside my tent, shared with the other officers of the company, Julian Martin-Smith in command, and Vernon Lewis. The former a very charming and good soldier and 'too like Apollo for words, my dear'. The latter rather older with a most commendable dry humour. Slightly to my left is the cook's trench with a petrol cooker roaring away like a furnace. This is the first sound that greets us in the morning (5.30). All around us are little wadis, filled up with quickly browning bodies, sandy and heavily dotted with rosemary and squat firs. In the evening, gathered in the dusk, sitting amongst the rosemary, we sing, sometimes in unison, sometimes in harmony, sometimes solo, those lovely Welsh songs which I shall introduce you to in years to come. Who would not have wished to experience all this at least once? The men are constant letter-writers; simple and emotional, they reiterate their love and desire for wife and home.

30 April 1943

Churchill's speech is attaining a good circulation among officers and men. It does not really say very much, but it does commit any government to fairly substantial measures of reform. We had a brains' trust this morning in which inevitably the Beveridge Report was discussed and I was able, I think, to allay some of their uneasiness. If it is not accepted *in toto* I feel there will be a revolution.

14 May 1943

The morning of May 6th opened with the crescendo of guns about twelve miles to our north heralding the attack of the infantry divisions. By seven o'clock we could see nothing because the air, from ground to sky, was filled with dust thrown up by thousands of vehicles. By midday, as the sounds of battle receded, we knew that things were going well. We moved at 3.45. Roughly, our functions are threefold, to take over ground already won, to prevent a counter-attack and to force a gap, or any high ground. The evening of May 6th found us motoring down the main Mejez–Tunis highway until we reached Massicault. Here indeed was the first of those scenes which bring tears to the eyes and which multiplied as we continued the push. A liberated village and the whole population lining the streets, cheering, making the V sign, throwing flowers, offering wine. And there was I, feeling rather emotional and victorious, standing up in the car, and acknowledging in a lordly manner the salutations of the populace.

By next day things were obviously nearly over. We bathed in the sea and at thirteen minutes past seven I got this message, 'The campaign is concluding; our side has won; all companies will concentrate round battalion HQ.' What did it feel like to be so utterly victorious? I was quite miserable and depressed and very tired. We celebrated that night by sleeping. Tomorrow I hope to go to Fourchville, where our dead are buried, and if possible to get photographs of the graves for their relatives. Their funeral, I hear, was royal.

24 June 1943

The *Horizon* with Koestler's article on Richard Hillary has arrived. I read it with great interest but do not feel quite in the right mood to discuss it. I can't decide yet whether Koestler is not romanticizing too much and making an unwarranted induction from the personality of a young man who had obviously not obtained that harmony in his life of which the Greek philosophers make so much.

11 July 1943

About Richard Hillary. I have been thinking a good deal about him and have sounded some of my friends. That so-called 'thinking people' have been searching for Something and have not as yet found it is, I think, quite true. That they desire a redeeming emotion or faith in which to surrender themselves is also true. You might describe the 1920–1940 era as a concentration on self, introvertive and egocentric, and leading in some cases to a certain amount of pleasure, but never of happiness. It was also quite obviously an era when old standards of morality, belief and conduct were rejected, but as in the story of the Seven Devils, the last state was worse than the first. You are also right in your references to pacifism and the great difficulty in readjusting oneself to a war. The cry during the last three years has been, 'We know what we are fighting against – but what are we fighting for?' Now do you suppose that if the belief in a God of love existed in the hearts of most of us that this search for an ideal, or something to fight *for* would be really necessary? As far as I'm concerned, God exists as the stars exist, or as the source of a river exists, and He has no effect on my way of life – this is what the majority of people have come to. One could express it succinctly by saying that 'God is no longer near.' And so some have been able to lose themselves in the course of fighting, some in social reform, and so on. I think that this generation is petulant; it expects a war to give it the answer to the old question, 'What is the meaning of life?'

28 July 1943

Bathing at Sidi Bou Said, a village just outside Tunis. A visit to the villa there of La Baronne D'Erlanger. This is a banking family equivalent in wealth if not in reputation to the Rothschilds. The villa was built about twenty years ago looking across the Gulf of Tunis to Cap Bon and Hammamlif. It must be by far the most beautiful in North Africa. There is one room, about 100 feet in length, which is constructed in the style of Kairouan. There are two tiers of fluted marble pillars with Moorish arches, banked one on the other, and the ceiling looks like gold and silver lace. A water-tank surrounds the whole and through this the sun diffuses a greenish golden light. Water issues from the mouth of a dragon encircled with rubies and emeralds. The Baroness was a stingy old thing and didn't offer us any refreshment at all.

Have been thinking that some of the place names could be

used for metaphors. I wonder if they would sound beautiful to you. They all contain the yearning of the long ōu and ā.

> As the plaster-work of Kairouan
> So was your delicacy
> As the dustclouds gold suffused on Zaghouan
> So was your hair
> As the waters of Oued Tahouna
> So was your tranquillity.

I was terribly depressed on arriving back at the battalion on Sunday evening. Why this depression? There is nothing so utterly boring, so utterly narrow and so utterly petty as regimental soldiering which lacks the accompaniment of a state of battle. I have done six months and it is enough. I long for an outside job, something broader in scope and requiring the application of one's mind in an intelligent rather than a routine manner. I suppose that the pleasures of stupid societies are mainly confined to picking the other fellow to bits. Certainly in this battalion there is no charity, no loving kindness, no loyalty. I am probably going to get a slightly different job very soon. That of training our reinforcements in North Africa. They are quite considerable. Among the officers, if not among the men, there are many problem children. The drafts? The drafts we get now are either 'old' or 'funny' or more usually both.

I want badly to know the composition of the new Italian cabinet. If Alberto Pirelli is in it in any capacity my bet is armistice within a fortnight. I hope to spend my winter with him in Northern Italy. Also I would like to converse with his arrogant son.

18 November 1943

The Welsh Guards have won the Drill Competition. We are very pleased. (That's the stuff that counts! It really is!!) We are celebrating tonight. Our choir continues but the choirmaster is every day on the point of going to Italy. We sing the Coventry Carol. We intend to challenge the battalion to an Eisteddfod. It rains and rains and is getting cold. Battle Dress is the order of the day (and pullovers). The prospects for winter are appalling. I have a sheepskin coat waiting for me in Constantine. That anyone should even be faced with such a pair of alternatives – to stay here or go and fight in the Apennines. Luckily, perhaps, the choice is not mine. How I hate airgraphs – it's like talking on the telephone in a crowded room.

6 December 1943

Ronald Lunt wants to go back to Oxford very much during the five years immediately after the war, hoping to find students of riper years, and wider experience than the usual undergraduates. Also I suspect he wants to try to found a fresh Oxford School of Philosophy – or perhaps rather to show the shallowness and failure of logical positivism. He has big ideas for building model communities on an agricultural basis. He is very much the fighting padre – intensely interested in military affairs.

Sartorially I have made some improvements during the last week. To begin with I have replaced my old motheaten khaki beret with a black one and on it there is a beautiful golden upstanding leek. Then I have acquired an American battledress. So much better than our own! Also an African Star, a cheap garish medal ribbon, typically American. At the moment I feel extremely well contented and relaxed. This afternoon I took part in the inter-company cross country run and lugged my 15 stone around fast enough to come in 26th out of a field of 75. So I am quite pleased with myself. The Welsh Guards won the competition.

But the real reason why I feel so happy is that the choir is going 100%. I have weeded out those who were there only to see what they could get out of it. By having a practice when everybody was rather tired and by giving the absentees the bird, I have got the publicity I wanted. Through the entertainments officer I have arranged for a tour by the choir round all the units during the week 12th–19th December. A block of carols, Noël, Wenceslas, Silent Night, the Coventry Carol, then an interlude of individual turns, impersonations, etc., then a block of miscellaneous songs, another interlude of turns, then a final block of sacred music,

'Bless this House', 'Jesu, Lover of my Soul', 'Finlandia' . . . You can imagine what fun (and hard work) it has been singing and arranging all this. In the blending of the 4 parts in harmony, and in the art of singing itself I find something sweet and creative.

We have some film people staying with us. They are here to take some shots for a big army film on the lines of *In Which We Serve* and it is very possible that in this you will see Captain David Elliot and his merry men taking up a defensive position!

Much love and best wishes for Christmas.

Boxing Day 1943

You will see from the address that my sojourn here is nearly ended. I am going back to the battalion as 2nd in command to a man to whom I have not addressed a civil word in three years, nor he to me! This I suppose is the penalty for bad tactics when the CO came down here recently and asked me if I had any grouses, expecting me to say that the only thing I wanted to do was to get back to his battalion, and I replied that I was quite happy. Comparing the battalion to the IRTD [Infantry Reinforcement Training Drafts] I came to these conclusions. Battalion – far less congenial friends, far less freedom in my job, a CO whom I dislike, a company commander whom I dislike, bad food, bad drink – and very cold and very muddy!!

I went to midnight Communion on Christmas Eve in a large Nissen hut. A Christmas tree with one or two candles shining from behind it and bunches and bunches of sweet-smelling narcissi for decoration. It was the first time I have ever done this and I am very glad indeed to have done so. It is really, I suppose, the most important service of the year. We sang to 12 wards in the local hospital and incidentally reduced three sisters to tears. Peter Ustinov was staying here. He is a character actor in the big army film called *The Way Ahead* and was quite brilliant, whether as a Colonial bishop or as an unknown oratorio of Handel's being sung by some amateurs near Macclesfield. When I get back to the battalion my ambition is to make its choir the best in the army.

My bed is giving out. Do you think you could get me a SAFARI camp bed and send it to me? Also could you send me a small accordion?

... One of the most disturbing things about the men is their complete distrust of their leaders. They are all convinced that they will be forgotten after the war as they were after the last. I have even got to the stage of telling them the war is worth fighting even if they *are* completely forgotten afterwards. They have got to the stage when they only believe what they can actually see and feel.

How does all this tie up? We want a redeeming emotion but we are incapable of believing in the nearness of God. So we expect a Substitute to give us the key to life. So far this substitute which people like to call 'What we are fighting for' has not given the answer, and hasn't even materialized beyond 'Freedom from want', 'Better conditions', etc. Can it, in fact, ever materialize? Can we fight for anything else? I don't think so. So I restate my belief we expect the mere fact of war to solve our own problems by its contact with us from outside. But it cannot do this because our salvation, or emotional health, or whatever else you like to call it, has got to come from within to without, and not from without to within.

What chances are there for a spiritual revival? I should say not for a long time. There is no evidence of it among those I know or those I command. The interest in C. S. Lewis and Dorothy L. Sayers I take to be largely academic, the increased attendance at church merely a symptom of war, like immorality. I don't think that 'the Spirit' has much to do with it. I should say that the Spirit is still numb after its strangling during the 1930s and that it will not recover in any appreciable way for at least 20 years.

What of the work of the army chaplains? They have a very great part to play during and after the battle, viz. helping the wounded, and seeing that the dead are buried with ceremony, that crosses are made for their graves, and that their personal belongings get back to their relations. All this is obvious. But if you only fight two battles in six months, what else should they do? Services on Sundays. The difficulty about any other religious work is that men do not respond – they do not open their hearts. They have a traditional belief in God, naïve, if you like, which for them is sufficient. They do not want to talk to the padre. Very different is the state of affairs with the RC padre, he never ceases to work. But unless the C of E padre is of such an inspiring and sympathetic character that people *want to go to him*, then, outside hours, his religious output is practically nil. He is not, nor can he ever be, except in unusual circumstances, the father of his flock. So he either does nothing, which is the most usual, or at best he busies himself with the entertainment and relaxation side. Ours doesn't even do that. The verdict then is that functionally they are necessary and you can't do without them. They can help enormously in the physical and mental recreations of the men but on the personal side it is very difficult for them and that usually they can't help failing.

I find extreme difficulty in believing in the nearness of God. That he has a plan for the world which is entirely dependent on the free will of men, this I do believe. That the Christian way of life offers the best way of life, I also believe. But things like the Crucifixion and the Sacraments have lost their nearness. The war presents no moral or intellectual problem. I do verily believe that Nazism presents the most diabolical, physical and spiritual enslavement of man ever known. I am fighting for conditions where a happy family life is possible, not only for me but for all those who work and fight. My attitude, I should think, is a very common one.

I have put in for a correspondence course in political economy. The thought of going into politics is definitely intriguing.

PS The letter I wrote to my Servant's widow has appeared *in extenso* in the Welsh papers as his obituary! Talking of heat, the Khamseen was blowing five days ago and it was 120° in the shade. Perhaps I was killed at Hammamlif and am now in my appointed place. Richard Lloyd has written an imaginative account of the battle. It should appear in the papers.

Desert Weariness

The sand-laden winds had ground its exposed surfaces to a pitted smoothness like orange-rind, and the sunlight had faded out its blue to a hopeless grey . . . We felt we were in an ominous land, incapable of life, hostile even to the passing of life, except painfully along such sparse roads as time had laid across its face.

T. E. Lawrence, *The Seven Pillars of Wisdom*

Private R. L. Crimp, who served throughout the North African campaigns, analyses the notorious ennui and depression which European soldiers suffered during long spells in this terrain. Like the poet Sidney Keyes, who wrote,

> The rock says, 'Endure',
> The wind says 'Pursue.'
> The sun says 'I will suck your bones
> And afterwards bury you',

Crimp found himself sometimes overwhelmed by the sand and the sordidness, the demands and threats. The desert did bury Keyes.

18 October 1941. Just lately I've been feeling a bit browned off. There's a sort of psychological complaint some chaps get after long exposure on the Blue called 'desert weariness', though I can hardly claim to have reached that yet. But for months now we've been cut off from nearly every aspect of civilized life, and every day has been cast in the same monotonous mould. The desert, omnipresent, so saturates consciousness that it makes the mind as sterile as itself. It's only now that you realize how much you normally live through the senses. Here there's nothing for them. Nothing in the landscape to rest or distract the eye; nothing to hear but roaring truck engines; and nothing to smell but carbon exhaust fumes and the reek of petrol. Even food tastes insipid, because of the heat, which stultifies appetite. The sexual urge, with nothing to stir it, is completely dormant, and there's nothing to encourage its sublimation except, perhaps, this crack-pot journal.

Then over and above the physical factors, there's the total lack of change or relaxation; nothing really certain even to look forward to, that, after a term of such vacuum-living, would make it tolerable. In civvy-street, when day's work is done, there's always an hour or two watching Rita Hayworth, a couple of drinks at the 'Spread Eagle', a chair by the fire and a Queen's Hall prom, or a weekend's hike on the North Downs. Even in camp there's Garrison Theatre, or Shafto's Shambles, and the ubiquitous NAAFI. But here there's no respite or getting away from it all. For weeks, more probably months, we shall have to go on bearing an unbroken succession of empty, ugly, insipid days. Perhaps, eventually, a chance will come of a few days' leave in Cairo, but that's too vague and remote to be worth setting tangible hopes upon. Anything might happen in the meantime. But the one thing that keeps the chaps going, that gives them a sort of dogged persistence in living through these interim days, is the thought of Home.

The immediate present effect, however, is extreme mental sluggishness, sheer physical apathy, and a vast aversion to exertion in every form. The most trivial actions, such as cleaning the sand off weapons, making a fire for a brew, or, when you're lying down by the truck, moving position into the patch of shade that the sun has shifted, seem utterly not worthwhile and require a tremendous effort to perform. It all seems so futile.

Then, of course, there are the flies. Lord Almighty, that such pests should ever have been created! Bad enough in any climate, the Egyptian sort are militant in the extreme, almost a different type, imbued with a frenzied determination to settle on human flesh. This may be due to the aridity of the terrain and to the fact that the only moisture available is human sweat. Soon after sunrise they arrive in hordes from nowhere, then plague us with malign persistence all through the day, swarming and buzzing around, trying desperately to land on our faces, in our eyes, ears and nostrils, on our arms, hands, knees and necks. And once settled, they bite hard. Desert sores, oases of succulence, draw them like magnets. In fact everything unwholesome, filthy and putrefied is manna to them. That's why we have to make our latrines completely sealed and burn out our refuse dumps with petrol daily. It's the devil's own job keeping our food from their clutches, and as soon as a meal's on the plates they always get the first nibble. At the moment of writing this there are five crawling over my hands and I'm spitting as many again away from my mouth. You can whack them a hundred times, and still they'll come back. It is a blessed relief at sunset, when, as at some secret signal, they all simultaneously disappear.

Private Crimp's account of routine evening and dawn patrols is low-spirited and tinged with the indifference and pessimism which had begun to spread through the British Expeditionary Forces, and which shocked Montgomery when he arrived to take command.

Evening. We start at sunset, on trucks, with the eastern darkness behind us. It feels strange to be perched on the back, bumping and jostling noisily over the rough surface, scanning in every direction, our own positions a long way behind, and getting nearer, mile after mile, the enemy's lines, somewhere out in the still sunlit west. But the Blue is a big place, and for patrols to meet in the 20-mile strip of No-Man's-Land between opposing front lines is supposed to be a chance in a thousand.

Our object is to recce an area where a German outpost is suspected to spend the night. After covering a dozen miles we dismount and leaving the trucks behind with the drivers, proceed a further 1,000 paces on foot, with loaded rifles at the trail, the officer in front and the sergeant swanning about in the rear. By this time it's completely dark – no moon. Eventually we arrive at a patch of desert which presents no distinguishing features at all, nor any sign of the enemy. So we turn left and cover another 1,000 paces directly south, marching in file strictly according to the compass open in the officer's hand. But still no trace of the enemy. 1,000 paces east brings the same result, not to anybody's regret. And 1,000 paces north brings us rather surprisingly, though according to schedule, back to the trucks, where George and his mate are getting a bit cheesed off with hanging about by themselves and confess they felt pretty windy at hearing footfalls approaching over the sand.

Our job deemed done, we set off 'home', bumping and jolting, with engines roaring, satisfied that nothing really awkward has transpired. Eight miles covered, we pull up and get down to a couple of hours' kip, then reach the Company area in time for breakfast.

Morning. The Company has to get up in cold pitch-darkness an hour before dawn. Accompanied by a battery of RHA 25-pounders, who've been in leaguer with us and some 2-pounder anti-tank guns, we travel forward several miles into No-Man's-Land.

By sunrise the small concourse of vehicles has arrived in a shallow depression. The guns are sited, and we in the infantry platoons take up protective positions on a ridge a thousand yards in front. A gunner OP is creeping about some distance ahead of us, and it doesn't take him long to find a target, for after twenty minutes of empty silence the 25-pdrs suddenly burst into action. They're firing super-charged at long range, barrels pointing high. The air is rent by rapid salvos, and the shells in flight overhead make a mewing and squealing chorus. Then as the barrage ceases abruptly we can hear the murmur of the shells landing a long way over in the west. Five minutes later there's another outburst. No response is forthcoming from the enemy, except for a couple of armoured cars which appear on the skyline and refuse to be lured within the few thousand yards' effective range of the anti-tank 2-pounders. After a third and even lustier onslaught – the guns firing in unison for several minutes – we all pack up and roll back to our normal daylight positions. The Battery Commander is very satisfied. Evidently his guns managed to surprise an enemy battery in leaguer, and brewed it up without retaliation.

The News Cameraman

Photography is truth. And cinema is truth twenty-four times a second.

Jean-Luc Godard, *Le Petit Soldat*

The demand for photo-journalism and film-journalism was insatiable. Some of the most popular cinemas in the West End of London and in other big cities showed nothing but newsreels, and shoppers, visitors and members of the forces would drop in for an hour or two's rest between late morning and late evening. They were long, narrow passages wreathed in tobacco smoke and usually packed, so that the doorman, impatiently watched, would have to indicate a single or a double, or three separates to the long queue by holding up his fingers. Inside, the commentary, boastful and reassuring, hurtled along as a lengthy procession of brief episodes roared away on the screen. The occasional lurching shot and scratchy surface only served to emphasize the authenticity of what was being shown. The principal actors in the theatres of war – the Führer, the Prime Minister, Monty, Timoshenko, Joe Stalin – received similar boos and applause to those given to the heroes and villains of pantomime. There was frequently a noticeable divergence of integrity between the film itself and the mannered gung-ho voice-over which accompanied it. There was too blatant doctoring of images and words, but no indignation. There was a war on.

The newsreel cameraman managed to be both a glamorous figure and an unknown one. He was often injured or killed. He existed in a welter of permits, tip-offs, bribes, bullyings from his distant boss and reckless personal initiatives. He was among the lone adventurers of the war, a hitch-hiker to the battlefield, staggering along with his heavy awkward equipment and seeing in his mind's eye what millions of cinemagoers needed to see, a bit of the action set to aggressive music and commentary. He was a barely tolerated intruder where some of the First World War fighting was concerned, being regarded either as a nuisance or as an ungentlemanly voyeur who would teach civilians to see what only soldiers should see. In 1939–45, however, things were very different and he was positively courted, fed facts and followed around. But it was a rough business and little of this impressed him or changed his nature, which was sardonic. He served up a raw view of events, places and people, knowing it would be doused in patriotism and cheeriness when it reached the cutting-room, though nothing could soften these photographic images of war at their best. Whirring round with the noisy ephemera which made up the average newsreel there were often strips of reportage so marvellous that they could affect millions of cinemagoers as much as the best work from Hollywood or Elstree. Considering the amount and quality of his films, the newsreel cameraman kept a low profile and had little personal following. David Prosser, a newsreel cameraman working in the Middle East during the summer and autumn of 1941, kept a journal in which he tells an energetic but quite unambitious tale. Like his lens, he reflects an undiplomatic view, picking up human vanity and human strengths equally. The Western Desert preliminaries, the navy and press corps itself are being observed by a man who has been around. Prosser writes as someone who has never had a moment to spare for life's little rituals. Nor, unlike most people, does he write more intimately in his journal than in his letters to his parents.

July 1941. On Saturday morning I came down to breakfast to find that Ben Hart had pulled a fast one on me and had sheered off on some story I knew nothing about. I guessed that he got it from Lee Ginsberg (*not* of 'Rides Tonight' fame). However, after a bit of hunting around I found that there was a rumour

about that the French had asked for an Armistice and that it was
being signed that day at Acre, just up the road, so to speak. I
chased round the PR people and found that a whole lot of them
had left early and had gone off that way. So I went to N. Sec
and asked whether he could confirm it, as I knew I'd only get a
bottle for going off up there if there wasn't anything doing after
all. Sec wouldn't be definite but finally he did say that he
thought we 'always chased off on these things' and, one way and
another, he gave me a good enough hint to make it pretty sure.
So I hired a car and tore off up there.

The scene beggared description. There were about fifty war
correspondents of all kinds, including Jewish ones – more correspondents than Army staff even, and that is saying a lot. The
site was Sidney Smith Camp, just to the north of Acre. The
Camp consisted of a series of low dark brown wood huts,
mostly with concrete verandas overlooking the beach, which was
a few yards away. The main conference room was one of these
huts. There was a good lawn running along its whole front and
reaching to within a few yards of the water's edge. At one end of
this hut was a large sandy square, with huts on the other two
sides, the Camp making the fourth side. In this square all the
vehicles containing generals and the enormous staff for the
Armistice were to draw up and disgorge their contents.

Early in the morning an Australian bugler was taken aside and
told that he would be required to blow the general salute –
twice. First on the arrival of General Sir Henry Maitland Wilson
– the conqueror – and secondly for General de Verdillac, the
plenipotentiary for General Dentz, the suppressed Vichy commander. The bugler signified his agreement and was left waiting.
Meanwhile, large numbers of British and Fighting French officers
had lined up all over the square with cameras, getting hopelessly
in the way of the official Army cameramen and the war correspondents, who were in a minority at this stage. As General
Wilson was due to arrive at any moment, the local officials of
the Camp thought they had better straighten things out, so they
ordered all but the official cameramen right back to the edge of

the square, leaving only two or three men in it. Then came the warning that General Wilson was on his way. No sooner had this message come in than three cars tore into the Camp road. The first two were dirty dust-covered station waggons bearing the scars of battle, the third was a new-looking well-polished car going more slowly. The first cars skidded to a stop in the middle of the square and two unshaven grimy men in dirty and rather ragged bush jackets leaped out with cameras, contrasting badly with the well-dressed figures standing around. The cars then went off and the cameramen, after a hasty word with another who had been there all the time, took up their positions, while the third car drove in slowly, majestically stopping in front of the group of senior officers. As its door opened, the general salute sounded off, the cameras buzzed and clicked, and General Wilson got out. Of course, the arrival of the two latecomers had completely disorganized all the arrangements for the others, although the only people who were worried were the welcoming staff and a few unofficial photographers who hadn't any right to be there.

Then another hiss went round. General de Verdillac was on his way in. Again an expensive-looking car rolled into the square, but as the Vichy chief got out there was *no* general salute. A staff officer rushed across to the bugler, who was standing blissfully correct with his bugle under one arm in the approved manner and looking skywards and stifling a yawn – 'Good God, man, what's the matter with you. Sound the general salute!' 'Aw,' said the Australian, 'rot 'im.' When all the necessary staffs and hangers-on had been collected, the whole group moved off to the main hut, both pursued and led by grinding cameras.

The entire morning was passed in discussion, although we had been given to believe that the signing was due to take place around eleven o'clock. Later we found that no terms had been printed out and that there was effectively nothing down on paper at all. Everything was being, first discussed, and then written down in longhand on masses of foolscap, to be typed out

later, and then signed. Lunch came, and various messes belonging
to the Camp were handed over to the Vichy, FF and British
officers. The war correspondents were left with the sergeants'
mess belonging to a Palestine Police group, as we were so
numerous by this time that we couldn't be accommodated as
usual in the officers' mess.

Of course there was a tremendous amount of bad feeling
between the Vichy officers and those of de Gaulle, and they had
to be kept carefully apart. As it was, the Vichy Navy and Air
Force officers were just plain bloody-minded about everything,
although their Army officers didn't seem to mind very much.
They felt that they had done a good job of defending their
country and that was all there was to it. They felt that they had
been conquered through insufficient supplies, or they might have
held out a lot longer. They were having a very difficult time
when they asked for the Armistice. But the Navy was different.
They had Oran and Dakar on the brain and these two operations
against a former ally, however necessary, rankled badly. They
never seemed to stop and consider how they had let down the
British in France after Reynaud had sworn to fight on from the
colonies if needs be. The Vichy Air Force seemed to be much of
the same mind. I never quite understood the underlying cause of
their resentment.

After lunch, which included something of a party with many of
the Palestine Police, and some very good sandwiches, coffee, and
an excellent brandy, we went out to see what the chances were
of getting anything done that day. They looked pretty small, for
they had only just started to type out the pages and pages of
terms and agreements, and the cameramen were beginning to get
a bit worried, for it looked as though the light would be going
by the time they got through. There were no means of lighting
the conference room artificially, and no one knew where they
could get lighting equipment in Haifa.

Gradually the afternoon wore out and, during a lull, General
Wilson made a recorded speech for the BBC Sound Truck which
was there under Richard Dimbleby. All this time the cameramen

were rushing about trying to steal pictures of the surly Vichy men and official Army photographers were persuading various high officers from all three signatories to make groups and have their pictures taken. Occasionally some civil servant would hurry through from the typing room to the main hut and dash back again with a handful of papers.

At last, just after tea, the Armistice papers were ready, or the first batch was. Once more they all filed into the conference room, and some Naval officers drifted out on to the veranda, and were pounced on by the correspondents, trying to get some idea of the terms. The officers didn't tell much. Cameramen were peering in the windows, despite the patrol designed to prevent this, trying to assess the chances, now fast diminishing, of getting any pictures of the final signing, and glancing over their shoulders anxiously at the fast-lowering sun. They decided that they *must* have lights, and so each went off to a different telephone and tried to get through to Haifa in order to discover some shop where they could hire some Photoflood bulbs, just to plug into the ordinary lamp sockets so that they could increase the light to a photographic value. One telephone booth was inside the main hut, at one end of the conference room and opposite the Gents. Various people kept wandering in and out, and every time the swing door opened you saw the heads of some of the Armistice-signers jerk up as they heard such remarks as, 'Well, for Christ's sake get me a photographer who isn't a bloody Jew. Or call a Jew at his private number or anything. I gotta have lights, see?' It was Shabbat in Haifa.

As the sun dropped into the sea, the cameramen convened another meeting, having failed to get any lights out of a Jewish town on a Saturday afternoon. They decided, with disgust, that the only thing left was to go round all the messes and officers' quarters in search of high power reading-lamps, and then to wire them all up on a piece of cable borrowed from Richard Dimbleby's sound truck. This was done, but the lamps weren't very powerful, though the best we could manage, and while they still meandered on with the drooling talks in the conference room, we did what we could to get the lights shipshape, so that we could take them straight in when the signing began.

Finally they said that only one cameraman could actually film the signing, though others might be allowed in to help him out with the lighting and so forth. By now it was quite dark, and *all* the cameramen filed into the conference room to set up the improvised lights, while one arranged his gear in a corner. Then the two sets of generals and their staffs entered and took up their positions so that the cameraman could focus on them. When everything was ready, cameramen were swinging by their legs from the ceiling in order to hold reading-lamps in the generals' faces, or clambering about all over the tables, or crawling around on the floor. Just as they were about to sign all the lights in the Camp went out; the powerhouse had had a breakdown of some sort. Somebody was deputed by General Wilson to go and get some candles, and the cameramen went mad at this. As the orderly reached the door, he was stopped by the sentry, who happened to be one of the Palestine Police sergeants who had been at the lunch party, and who was now somewhat bottled. He had been told that he was not to let anyone pass in any circumstances *if the lights went out*. After a long argument in hushed whispers he reached the conclusion that the General *had* ordered the candles and so he let the orderly pass. When he came back he had a bundle of candles under one arm and was holding a lit candle aloft. The sentry, now reeling, announced to the Armistice conference, 'Lead, kindly light!'

The candles were soon found to be insufficient and so it was suggested that they might bring cars up to the windows and shine their headlights in. It was obvious that the windows were far above the level of the highest of headlights, but they had to try it before they dismissed the idea. Then someone thought of bringing in a motor-bike and standing it on the conference table with its headlight on. This seemed pretty good after all the other efforts, so they did it, only to find that there was not enough power in the battery to keep the light up without the engine running. So they started it, and when the room was filled with exhaust fumes found it 'wasn't quite dignified' and gave that up.

During all this a captain from the Palestine Police was striding in and out of the swing doors by the telephone booth from which an orderly with a Lancashire accent could be heard saying, 'An' the General says the lyhte *moost* be on in ten minutes . . .' Meanwhile, cameramen were disgustedly evacuating their gear and cursing quietly as their wires got caught in some frightened Vichy man's feet, the latter now beginning to wonder if the whole thing hadn't been staged as a plot to assassinate them. At length the only conclusion the conference could reach was that it had better postpone matters till the morrow and ratify the pact on the Monday. Dinner-less and disgusted, we made our way back to Haifa, while some returned to the Front, where fighting was still going on in sporadic bursts. The two who had dashed in ahead of General Wilson had come straight from battle, hence their scruffy apparel.

Tobruk, 25 November 1941. As soon as I got back from the first bombardment I put in to go up to Tobruk-on-Sea, as that was the only way to get there, as I felt that there might soon be a battle worth watching ashore, and that anyway it ought not to be long before they started sending supply convoys up there for the Seventh Army. I filmed the first preparations and loading of one of these convoys and then, after preparing to sail with it, I was delayed, and so I went to Tobruk in one of the light destroyers in the ordinary way, slinking in by night.

I joined this destroyer late one evening and we left about 0200 hours. As we had a rather slow ship with us, we couldn't make the usual fast time over the run, and so we resigned ourselves to a thirty-six hour trip. The afternoon before we were due to arrive there, we had our first proper air attack. I had been on the bridge all day and had just gone down in a quiet moment for a cup of tea. When I left there was no sign of aircraft anywhere. But when I got below the successive 'A's sounded off on the alarm bells. Dashing up on the bridge again –

a matter of a few seconds – I saw a ship hit by a torpedo, one of a pair launched from two aircraft which had somehow eluded us until they came in to make their actual attack. Immediately, from nowhere, apparently, two Grumman Martlets appeared and gave chase to the enemy, shooting down one of them and damaging the other. However, we heard that another flotilla was approaching from the opposite direction and so, after collecting some survivors – none was injured – from their boats, we put on speed and went for the port. We couldn't afford to waste any time on the way and had already been hanging around the stricken ship for nearly an hour. Our destroyer had to get in and out of Tobruk harbour, unload the cargo, which contained ammunition and stores as well as troops, and then try and get clear of Axis attacks on the way back, and before daylight broke.

We felt our way in to the harbour, for once without an airraid. I was, as usual, disadvantaged with all my gear, as every man has to carry his own stuff on these occasions. I had about five journeys to make, and these were only to get the stuff on to the jetty. By the time I had located the jetty, the ship was nearly ready to go, and I found that about half of my gear had been brought ashore by someone else, well meaning, no doubt, except that I couldn't find these missing items anywhere on the jetty. I gave up searching eventually, for it was getting on for 0200 hours, and I was fed up with kicking around in the dark looking for something which had either been stolen already, or else had been taken away to somewhere fairly safe from whence it might turn up in the morning. After carting my half of the gear to the end of the jetty, I was shattered to find they hadn't got any trucks there for us, but that we had to walk all the way up a hill on a winding path and join them at the top. By this time I was sweating blood and staggering under the weight of all that I could carry. But just as I was going down the hill for the last two loads, some very decent RNR officer who was arriving without much gear came along and gave me a welcome hand. Together we searched everywhere for the missing cases, but vainly.

Finally we set off in this truck, sitting atop our baggage. The road was hellish and, of course, had been bombed and shelled to a ruin. After going so far that we thought we must be coming outside the perimeter and into enemy territory, we found that the driver had actually lost his way and hardly knew any better than we did where we were. After much wandering, he hit the right track, finally getting us to the top of the wadi where we were to be billeted for the night. When I examined the route by daylight, I don't know how he made it at all. I felt that we ought to have gone to Navy House and been put up there, as it was hard by the harbour. Instead we picked up what we could carry of the gear, being told that the rest would be all right there at the top till morning, and staggered down yet another of these awful mountain paths which seem to abound in Tobruk. I just took a bedroll, lurched into the orderly room and gave my name, pretty well desperate by now with loss of my gear and with fatigue. To my astonishment, they gave me in return for my details a large cup half-full of Navy issue rum. That just about saved me and I went off to pitch my bed in a tent and turn in.

On rising in the morning about seven to go to breakfast, we went and washed in the salt showers – the helpful Navy lieutenant had shared the tent with me – and went straight over to the mess. Somewhat to my surprise, as I walked, I realized that I was definitely reeling, if only slightly, though it needed a tremendous effort to avoid doing so. After breakfast it was even worse and I began to realize with some misgivings that the rum I had been given the previous night had made me somewhat pickled, and that it hadn't had time to wear off. However, after packing up the gear again and preparing to go and live at Navy House, I began to feel better.

This camp, as the growing daylight showed, was set in a flat palm grove at the bottom of a wadi, or deep inlet in the rocky coast. The tents were well dispersed and dug four feet deep into the earth. This was for a measure of protection against the almost continual air attacks which Tobruk used to suffer, though the wadi itself was not often attacked. The northern end of the

wadi reached out to the sea and later on we used to go down
to bathe there before breakfast, and again before supper. The
water during November–December was chill but intensely
refreshing. The upper end of the wadi forked into two just
beyond the camp, the eastern fork being the one down which
we had walked the night before in the darkness – a descent of
about two hundred feet with a mean gradient of one in three!
There had been a track down which one could take a vehicle,
but it looked as though it had been shelled and was now
quite impassable. The other fork did carry a very roundabout
way to get a vehicle down into the wadi. It had a frightful
surface but was just passable to a driver well versed in the
terrain of Tobruk.

I remember the morning we heard a news broadcast from
London announcing the start of the offensive in the desert, when
it was also announced that Sir Dudley Pound, First Sea Lord,
had commented, 'It will not be long now before we are relieving
Tobruk.' And how this had struck all of us as a very foolish
thing to say so soon in the show, for as yet we hadn't even made
much of an advance. It was the way in which we always seemed
to go about the war, making foolish and fantastic boasts before
counting our enemy's strength.

At breakfast on my first morning in Tobruk I met several war
correspondents, one of whom was Desmond Tighe. He
remembered me from Syria, although I had by this time grown a
colossal beard. Also there was William Forrest and an Australian
called Ron Monson. They were all very good chaps and offered
to take me round, as they had been in Tobruk from three to
six weeks. They had with them a conducting officer, Captain
Roy Oliver, who was also an extremely good fellow. After
chatting, it seemed a sensible idea to stay with them at the camp,
as there was no transport for me at Navy House and I could
always tack along with them, and thus get right out to the
battle. This was imminent, for the plan was to break out of
Tobruk with tanks and to join up with the other main force of
the Eighth Army down to the south-east.

After locating the gear which I had lost on the previous night – it had been taken to Navy House by some kind soul – we went out to Battle HQ to learn the latest news from the General, and also to visit Brigadier Willensen, who was in charge of the tank forces there, many of which had been brought up to the garrison by the Navy in large flat-bottomed motor launches under intense fire and bombing from enemy aircraft. Near the Battle HQ there was a tall observation post, climbing which I wanted to photograph the General. But he was too busy that morning to leave his dug-out and so we passed on to the headquarters of the Brigadier. As we got on to the main road his car flashed past us, and so we gave chase and followed him to his desert tank park. I was hastily introduced to him, being the only member of the party that he had not met nearly every day for the past few weeks, and then he apologized and said, 'Well, chaps, I'm just going to have my wash and shave, but you can talk to me meanwhile, and I will try to give you the plan as best I can.' This seemed amazingly reasonable to me, and was the first sign of the remarkably good co-operation that we all had up there. While the others got the plan from him as he sat in the back of his car shaving, I filmed him. He was preparing to go out on one of the most spectacular battles ever fought. It promised to be the first break-out from that state of semi-siege which would be successful. The Brigadier told us that he couldn't say just when we war correspondents could come in to the battle, but that we should be kept in touch by Division HQ.

The Tank HQ was no more than a spot in the desert, a mere parking place. The men all slept simply on the ground in their bedrolls beside their tanks. A few hasty slit trenches had been dug nearby as a precaution against air attack, although there wasn't much of that at this time – the enemy was much too busy moving back fast. The Division HQ, however, was a wonderful place, built, I believe, by the Italians. It was like a large fortress, all underground and lined with concrete, fully bomb and shell proof, and set under the side of a hill – or as

much of a hill as one ever saw in that part of the desert, which
was only a rise of some forty or fifty feet.

As soon as the Brig, as we called him, had finished his toilet
he had a short conference with his staff officers and checked
exactly how many tanks he had, and he congratulated one major
on getting so many back into action so quickly. Many of these
repaired tanks had been knocked out in action during the
previous day's fighting, and it was certainly a matter for praise
that they had been recovered and mended so quickly. In this
isolated garrison salvage was, of course, the most important
word. All vehicles had to be run to the very last and when some
important part wore right out, then the whole machine was
turned in for what was known as 'cannibalizing'. This meant
that they were turned in to the workshops as a source of spare
parts for other vehicles, and nothing else. This often happened
with vehicles that were still serviceable up to a point but which,
after careful consideration by the experts, were deemed more
valuable as spares.

After the Brig's conference, he leaped into his tank and drove
off towards Tiger, another spot on the map which was the
advance base of his tanks. Flying from his radio mast the Brig
had his usual squadron pennant and, below this, his own personal
pennant, a silk stocking rigged by the top. This I gather was a
present from some admirer of his and was always flown into
battle from his radio mast. It had the advantage that one could
always pick him out at once from a mass of tanks. We followed
him in our car, trying to keep on his tracks as far as possible,
for, soon after we left the perimeter – the original main defence
around the area – the terrain was likely to be full of mines. In
fact, the Brig had been blown up on one only the day before. It
wasn't too bad sometimes in a tank, but in a car it was no fun at
all. These mines were designed to blow up armoured tanks.

On reaching Tiger, we met two officers of the AFPU – the
Army Film and Photographic Unit. Both of them I had met
before but they had left the staging camp the day I arrived. They
said there wasn't much doing at the moment and so they were

going back to the camp for the night and were coming out again early in the morning. We confirmed this and also decided to go back, collecting our bottle of whisky per head that we are now entitled to from the NAAFI. Generally there was never any liquor in Tobruk, but they had just got a new store in from a destroyer and had announced that each officer might have his ration pro tem. By the time we got there the ration had been reduced to half a bottle, but we took that gladly and went back to lunch to sample it.

Late that evening a telephone call came through from Division. We were advised to get over to El Duda about seven the next morning, as the link-up with the Eighth Army was expected that day. A battle was going on at the time and some of the New Zealand tanks were slinking in under cover of darkness to give some support if it came to be needed. So we all prepared to turn in early, while it was arranged that I should go in the truck with the AFPU boys in the morning, as they were more likely to be going in sight of the battle than the correspondents, they having seen enough of actions to get the background. The war correspondents were going to hang around the Intelligence Office at BHQ to see what direct information they could get from the Intelligence Officer, who, an excellent man, was a Count in some country — I never found out which. Nor can I remember his name but it sounded Hungarian.

Rising several hours before dawn, we found that the mess orderlies had been good to us and had managed to get some breakfast together, which was mighty welcome. For the nights were cold in Tobruk and the early morning colder. About first light we loaded my gear into the truck and departed up the long, maddening track to the top of the wadi, then down the road, along which we raced east to get to the break in the perimeter, and so out to Tiger and El Duda. To say we raced is misguiding, for the road was shell-holed to pieces and one was lucky to get up to more than thirty in the best stretches. But the captain who was driving us was like a madman. He raced the protesting truck along this broken surface, with the real driver, who was

batman to the others, and myself being thrown heavily from side
to side in the back, where we were mixed up with all the gear –
cameras, film, bedrolls, crockery and food. It wasn't long
before the coffee and sugar broke loose and spread all over
the interior of the vehicle like a sticky shower. When we
turned off the road into open country it was even worse, for
it was either hard rocky ground with a very uneven surface or
else it was sand or hard mud bound with camel thorn hum-
mocks rising five to ten inches from the level. The consequence
was that the only real way to take this track was to roll over
it very slowly in second, or even in bottom gear, steering
carefully to avoid the worst bumps, for if one did finish a
vehicle in Tobruk one was very lucky if another came one's
way. Though not the mad captain; he just kept our truck in
mid-air for about two thirds of the run.

As far as one could see from this point the land was quite flat,
so that one's horizon was about two miles away. Back on the
coast road, all the telegraph poles had been cut off on either side
of the perimeter. This was to prevent easy ranging on any
temporary target. At various intervals there were these forty or
fifty foot observation towers from which one could watch one's
shells falling, again on both sides. Some showed originality by
having a patch of canvas running up the whole height of the
tower, so that the enemy couldn't tell which one was being used
by a sniper. But generally they were just plain four-legged
wooden towers with a small railed platform on top where two
men could stand. These, of course, brought the horizon up to
seven or eight miles.

Suddenly, as we breasted a low rise, we saw the flat of El
Duda laid out before us. There had been a little sporadic
shelling from the enemy as we came across, but now we saw
it going on with a slow but steady intensity. The area was a
slight depression, flanked to the south by a low escarpment, at
the top of which lay the Axis highway which they had made
to bypass Tobruk while we held it. To the south-east, the
enemy still held this ridge and were firing from it. The

depression was filled with a large number of dispersed tanks of all types with their crews sitting round them taking shelter from the shelling as they ate their breakfast. The enemy was using eight-inch anti-personnel shells fired from mobile guns that they had been employing to shell Tobruk harbour from the so-called 'Bardia Bill' position. Enormous mushrooms of smoke kept rising from the depression. We tried to pick a likely-looking route which might not be shelled during the next 'bracket'.

We pulled in under the ledge of the escarpment and parked the truck alongside a tank, so that the latter would shelter us from any shells falling short of us. The Army Lieutenant, who was a film cameraman like myself, got out and prepared his camera. I did the same, and we started off, photographing a few bursts now and then from the shelter of tanks as we made our way across to the wadi in the side of the escarpment where they had made a little HQ. The Brig's tank was there, alongside that of a colonel and another brigadier whom I didn't recognize. I assumed that they had come through during the night. We had a word with them and found that the Seventh and Eighth Army link-up had been entirely successful, and that many of these tanks with us in the depression were New Zealand ones, having come through with this colonel. His was rather a sad tale, so typical of the war. He had a son in the unit coming out from Tobruk and, of course, had not seen him for some long time, and had been very excited at the thought of coming to meet him in so spectacular an operation. But when the colonel finally met Willensen's outfit, the latter had to tell him that his son had just been killed that night during the break-out. The only consolation was the success of this operation. The galling part was that the colonel's squadron had suffered no casualties at all.

By this time the captain who had brought us out had completely disappeared, so we set off on our own, the Lieut. and I. He was lucky. He had only a small light camera of a type which I had wanted for a long time for this job. Instead,

I was equipped with a large and extremely serviceable machine which weighed over thirty pounds, added to which I had to carry another fifteen pounds of spare film and lenses. These I slung in a haversack attached to my Sam Browne belt. We wandered around a little, taking pictures of tanks being shelled, and of prisoners who had been brought in, some of whom were arriving voluntarily, having been left by their own units to fend for themselves as best they could. They looked just like a great flock of sheep coming over the horizon. They wandered along in a trailing mass, apparently without escort. The Italian prisoners seemed quite happy that the war was virtually over for them, but the German prisoners were really miserable, though some were still arrogant as usual. They said that we had done to their forces what they had done to the French. In other words, they had just been broken and were running. They took a low view of the shelling which was coming from the top of the escarpment and those who still had their little trenching tools hastily set to and made themselves some good slit trenches to lie in. Most of our tank crews had done the same thing and dived into them when they heard a shell coming uncomfortably close to them. Occasionally a direct hit from one of these heavy shells wiped out a tank. It looked horrible. An officer from the unit then had to go over and collect the papers of the dead men, delving in that frightful mess.

Sometimes a man would be struck down beside you by a stray splinter or burst. The difficulty with these shells was that their splinters went such a very long way, so that you might stand up a few seconds after a burst in the distance, thinking that they would have settled by then, only to hear a heavy smack on the ground alongside, and to see a splinter as big as your fist drop at your feet.

We strolled back to our vehicle, hoping to find the captain. By this time I was definitely scared. It was my first experience of really personal shelling on land and I found it too accurate for my liking. I have always thought since that I far prefer to be shelled or bombed at sea than on land. In the open desert like this a splinter travels too far from either type of missile. At sea, a shell or bomb which falls in the water is almost harmless if you are in a ship – especially a warship. And even if the ship gets hit in one place, the chances are that you get away with it on the bridge. Whereas a bomb in a street could bring down a whole block on top of you even if you were fifty yards from where it burst. We found the truck but no captain. The driver–batman was having tea with a tank crew nearby, and we were invited along. Tea seldom tasted so good. They also offered us some of the captured food that they had got that morning. It too was extremely good. After bully beef and dry biscuits, the fresh bread and butter and cheese was a mighty fine change.

Wars are for Photography

I am a camera with its shutter open, quite passive, recording, not thinking.

Christopher Isherwood, *A Berlin Diary*

Wars are for photography. Brownie images of home, of love, of connection. Utmost respect was shown to these images when the little packet of snapshots was opened up to a colleague. 'My wife', 'our house', 'my dad'. Girls were different and a certain speculative response, even to a fiancée, would be taken as a compliment. Once abroad, there was virtually no home leave, so pictures passed to and fro showing sons growing up and husbands beginning to look like strangers, and back gardens, viewed from Tobruk or Sicily, taking on the quality of some Eden which might never be regained. His photos of home, and also of himself, became a serviceman's most treasured possession. Wherever possible, they would be scrupulously returned to his relatives should he die. They were the icons through which he had stared countless times to make contact with his true identity, sepia faces crammed with incidents. The most poignant literary assessment of the wartime snapshot is in Keith Douglas's poem 'Elegy for an 88 Gunner', written in Tripolitania in 1943. Wandering over the battlefield three weeks after the fighting, the poet finds the corpse of a German soldier 'sprawling in the sun'.

> Look. Here in the gunpit spoil
> the dishonoured picture of his girl

who has put: *Steffi vergissmeinnicht.*
in a copybook gothic script.
. . . .
But she would weep to see today
how on his skin the swart flies move,
the dust upon the paper eye
and the burst stomach like a cave.

Wars, with their hyperbole, uniforms and stress on physical fitness, make men narcissistic, and it was not just the desire to have a picture to send home that filled the photographer's shop with sitters. In his 'The Middle of a War' Roy Fuller thinks of what it will be like to see his portrait in the family album:

My photograph already looks historic.
The promising youthful face, the matelot's collar,
Say, 'This one is remembered for a lyric.
His place and period – nothing could be duller.'

Both the Brownie snapshot face and the photographer's parlour face were to make way for the Polyfoto face, the multiple image of oneself which provided horror, acceptability and choice. Polyfoto booths, covered outside with funny and beautiful faces, were packed with customers, especially where there were barracks and aerodromes. John Guest tells of his pilgrimage to the source of the many-faceted self in his war journal *Broken Images*.

Yesterday, Saturday, I had another taste of madness of a different kind. My mother had hinted that she would like a photograph of me in my uniform and gold-braided hat so, being in Glasgow for the afternoon, I thought I would go and get 48 (or is it 96 or 192?) of those tiny photos taken by a machine; surely *one* would be good enough to enlarge. I made inquiries and was told that there was such an apparatus at G——'s. This proved to be a nightmare emporium. What I can hardly describe to you are the crowds. The pavements on a Saturday afternoon are so jammed that the normal mode of progress is to be pushed, jostled and knocked along. As I came within the cliff-like shadow of the place, the crowd thickened to a solid stream of hot flesh divided into cells by partitions of clothing, and I found myself being sucked through bronze and marble doors, all identity gone.

Inside it was Wellsian. Noise – the rumble of feet and voices, escalators, the racket of the world market, and music. Colours – electric lights like the Milky Way, cascades and fountains of material, sky-scrapers of tins and boxes, a thousand counters and stalls all screaming to catch the eye. Everything suddenly became unreal. I saw a sea of women's hats like brooding hens, rockets, piles of oily rag, coloured lids and surgical dressings. There was a man with a carrot in his ear and an ape with a scent-bottle, a mad gang of female furies smashing up a counter with spades, a flood of sewer-water pouring out of one of the lifts. As our lava-flow of flesh oozed past a kiosk (which had 'SNOWSTORM' written on it for some unfathomable reason), I managed to shout to the woman in charge: 'Polyfotos?' and she pointed to an escalator. Five minutes later I'd made it.

It was comparatively cool and quiet up there, but I found myself in a Hampton Court maze of cabin trunks. Having got free of that, I set out on a fantastic journey. First a Walt Disney fantasia of down cushions, quilts and satin cots; then into a forest of hats on bare wooden sticks; then through a vile-smelling jungle of hanging chintzes. Finally, I arrived at a green log cabin with snow-laden fir-trees and mountain peaks rising into a blue sky beyond it. Along the whole length of the roof was inscribed the word 'POLYFOTO', and in front of it stood a silent, glum queue of perhaps twenty-five people waiting to be polyfotoed. It was too much. But I went so far as to ask the attendant if I could book an appointment. 'Oh, yes,' she said brightly, getting out a ledger. I then asked whether, if I turned up at the appointed time, I could be *sure* of being polyfotoed. 'W-e-ll, I'm afraid *not*,' she said. 'It all depends . . . you see, sir, *portraits* nowadays are in such demand . . .' I fought my way out.

Susan Sontag was to write, 'A photograph is not only an image (as a painting is an image), an interpretation of the real; it is also a trace, something directly stencilled off the real, like a footprint or a death mask.' It was such traces of personal actuality which were carried next to the heart through campaigns, concentration camps, in the air, below the oceans and back home, or to the grave.

Conchie

'Look at that Hungarian fellow there by the window, chaps,' said Vodička. 'See how the bastard prays to God that everything will go well with him. Wouldn't you like to break his mug open from ear to ear?'

'But he's a decent chap,' said Švejk. 'He's only here because he didn't want to join up. He's against the war, belongs to some kind of sect and he's been gaoled because he didn't want to kill people. He keeps God's commandment, but they're going to make God's commandment hot for him. Before the war there was a fellow called Nemrava living in Moravia who didn't even want to take a rifle on his shoulder, and when he was called up he said that it was against his principles to carry a rifle. Because of that he was gaoled until he was blue in the face and then brought up again to take the oath. But he said he wouldn't do it as it was against his principles and he held out so long that he got away with it.'

'He must have been a stupid chump,' said old Sapper Vodička. 'He could have taken the oath and then shitted on everything and the oath too.'

Jaroslav Hašek, *The Good Soldier Švejk*

The man who refuses to fight because of his pacifist convictions is at his most vulnerable at the beginning of a war. It is then that a country is most wildly united in doing battle and most intolerant of those whose refusal to take part seems to it despicable. During the thirties, pacifist societies like the Peace Pledge Union attracted vast memberships which disintegrated as the Fascist threat to civilization became apparent. But out of the short-lived popular renunciation of war as a way of settling the arguments of nations, there remained a small group of people whose principles, religion and common sense combined made them stick to their guns, as it were, and refuse to take up arms of any kind. However sincere they were, they often made a poor showing before some examining board or other and were forced into uniform. It was then that to have the courage of one's convictions was to possess very great courage indeed, for to be a conchie in the barracks was like being a sex offender in a gaol, the object of all abuse. As the following letter reveals, the bravest spirits could collapse under it. It was written to Dr Soper by F. B. Breakspear, a conscientious objector, in September 1940.

Last Wednesday I was charged with another CO named Leslie Worth with not *complying* with an order given by a superior officer. We were sentenced to fourteen days' detention. Another CO has drifted in and we went before the RSM this morning and gained the following information. The RSM had captured a copy of the *Court Martial Guide and Friend* from Leslie Worth and had studied it pretty well. By charging us with not *complying* with an order, as apart from *disobeying* an order, he says that we cannot ask for a court martial. Also, of course, a sentence of fourteen days does not allow one to make this request either. Their intention is to keep this up until the war ends.

... I have given in. I could not continue with the prospects of the future being a repetition of the past.

I will try and give you a little idea of the treatment given to us in the last few days. It is quite on the level of what you can read of in Nazi concentration camps – and it happened here in England. I arrived at Dingle Vale School on Thursday 12th September at about 6.30 p.m. and went to the reception office, and after some talk refused to sign the Attestation Form. This is not of any significance but it was disobedience of an order. The reception officer was very decent; he warned me of the consequences and after a final trial put me under arrest, and I was placed in the Guardroom for the night. The next morning I had the normal breakfast which leaves nothing to grumble about. During the morning, Sergeant Cullins, of whom I will have more to say later, dressed me. At 11.45 a.m. I went before the Colonel and was told a story which he fires at everyone about a German soldier in the last war securing a woman to a wall with a bayonet, and then raping her daughter. He tells this story to every CO and his final roar is, 'And I shot the bugger dead on the doorstep!' This story, and variations of it, seemed to spread through the whole company after a while. Anyhow, I was not given a chance to say anything before I was chucked out and put in a cellar in solitary confinement on bread and water. I received only one meal of this. It seemed a novelty and I rather enjoyed it. I was in the cellar until Monday morning. During the weekend a number of people, including the Padre, Captain Kemp, and members of the Regimental Police, dropped in and argued with me, and tried to talk me round. On Saturday, I was given another dose of the Colonel to help matters along.

I spent the weekend reading the Bible and the Weekend Book, and was fairly happy. On Monday I was taken back to the Guardroom so that a tough egg called Foster, a political CO, could be put in Solitary. He got a pretty good bashing up for refusing to put his uniform on. In the Guardroom I met Leslie Worth, an Objector rather like myself approaching the question from all angles, his predominant approach being Christian. As far as I can remember, Monday and Tuesday passed without much happening. On Wednesday morning we were led off to work and were then taken, on our refusal to work, before the RSM, who let fire at us in no uncertain manner. We eventually managed to get a word in and complained that we had neither been tried nor sentenced. This seemed to have some effect because we were then taken before the Commanding Officer and then, much to our amazement, given fourteen days' detention and chucked out of his room. We thought at the time that this was for observation purposes, and so we decided to work without further protest. The work was never hard, but rather dirty, but we did not mind this as it passed the time away. The most we did was five hours a day, although it was generally less.

About Thursday Peter Thornton arrived from Glasgow Military Prison. He was an Objector on Christian grounds. On Friday and Saturday we worked as usual. The whole week we had as company some Army Military Police who had overstayed their leave. In themselves they weren't too bad but we never had any peace. They used a certain word, very obscene so that I will not quote it, between every other word. Their conversation was entirely sexual. It got so much on my nerves that I almost howled at them to stop.

I think it must have been Saturday when Foster was put in the Guardroom and received a bashing up for refusing to work. On Thursday night we were lugged out of bed by the guard and told that we were supposed to work. On Friday night another RP did the same thing, but we refused to get up. In the end, after a bit of a row, we went and cleaned a dozen wash basins for half an hour. This was about 2 o'clock. At 4 the RP returned to dig us out again. There was nearly a fight this time, the guard was called and we were dressed and made to mop up the Guardroom. While we worked the most abusive language I have ever heard was poured on us. To get back to Saturday. A letter giving the details of the past couple of days fell into the hands of the Police Sergeant, who opened it and read it. He at once promised me a fight with gloves on in the Gym in a couple of hours' time. He is an ex-professional boxer. That date was never kept, thank goodness!

About 5 p.m. we had two new arrivals, Ted and Bert. The former, a great bloke from Lowestoft, filled us with pep and we decided that we would all make a stand together and support Foster, who had had a pretty tough time. On Sunday morning at 8.30 we were asked to do a couple of hours' work. When we refused we were put on bread and water and promised a boxing contest with the Sergeant. Sunday passed with one slice of bread for breakfast. On Monday, about 9 four or five RPs turned up to ask if we would work. We, Leslie, Peter and myself refused, and then the trouble began. We were knocked about and then dragged to the butcher's shop. Here we were bashed up a bit more and Leslie had a bucket of water thrown over him. We stuck it and were only returned after the hottest half hour I have ever known. Later that morning we went before the RSM. He gave us the choice of doing an hour's exercise or an hour's scrubbing, so of course we chose the former. We were placed in a squad of soldiers and marched around with them. They continually kicked us and gave us hefty bangs with the muzzles of their rifles at every turn. After one terrific wallop I went down but managed to get up and continue. It came on to rain and we were taken into the Gym and made to do more exercises, including a fair amount of running. An NCO went along the line [of four Conscientious Objectors] and brought his knee up under our legs with such a crack that mine was so bruised that it is still stiff today. We managed to stick it out for an hour and were then marched off to dinner. One slice of bread and some water.

During the afternoon we were given another hour's hard exercise. I don't know how I managed to keep up, but I did. Tea was two slices of bread. After tea we were each shut up by ourselves in little cupboards, the windows of which had been blacked out. Only in my case a very dim light filtered through. Hardly enough to see how to get to bed. We had no bedding at all except one blanket. That evening we were given another hour's hard marching. You will believe me that by this time I was ready to drop. More or less in a daze, I managed to get to my black room and wrap myself up as best I could and get to sleep. We were supposed to be dug out and marched around the square at 12.30 the next day but the RP let us off. He was a good chap. None the less, I was pretty well out on Monday evening.

Tuesday came. Breakfast, one slice of bread. During the

morning we had some hard PT with some more soldiers. They had slippers on, we wore boots, and it was pretty hard going. Dinner, another slice of bread. Then we were marched to the Public Baths and back again. On the way we went for a walk around the park – for exercise! Tea was better, with two slices of bread with our water. On Tuesday night we were made to get up at 12 o'clock, 2 o'clock and 4 o'clock and walk around the yard in our shirts. Then back to the blanket on the floor. I could not sleep. On the 2 o'clock walk I collapsed after a hefty shove from the guard but they kicked me to my feet again and I managed to get back to my cupboard. Wednesday morning, up at 6 – you can guess that I was pretty down by then. We were given an ordinary breakfast and I felt a bit better. Afterwards, the Sergeant came round and demanded to know if I would work or eat bread and water again. I said I would work and was led away to peel potatoes. I just could not refuse again, and so I was compromised on this question. But the others refused to work. After a while the barber came along and said he had instructions to cut our hair, and that it was not his idea of hair-cutting. Anyhow, he took the lot off and so now I have a convict's crop. The humility of this last blow broke me and I was taken back to my cell and just sat around and cried.

After a while the Sergeant came along and said that even if I did work I would only get bread and water. He also told me that Foster had given in. I could not take any more. I gave in. I think it has nearly broken my heart. I never felt so unhappy in my life. People are trying to cheer me up. Foster says we must be philosophical about it, and that we should be proud to have stood up to them so long. The Padre has been chatting with me. He says I can do more good spreading the Gospel in the RAMC than dying on bread and water. There is only one CO standing out now and he should get his appeal next week. He has been imprisoned for three months, and is all in. He doesn't know if he can stick it out until next week . . . I will never forgive myself for giving in. Yet the consequences of not doing so would have meant complete physical collapse.

Brief Encounter

Now cry your heart out if you can,
Cry for many a simple man.

G. S. Fraser, 'Poem'

The pen-friend or pen-pal was a busy contributor to the writing of the war. Much was said about the loneliness of servicemen; pen-pals were encouraged by schools, churches and especially the women's press, which also taught its reader how to put a damper on a correspondence that threatened to get out of hand. Like having a soldier for Christmas, or volunteering to partner Americans at the local US base, writing as a pen-pal did not commit a girl to anything more than 'friendship'. Photographs were exchanged but in many instances actual meetings never took place. Marriages based on a lengthy pen-friend relationship could be disastrous. Classic epistolary novels such as Jean Webster's *Daddy Long-Legs* (1912) lent excitement to the letters-to-an-Unseen custom and allowed the young writers a pattern of possibility. A pen-friend's letter would often seem more tender and intimate than one from the boy or girl one had been out with. The pen-friend needed to be the author of a 'good letter' because all that its recipient would know of him or her would be contained in it. It was important too that the letters should be correctly set out. Pen-friend letters of the period are a tribute to the teaching of letter-writing in elementary schools and of 'composition'. Sometimes the formal structure could be a cage from which a writer would struggle in vain to escape. But often it provided just the right amount of etiquette for being 'personal'.

In 1943 the girls in an ATS barrack-room somewhere in Kent were told that the sailors on HMS *Intrepid* were lonely. Jill pen-friended Danny, a cadet. They never saw each other. He did once arrive at the ack-ack battery but she was on leave. She kept his letters all her life. 'Suddenly they stopped coming. Either his ship went down or, hopefully, he went on leave and met a "real live girl" to write letters to.'

11 February 1943

When we arrived back in port there were nineteen letters waiting for me, so I reckon my popularity is on the up and up. The round trip was highly successful but the weather was deplorable and we had more than our share of pitching and tossing. At the present moment I am fed up and to crown all my mate has just got a draft back to barracks. Once again I will be on my own, one Scotsman among twenty-two Englishmen. I will miss him a lot for he is grand company and many a pleasant hour we have spent together whilst in dry dock. I believe I rather envy you being stationed ashore for sea life is not all it is cracked up to be. How about swapping jobs for a month? That is if you don't mind eating your food with one fork. During the last trip we had to do without a wash for over a week because of a water shortage aboard.

I have an idea that before long things are going to happen, and then the enemy will be smashed to bits. I am looking forward to a lot of excitement when the invasion comes off, for one gets tired of waiting. You and I seem to be of the same opinion concerning the length of the war. My guess is October of this year, so keep your eyes on the calendar.

19 April 1943

I have passed on your regards to the cat and you will be pleased to know that the family is coming along fairly fast. They have all homes to go to, thanks to the kind-hearted sailors.

Owing to Scotland's relapse on Saturday I am now ten shillings out of pocket, but it was worth a chance, for we were playing at home. You have no idea what I had to go through when we sat listening to the commentary on the wireless. Thank goodness I have a thick skin.

I suppose the new girls will be in your bad books now that you have more duties to do, but don't forget you were brand-new when you joined up – or should I say volunteered.

I have never been through the House of Commons on a visit, but I would like to ever so much. I bet it was interesting and fascinating, and one doesn't see so many famous figures every day in the week. Just think, you were sitting in a place where the heart of a great country beats and controls our everyday life! If we ever go up to London for a refit I intend visiting all those places dear to the Englishman, Westminster, St Paul's, Hyde Park – gosh, I could go on till doomsday.

Yes, I still have the pleasure of being cook once a week and I honestly believe that I could turn out a Sunday dinner suitable for human consumption. I always put salt in the potatoes (experience again), not forgetting the little piece of soda in the peas when soaking over-night. I can carve up the joint like nobody's business. During long sea trips when fresh greens are not available we fall back on tinned goods, and, as you know, they don't need much looking after. Can you picture Jolly Jack sitting down to custard and pears (one tin to two men) after a dinner of meat pie, roast potatoes and greens?

So you don't intend doing any more washing-up after meals when this lot is over? Surely you are forgetting one important item (marriage), but maybe that question is not hard to answer. I should hate to think that all women have the same idea. But then crossword puzzles take a lot of thinking out.

Books! Funnily enough, I have just written home for some, for our reading material has dwindled away to a few tattered old magazines, well thumb-marked. I can assure you that a few books would be well received in the mess just now.

*

31 July 1943

The snap is grand and it came at the right time, for I was absolutely fed up with life in general. The mail I received today was the first in six weeks and although the news was rather old it was more than welcome. I had an idea that the censor would be busy with my last letter, but one has to take a chance now and again.

The few hours I had at home will have to last me many, many months, owing to the course of this war. As you will have gathered, we are out in the Med. and have taken part in recent operations. We are doing plenty of sea time and sleep is a thing of the past owing to continuous action stations night and day. No doubt you are familiar with the same. We have carried out bombardments all along the coast of Sicily and inflicted great damage on enemy positions. My first impression of Malta was one of pity, for some of the buildings were in ruins and others were beyond repair. In peace-time the capital must have been beautiful, for the majority of the big establishments are works of art, and the churches take one's breath away with their sheer beauty. We have touched many famous ports since coming out here, names made famous by our wonderful 8th Army. Gosh, it makes one feel grand to be British through and through.

Our library has started to function again after a month's silence, but we don't have much time now to enjoy a decent tale. I have read the *Woman's Own* at home, also the *People's Friend*, *Red Star*, *Red Letter*, etc. Don't blame me, when I have two sisters in the house.

Gunfire is the only musical note we hear now in the evenings, but this lot must be carried out if we are ever to get home.

You see, I detest Nelson Eddy and Jeanette MacDonald, not forgetting Alan Jones. I love to listen to Vera Lynn. She has something in her voice, a sort of throb, that is very attractive. Give me a contralto and a soprano together and I will be in seventh heaven.

When in Russia I had a drop of Vodka. It looks like clear water and tastes something horrible. I haven't been to a picture show now for months. You see, we have to rely on the big ships inviting us to the shows. I see you are a Boyer fan. Goodness knows what you see in him. Give me Spencer Tracy; he is a grand actor in every sense of the word. My choice of actress goes to Claudette Colbert, with Myrna Loy a close second.

I should have loved to see your performance of *Love on the Dole*. By the sound of things it went over a hundred per cent. As you say, unemployment is a dreadful thing. I sincerely hope that things turn out the way we want them after this relapse. The dialects in *Love on the Dole* would cause a lot of trouble, but no doubt everybody spent the night translating Cockney into Scotch, Yorkshire into Tyneside, and so on.

So the bathing-pool is still an imaginary one. Do you know that I have been over the side swimming since starting this letter? Gosh, the water was glorious, and I swam out to the buoy and sat there sunbathing. I have a lovely tan from head to foot, such a difference from being in the Arctic Circle where one has to keep well covered up. What is it they say, 'All handsome men should be slightly sunburnt.' Please, don't say it.

Thanks again for the photo ... Height 5′ 4½″, hair brunette, eyes hazel, mouth generous. I detest a woman with narrow lips ... The eyes are your number one attraction, they seem to speak of their own accord. If I have taken a liberty with our friendship, please tick me off. Tons of luck.

28 August 1943

This island [Sicily] would just suit you, for there are dozens of small secluded bays ideal for swimming, and nobody to disturb the quietness. But for all that I would rather be anywhere along our own coastline. The heat is terrific.

Jeanette MacDonald has been given a draft chit and Doreen Villiers has taken her place. She [Doreen] is tip-top and is a grand singer without too many frills. I simply detest the Cavendish Three for they are third-rate stars compared with the Bothwell Sisters, and not in the same class as the Andrews Sisters. Oscar Rabin is on the air just now — from the

Playhouse, Glasgow – about a penny car ride from my home.
My messmates from London spotted your snap in my ditty-
box and wanted to know what part of the world you came
from, and I told them that you were from the big city. Gosh,
did I start something!

I will try to give you a fairly accurate description of myself.
Please don't expect too much. I am five feet nine inches tall, slim
built and not too bad in features. Hair brown, eyes brown, sharp
nose nicely shaped, wide mouth, good teeth, but one of my front
ones is very black owing to an accident ten years ago. Big ears,
but not very noticeable, small scar on nose through bike accident,
and one large dimple on my chin. You know the old saying,
'Dimple on chin, devil within.' But it doesn't apply in this case. I
am twenty-three years of age and have got over my early love
affairs without a broken heart. I was courting strong over a year
ago but my young lady preferred the company of a war-worker
earning £8 a week to that of a poor sailor earning 4/- a day and
not often at home. Just think of my lucky escape.

There are dozens of different wines out here, plus the usual
spirits and cocktails. The latter have some queer names, Boiler-
maker, Block-buster and Hun-chaser being a few of the
favourites. Grapes, plums, figs, tomatoes, lemons, oranges are
plentiful, especially all along the Sicilian coastline. The people of
Sicily are a queer lot and filthy beyond words. The army detests
them and all their dirty habits.

  Tons of luck
  Danny

                           17 December 1943
If I get an opportunity I should like to meet you in person, so
first of all I had better find out whether the idea is suitable to
you or not. I couldn't possibly manage it on a night leave but
week-end leave would be ideal. I will leave all arrangements
about the meeting-place, etc. until I hear from you. Till then I
shall live in hope.

Go Home, Yanks!

War has always been against the marriages it makes and
intimate relationships of any kind.

Patrick White, *Flaws in the Glass*

The faithfulness of long-parted husbands, wives and sweethearts became
a tortuous issue. For many a serviceman the arrival of 'the Yanks' on his
home acres could be pretty near as worrying a fate as an invasion by the
enemy. The descent of the Americans on a mainly rural Britain was among
the most devastatingly emotional occurrences of the Home Front. The
pictures had come to real life. In reality, two contrasting states of
innocence came face to face in the dance-halls and pubs. That of men who
knew almost nothing of the world outside their remote townships or city
districts, and that of women who knew nothing of America save what
Hollywood had taught them twice a week for years and years. The curious
thing was that the cinema seems not to have let them down, rather
prepared them for the role they were to play. The Americans from the
local airbase were rich and classless by British standards. The lowest ranks
wore collar and tie and brown shoes, and status, education and accent
remained a closed book. They were open-handed, friendly and unblush-
ingly romantic in approach. On their part they were intrigued by British
manners and complexions. Contrasting mating rites were to benefit, not
hamper, relationships. The reticence of British courtship had to battle
with dating and heavy petting, and there were often more pleasures than
either side had previously believed possible. There was a moment mid-
way through the war when British women and American men were much
in love with what each romantically represented for the other.

Various efforts were made to keep the romance respectable. Young ladies were vetted and chaperoned as dance partners for the local base. Americans, shining in their best uniforms, were detailed for Sunday tea or cocktails at the best houses. But such refinements bore little resemblance to what was actually happening, which was the sweeping away of caution and inhibition and convention. The black-out, the blessings of the PX (Post Exchange) in the form of seemingly limitless Lucky Strike cigarettes, nylon stockings – the price of these above rubies – sweets and canned food, and strong sexual attraction created their own reckless ambience in the countryside. There was a war on, so make the most of it. Many women continued to love their husbands and fiancés but placed a moratorium on sexual faithfulness for the duration. They were young and lonely. So were the Americans. So were the distant spouses and boyfriends. There was guilt everywhere but little exchange of it. Men expected their wives and girls to be faithful. Women fought against their men turning into strangers.

Male notions of the sexual invader are nicely summed up in the journal of a Welsh soldier, A. J. Lane, who is enraged to discover Americans on his sacred home territory but whose account of fraternization with a German girl during the Allied occupation (*verboten!*) shows no sign of trespass. Indeed, as with the often brief love affairs between American servicemen and British women, Lane's night with his silent German has become, in the writing up, an accepted passing but unforgettable sexual experience. He was twenty-three.

Early January 1945, with a Continental winter at its worst, was a time and occasion when I was to find myself in the peculiar state of being happy and miserable at the same moment. A kind of not knowing whether to laugh or cry situation. I was happy at being one of the soldiers taken out of the front line of battle for a spell of leave in the UK. Earlier, a sudden military decision had been made, because of the favourable turning of the war tide, that a small percentage – at any one time – of the troops of certain combative units in the field be allowed, or granted, periods of leave at the OC's discretion.

An adapted system, in the case of my own unit, was to pick out a few names at a time by lucky draw, and I was fortunate enough therefore in being one of the early privileged few. Such luck could be a life-saver since fighting at the front was furious, and with yet more battles to come. But escaping the shot and shell at the front line to run the risk of freezing to death behind the lines was something I had not reckoned with, and therefore I was miserable because, although moving happily in the right direction, I was travelling on a slow, war-damaged train and feeling intensely cold. I sat on a hard wooden seat by a very draughty broken window and watched the ice form from the powdery snow which blew into my compartment. There was no heating, comfort or speed to be had from an old German locomotive which seemed ancient enough to be an early successor to Stephenson's Rocket. I wrapped up, curled up, shivered and cursed during the long cooped-up hours of travelling which, as I was to learn later, were to result in a number of fellow travellers having varying degrees of frostbite. But cruelly painful though the journey was, its purpose for me was the best of all reasons – to get back to Wales. My leave of absence had been a long, long time ago because so much had happened in the meantime. I had, for the most part, given up hope of ever seeing Wales again because seeing the war at first hand had made me more fatalist than optimist. Unbelievably, it was about to happen.

I had always thought a great deal about the old folk back home, as they did about me, and we corresponded regularly. My old Dad especially was painstakingly diligent and faithful with his usual two long, witty and informative letters. He was a scholarly man whose beautiful handwriting was an admiration and pride to me. A great morale booster, to be sure, and never once did he let me down in the three and a half years I had served up until that time. I knew too that he was equally consistent and loyal with my elder brother who, like myself, was also an overseas campaigner. In this way dear old Dad was able to keep us both informed about the other's circumstances and situation. James, my brother, was a longer serving soldier than I and, as one of Wingate's chindits in Burma, had suffered a much tougher time than myself. Because of our different theatres of war, James and I never communicated directly and were therefore totally reliant on the old fellow back home in Wales for news of each other. I had not seen my brother since late 1940 but I knew that he had done exceptionally well to have made the rank of Regimental Sergeant Major (WOI) [Warrant Officer Class I] in the South Wales Borderers. Considering that he was a militiaman and barely two years older than myself, such rapid promotion meant that he was one of the youngest, if not the youngest, infantry RSM in the British Army. I knew too that he was paying a high price for such distinction. In the jungle war against the Japanese he had overcome a couple of lesser wounds, only to fall victim to a third, a wound which was most serious. I remember getting the sad news from Dad saying that James was fighting for his life with a bullet in his heart. Later, I learned that he had miraculously pulled through.

As I sat on the train I wondered about my brother's complete recovery. Would he be seriously disabled for life? I tried to imagine the kind of jungle situation in which he had caught such a 'Nip packet'. He and I had always been close and I knew from my days of sparring with him that in a scrap he was the tough terrier type. As I endured more of the painful journey I sought comfort in thinking about my approaching reunion with the other members of my family. My parents must have gone through a period of great anxiety since I last saw them and I wondered if they had changed much as a result. Maybe they would find a change in me! I thought also about the one peaceful little spot on the globe which was the destination I yearned for – my home village in Wales. Living close to death in war has a sentimentality all its own and I dreamed often enough of arriving at the village station, to cross over the quaint little bridge, as I had done so often before. I had a clear picture in my mind as I recalled and anticipated the details of the bridge, and I determined that, when I got there, I would stand in wonderful reality at its centre and offer a prayer of thanksgiving for having made it after all.

The following day saw me looking and feeling less like a

traveller in Siberia and more as one who was on good old British soil again. Back home for the first time since I left for the initial assault landings in Normandy on D-Day. It was late in the evening when I neared the end of the journey. A few miles beyond Llanelly – the once so familiar place-name was somehow different and strange – and my destination was at last reached. There was a lump in my throat as I stood on the little bridge. I could see the platform below and the dimly lit street alongside the railway station. I expected and hoped that nothing had happened to change the much yearned for simplicity and tranquillity of the village but, alas, already I could see and hear something that disappointed and displeased me greatly. The noisy, staggering figures and groups of American soldiers, some with local girls, and all obviously the worse for drink. I was angry. My village contaminated! Polluted! Violated! At that moment I hated not only the American soldiers, but all soldiers, all uniforms, all and everything associated with war. I could readily have charged with a machine-gun to rid them from my most cherished piece of Welsh fatherland. It was at that moment that I had some real understanding of German fanaticism by young and old people alike defending their homeland. But as I sped homewards, my anger and disappointment gave way to more reasonable thoughts. There were few, if any, places left in Europe which were untouched by the war. As for the Yanks, well it was good to know that they were on our side. There are big wars up front on foreign fields and little wars on the soil of our own backyards.

[Later in his memoir, *What More Could a Soldier Ask of a War?*, Sapper Lane describes his own passing affair with a girl of the kind experienced by so many servicemen far from home.] There was a particularly strange and memorable encounter – the result of some audacity or downright cheek on my part. It started simply when I gazed down one afternoon from the window of our temporary Military Quarters. Across the road I could see a German girl in the company of two boys who seemed to be shouting and swearing at her for some reason. That she knew them was obvious. As they stood in a group I became more and more attracted by her beautiful body. As if hypnotized, drawn by her sensual movement, I moved to a position of being more than an observer and wandered across the street. It was a bold move. The two young Germans were little more than youths who, like most of their kind during those submissive days, found it hard to compete with victorious and better provided for Allied soldiers. They soon pushed off, leaving me with a clear field. There was a gesture or two, a 'you and me' signal. I was led by her along a ten-minute stretch of roadway until we came to her place of residence. Hardly a word had been spoken or a sound uttered.

With such little communication between us, I was a little shamefaced and uneasy about what to expect. All I knew up to that point was the uncertainty of whether I had gone along with her, or whether she had gone along with me. I had observed a natural reserve, a strong intelligent character and a refinement about her that was in keeping with her stylishly smart appearance. So much so indeed that I felt a bit of a fool for having so crudely introduced myself in the first place. I knew so little about her, her thoughts and feelings, that I was apprehensive as to what was to happen next as she rang the doorbell. It could be that somewhere in the background a big brother, or husband even, had the wrong kind of treat in store for me. The bell was answered and the door opened by a stern-faced old frau who also had nothing to say as we entered to climb a good flight of stairs. I discovered, much to my surprise, that she had her own flat. It struck me as being an exceptionally tidy and cosy place for a single girl. I was at a loss in knowing if, how and when a more positive reception was in the offing for me. I sat down on a sofa whilst she disappeared into another room.

I was left alone for a fidgety long time. I thought I heard the sound of a running tap and wondered for a moment or two whether she had chosen to ignore me by washing dishes, or clothes perhaps. I was puzzled but not without a feeling that, despite the lack of communication, we had something going for us by way of the unspoken language of sexual attraction. I

waited patiently and was surprisingly rewarded. She had taken a
bath for our mutual benefit. She stood in front of me in a
bathrobe which was loose and open to reveal what was perfect. I
saw that, as well as having said little or nothing, she smiled not
at all. She was, I guessed, a serious kind of person. A result of
the war, perhaps, as with so many Germans who, for so long,
had little to laugh and cheer about. She appeared before me as if
it were her duty to do so and as if waiting the nod of my
approval. In her hands she held the cushions which I was soon
to discover were to be carefully patted and placed for lift and
support during our love-making. There could now be no mistak-
ing of my own burning desire to get to grips with the business
now almost in hand. I waited thrilled and fascinated as she
settled herself slowly and deliberately on the cushions, so that
her body was arched and ready for the thrust and attack. I was
left in no doubt that her needs matched my own. It was a time
when the action did all the talking. I departed in the early hours
of the morning. I couldn't have asked for more by way of
(bodily) communication but I was still puzzled by the absence of
words, of conversation, by this loveliest of girls. At best all I had
managed to get from her during my attempts at talk was a slight
word or a shake of her head.

It crossed my mind that she was a born mute or maybe had
been made speechless in some way by the war. The more I
pondered the matter, the more likely this seemed, and that she
had preferred not to reveal the fact. I turned over our last
moments together and thought about her final parting gesture to
me when I wanted to express my feelings before parting. What
she did then was to put the fingers of one hand over her mouth
and the fingers of her other hand over my mouth. I took it to
mean that there should be nothing said or told, and that she was
happier with the unspoken word, perhaps because of the
language problem. But as I made my way back to the Quarters it
struck me that I had probably got it wrong. I was never to see
her again because of another move.

The following handful of letters tells of a commonplace wartime adventure with a kind of helpless eloquence. An American GI and an English girl have a brief affair and she becomes pregnant. Her family and his superiors then appear to insist that he should 'stand by her' for the child's sake. So they are married in bothersome circumstances and then, with equal indifference to his feelings, he is deserted, having done the right thing. It all takes just a year. Now in France, he doesn't know where he is either legally or emotionally, and he writes beseechingly to be put into the picture, but his wife has decided, or been persuaded, to have nothing more to do with him. The dreadful postal silence traps him into revealing shortcomings which he may not have known he possessed – stinginess. Now a married man with a baby on the way, his pay is docked, leaving him so short of cash that he cannot pay back the money he had to borrow from his mates for the fare from France to England when he had to return for the wedding. The fuss he makes about this gives his uncommunicative wife some cause for what she has to do, which is to get herself out of a muddle. But if she is cruelly silent, he is strangely so on the important matter of who and what he is, other than an American private stationed abroad, for although he writes with fluency and charm there is never a word about his home town, people, job, etc. American personnel were notoriously attractive to British women, for whom they were often figures who had stepped down from the local cinema screen. The soldiers in their turn were said to have found the women easy because they had no knowledge of American teenage customs, British 'courting' and their 'dating' not being at all the same thing. The US military authorities had a policy of making marriage between often very innocent youngsters, unintentionally mutually deceived, not easy. Because of their reputation, it was enviable but not wholly respectable to be seen around with Americans, and to get pregnant by one of them was a subject for ribaldry and moralizing. A social disaster.

Private Ted Seckle assumed as best he could the roles of responsible lover and husband. He acts practically and honourably, then with consternation, then with a resignation which shows that he is not exactly heartbroken. The army will get him out of it, as it got him into it. Face has been saved in the West Country. A war-baby has been legitimately born.

21 August 1944

Dearest Stella,

Sorry I couldn't write before but we've been moving from place to place so fast that we couldn't send or receive any mail. We've been in France for a while now and believe me the war is really on over here. These French towns are really shot to hell. Every town we pull into, the people swarm all over you. If you don't drive careful you would kill about a dozen. Where they all come from I don't know because all the houses are in ruins, but they are there all right – by the thousands. They offer us all sorts of things like wine, cakes, etc., but because some of them are German lovers we can't trust them. The wine and stuff might be poisonous. There are snipers all round us and we never go anywhere alone, or without a loaded rifle. We sleep with our rifle over here. I can't tell you where we are – but you'd be surprised if I could.

Did you go to see the doctor yet? Please take good care of yourself, honey. Don't let anything happen to yourself. We'll be together before long, I hope. I miss you more every day, darling. I wonder if you still think about me? I wish we could have that last day at Ivybridge over again. That was swell. Write soon, Devil, and let me know how you are. Keep up the prayers,

All my love
Ted

26 August 1944

Darling Stella,

There isn't much news. I'm busy every day hauling rations, water, etc., to our camp, usually a trip after supper. I can assure you that there is no time to play over here. I've only had two drinks since we landed. Pretty good for me, no? I still haven't received any mail, so I still don't know how you are. All right I hope, darling. I hope when the mail does come there are a lot of letters from you. I am looking forward to the day when we can be together again. I hope you'll be able to stand it. Are you still true to me, darling? If this letter sounds jumbled, don't blame me. I'm writing everything as it comes into my mind. It has rained almost every day since we landed. Can't even get my laundry done. Afraid it wouldn't dry because we never know when we are going to move to some other location. Like a band of gypsies.

Write to me every day, darling, so I'll know how you are and won't have to worry so much. Goodbye for now, Devil,

All my love

Ted

12 October 1944

Dearest Stella,

Will start right in on the latest dope about the marriage. My Company Commander talked to me yesterday about it and the news was good and bad. The good news is that everything is really OK as far as permission is concerned. Nothing more to worry about on that score. The bad news is that it is impossible to be married by proxy. No one knows when but maybe in the near future we are going to be able to get furloughs. *But*, if I get one I still have to find a way to get back to England on my own. The government can't help me on that at all. If it is possible, it might be a good idea for you to get the license right away, because I might pop in on you any day. I don't know anything about the English law, and as I won't have much time we can't afford to have a long delay because of the law. The CO said that when the furloughs are issued I'll get one of the first.

I was sorry to hear about Hilda being to see you. I don't like her and I don't think she makes a good companion for you. I've enough to do here trying to keep alive without worrying about her. Do me a favor and stay away from her. Are you still staying true to me, darling? Don't ever stop, Devil, because I love you more every day. I can hardly wait until I see you again.

Ted

22 October 1944

Darling Stella,

Well, this time I hope my news is good. Nestling in my pocket at this moment is the approval of my commanding officer. So that worry is over for good. I am sorry it has taken so long, honey, but it is regulations. Hard to understand for a civilian, maybe, but everything is done according to regulations in the army. Your job now is to find out all you can about the marriage laws of England . . .

Boy, I can hardly wait to hold you in my arms again. It seems like ages since I've had the opportunity. You're my whole little world, darling, so take good care of yourself for me until I am in a position to take care of you myself. I don't believe that day is too far away now. I still think I am dreaming sometimes when I think I have a nice girl like you worrying about me, and waiting for me to come back.

I can't tell you what we are doing over here but I can assure you that it is not pleasant. War isn't pleasant, but still, if it wasn't for the war I wouldn't have met you. (Good old war.) I haven't thought of the names yet for the baby; you can have first choice, provided it isn't Malcolm. How does it feel to be an expectant mother? I hope the baby waits for the war to end so that I can be there when she or he or they are born.

All my love to you
Ted

7 December 1944

Dearest Stella,

I am sorry I couldn't write before, darling, but the truth is I didn't return to my outfit until yesterday. It feels fine to be married, how does it feel to you? I sure hated leaving you, darling, but the way I look at it is that we were lucky to be together at all. They were five days I'll never forget. There will be a lot more after the war is over. It is just three years since Pearl Harbor. It really shouldn't be much longer now. Darling, please write as often as you can.

All my love
your husband
Ted

8 January 1945

Dearest Stella,

Received your second letter today. What has been the trouble? Surely you can average more than two letters a month if you try. I thought sure you had been bombed out or something. There isn't much to write about from over here. What I want to write about I can't. I'm glad to hear that you are all right. Does the doctor still think it will be in April? I'll be glad when it is over and I guess you will too. Wish I could be with you . . .

I didn't get much time to see Paris but what I did see was really nice. Yes, we had turkey at Christmas. I've got a dog now. He attached himself to me about three weeks ago and follows me everywhere I go. He is nuts about the truck too – rides every place I go. When I eat or sit down he lays by my feet and never moves until I do. Take care of yourself, Stella, and *please* write more often.

Ted

12 January 1945

Dearest Stella,

How is everybody in London? Are the rockets and bombs still falling? If they are, keep on ducking. We have moved again, but naturally I can't tell you where. It is really a hell of a married life we're having. I couldn't love you any more if I were twins, darling. I miss you more every day.

You should get your first check very soon, if you haven't gotten it already. It should be for two months of $100.00, equal to 22 pounds 10 shillings. Write more often *please*.

Ted

27 January 1945

Dear Stella,

I received your very fine letter today and will say that as a morale builder it was tops. Just what I needed to cheer me up. I guess I should have realized you would be too busy to write, but for the life of me I can't see what keeps you so busy twenty-four hours a day. Don't you think I'm important enough to take maybe half an hour off to drop a few lines? I can easily see that the answer to that is no.

Now for the money angle. I was told the allotment wouldn't start until January. Later on, they informed me, the money would start as of December. So this month is a double dose, coming out of my check, so you can figure out where that leaves me. It won't leave me enough to pay my laundry, but I'm not complaining about it. There isn't anything I can do about the allotment now, but you should get a check for $100.00 about the first of February. That will take care of December and January. From then on you should get fifty dollars on or about the first of every month.

I don't see much use of us fussing about. As long as you feel the way you do about writing I think the best thing *we* can do is to stop writing altogether.

Ted

March 1945

Dearest Stella,

We are in Germany now with the Ninth Army and as you no doubt probably know are on the move. It would sure please you people in London if you could see what we are doing to these German cities as we go through. Just Aachen alone would almost compensate for the damage done to London. I guess it won't be long now until the little sprout gets here, will it? I guess you are as big as a house now. Hope you don't lose that million dollar figure. I want to gaze at that plenty often after the war is won. It seems like you're on my mind all the time. I know there is no way I could help, but I sure would like to be there for the arrival of the new Yank.

I guess one of these days soon I'll be shaking hands with Russians and writing you from Berlin. Since they took the allotments out of my pay I haven't been able to get any money ahead, what with paying the boys back for my honeymoon trip and my rations I'm always broke. Will you please send me fifty dollars as soon as possible so that I can get out of debt. I've never had debts before I couldn't pay and I don't like it. My pay is now so small I can't make it go around. Speaking of money, be sure and send me a copy of the birth certificate as soon as you can. It will mean thirty more dollars a month for us.

Say hello to your folks for me and keep a stiff upper lip, Butch. It won't be long now. I hope it doesn't hurt too much.

All my love

Ted

22 April 1945

Dearest Stella,

I suppose this letter will find you a mother. How does it feel to be a parent? Did you have a very hard time, honey? I certainly hope not.

You will know I am now across the Rhine. Boy, that was a sensation. I'll never forget the day I crossed. It's something you feel inside – I can't describe it. I don't think the war will last much longer now. Maybe we can be together sooner than we think. I can hardly wait for that day. Better be ready.

The Germans are surrendering so fast we are up almost 24 hours a day. The end really is in sight. Received your letter today. Words can't express my feelings, darling. Write me more what your post-war plans are. I don't know what the Army discharge plans are and maybe I might go to fight the damn japs [sic]. Yesterday we turned in our record of service, number of months overseas, number of decorations, awards, and number of dependants. By the way, you didn't tell me the baby's name. The last two days in the sector that we're in, about 100,000 Germans surrendered at almost the same time. They came in buses, trucks – almost anything with wheels. This morning one tried to escape. He wouldn't halt so the guard had to kill him. Too bad, but necessary. Well, darling, take the best care possible of the both of you, especially yourself.

All my love for ever

Ted

France
3 June 1945

Dearest Stella,

I can see you don't intend to write so will make this last attempt. We made our trip from Germany without any mishaps of any kind. The entire journey took about four days. It rained almost all the time, but still it was good leaving Germany behind. We're spending our time just now doing anything we want to. We play football and pitch horse-shoe all day. I'm really getting plenty of sleep now. Yesterday we turned in all the trucks to Ordnance. I hated to see mine go because it was working better than it ever did.

Love
Ted

30 August 1945

Dear Stella,

Well, darling, I don't know what to think about you. I haven't had a word for three months now. Down in your heart, do you really think you're being fair? Where you are concerned, at least I have done my share. I was man enough to go to a lot of trouble and expense to come all the way from France to London to marry you. I certainly didn't have to do that if I didn't want to. I don't imagine you care to go to the States with me. If not, what do you want to do? Are you going to get a divorce? I could have had a furlough to England about a month ago, but the way you are carrying on I turned it down. I wasn't sure I would be welcome.

I'm to leave for home, if nothing happens, in a few days. The plans are now we are to fly. Please write soon and let me know what *your* plans are. That's all I ask of you, and it isn't much. I'll admit I wasn't much of a husband, but I didn't have much of a chance to be one either.

All my love
Ted

Miniverism

> When people say to me: 'Oh, so you're Mrs Miniver!' I always draw myself up to my full height and say: 'No – I *write* Mrs Miniver.' But lately I've begun to wonder rather bitterly whether it wouldn't be truer to say: 'Mrs Miniver writes *me*' ... There have been moments when I found myself exclaiming: 'Oh Lord, I think I shall push this woman in front of a bus!'
>
> Jan Struther, Lecture to the English Association,
> November 1939

For some, the war was a celebration of the brave little lady. Her husband abroad, her staff depleted, children in Canada for safety or away at school, she did her bit with zest and aplomb. Patriotic and snobbish, she was irrepressible and could drive a village mad. Queen Victoria's reproach to Arthur Balfour during the Boer War, 'We are not interested in the possibilities of defeat', hung framed in her dining-room. The novelist E. M. Delafield's *The Provincial Lady in War-time*, a very funny book, showed her at her most tolerable, Jan Struther at her most insufferable. Jan Struther called her 'Mrs Miniver', a name inspired by seeing a man carrying a bundle of furs out of a warehouse in Upper Thames Street. Miss Struther (Mrs Anthony Maxtone-Graham) was a writer of what were known as 'light middles' for *Punch* and other papers when Peter Fleming invited her to contribute a series of articles about 'just an ordinary sort of woman, who leads an ordinary sort of life – rather like yourself' to *The Times*. Thus was born Mrs Miniver and Miniverism, the complete class-conscious Home Front lady battling it out with total social confidence. In 1942 William Wyler's *Mrs Miniver*, with Greer Garson, placed this paragon before millions of filmgoers in the States, lending a curious view of the womanhood of Britain.

At home Miniverism was attacked with such vehemence that Jan Struther was obliged to defend her creation, which she did in a witty lecture to the English Association in November 1939. *Times* readers found Mrs Miniver too trivial for their sacred Court Page and had protested. Then, when her upper-class soap became an establishment entertainment, more serious objections were voiced. Mrs Miniver was denounced by Rosamond Lehmann in the *Spectator* and E. M. Forster in the *New Statesman*. Jan Struther did her best to prove that it had never been her intention to promote 'the Struther–Miniver axis' as a 'howling snob'. Forster's anger bewildered her. 'I don't agree with him at all. It seems to me that he is confusing class-consciousness with class-hostility. This is a mistake which is only too often made ... Class-consciousness is not in itself a bad thing, any more than any other form of consciousness is a bad thing. On the whole, there is far too little consciousness about in the world.'

The influence of Jan Struther on letter-writing was considerable. Her Mrs Miniver, unflaggingly cheerful, indomitable and insensitive, authorized a certain social tone and attitude. In 1941 the following letter from her anthology *Women of Britain*, published in New York, would have shown the lady at her ineffable worst.

Surrey
18 August 1940

Darling B,

Well, John spent a week here putting up K's and our shelters and a lovely job he made of them. K's is in the barn and ours is partly in the ground by the back door and joined on to the wall of Mrs B's bedroom. It has electric light, shelves, a long seat, a concrete floor, and holds 5 quite easily, and 9 or 10 at a pinch.

Roses trail over the sandbags and in fact it is a very dainty and Ideal Homey affair, and doesn't take up too much room to allow cars to turn round by the barn. Two days after it was put up, air raids began in earnest and *did* K and I pat ourselves on the back and put out our tongues (metaphorically) at the neighbours and tradesmen who had smiled at our sandbags, etc.

As I expect you've heard *ad nauseam*, there have been incessant raids this week. The most exciting was on Thursday when about 50 German bombers came right over us and dropped bombs (which hurt no one except a few chickens) in R— and at B— Court, about half a mile from here. It was about 7 and a most lovely evening. I'd just given Sue her bath when I heard a deep droning noise, no siren, so I went out to see, and Christopher, who simply haunts the house and is always using P's Zeiss glasses, rushed up to me and said in a voice quite trembly with delight, 'Look, LOOK, there are hundreds of great German Junkers.' So I wildly looked up through the glasses and, my goodness, it was magnificent. There were the bombers coming up in a great V-shape out of the South-East (we heard after that they were only about 50, but they looked at least 500!). And suddenly two little Spitfires came diving down right under them and up the other side, firing like mad, a sort of tat-tat-tat against the deep droning noise. They looked so tiny and heroic, rushing at those great bombers, it made you hold your breath. Then the anti-aircraft guns began to fill the air with big black blobs of smoke and I suddenly realized what I was looking at, grabbed Sue, shouted to Christopher and Mrs B and was in the shelter in about two seconds. As we got in the noise was all up and down the scale, and one big BOO-OOP like somebody giving you a bang on the ear (the bombs at B— Court, I suppose). Poor Sue burst into tears, trembling so that I had to hold her tighter and tighter, and wetting my dress right through, poor lamb. Christopher was splendid. He grabbed our new kitten, Darkie, who'd followed us into the shelter, and held him up, all purring, and said, 'Look, Sue, Darkie is purring, he *loves* air raids.' Then Sue laughed and in a few minutes she was quite happy, and ever since she hasn't turned a hair, just bustles into the shelter and starts reading a book. And she isn't frightened at night or *anything*. And Janet and Sally are the same, so K and I are very happy. Christopher of course just adores raids.

I must say I am glad that I saw that sight, and K and I agreed it sort of satisfied something in our souls to hear those noises. I shall never forget the terrific droning as the bombers came up out of that lovely evening sky, and K felt her whole house shake as the bombs exploded, and to feel the children had seen and heard it too, and come through quite happy.

Apparently, as a squadron of our fighters came from the Dorking direction, the Germans swung right round over the pig farm next door and made off for the coast. They looked so invincible, and yet all they did was to kill a few hens and make Sue cry and wet her knickers, and then our fighters chased them out to sea. Oh yes, they put our telephone and electricity out of action for a few hours by making some holes in the road and knocking down a few telephone poles. That was the day we brought down 160 German planes, and we haven't had anything as exciting since, though lots of alarms, and AA fire. The anti-aircraft guns, by the way, have done superbly; 57 planes this week. As soon as our fighters are in action the AA have to cease fire. Today we had to have lunch in the shelter, Dad and M and Mrs B, R, Sue and myself, with P and P—r standing outside and handing in claret and cider!

P—r is doing a special gunnery course in Kent for a month and had two days' leave. M—l was here too, hobbling most painfully with a bullet wound through the ankle from a raid on some aerodrome where he was working.

PLUMS – B, I feel I shall never be quite at ease in face of plums again. I've bottled and jammed and jellied and pickled them till my feet are flat and my hands gnarled with stirring and still the trees are *loaded*, and plums come plopping down on the lawn and are eaten by wasps and blackbirds. If I dealt with every plum on my two trees, I could feed a regiment for a year, and K has NINE similarly loaded. We've also packed about 20 lbs of beans in salt. I go over to K's for the News most evenings and we go bicycling, sometimes into R— to shop, and sometimes just for rides, and it is lovely. The children pedal away in front and K and I trundle along behind, gossiping and laffing.

Oh, B, a Frenchman is *singing* Verlaine's loveliest (in my opinion) poem on the radio, 'Le ciel est, par-dessus le toit, Si bleu, si calme' – singing it very well, as a matter of fact. I remember reading it at Bowen's Court two years ago, and what millions of years ago that seems.

PS Just got your letter offering to take Sue. Bless you, my dear, but I can't let her go – and now that the air raids have begun, we have our shelter, and I feel sure I must keep her here.

Writing in a Blitz

Miss Dorothy Thompson made a broadcast to Britain to-night. Her audience was somewhat reduced, since the air-raid siren sounded just after she started speaking. She informed the British that the poets of the world were lined up on their side. That, she said, was a matter of consequence. I'm not sure that Londoners agreed that the poets would be of much assistance as they grabbed their blankets and headed for the air-raid shelters ... She predicted that ages from now mothers and fathers would gather their children about their knees and tell them about these days. Well, mothers and fathers have their children about them tonight – underground. They're sustained in part by folklore, tradition, and the history of Britain, but they're an undemonstrative lot.

Ed Murrow, BBC broadcast to America, 12 September 1940

The blitz (*Blitzkrieg* = 'lightning war') produced three eloquent and distinctive strands of writing. Partly due to the number of London-based poets and novelists working in civil defence, and especially in the Auxiliary Fire Service and at the BBC, the blitzed capital with all its grim humour, poignant architectural destruction and tragedy received immediate literary attention. No less attracted to the national character so nakedly exposed by this event was the Mass Observation recorder. MO, as it was called, was three years old when the *Luftwaffe* threw the classes together in a necessary camaraderie, providing unprecedented material for the oral historian. And, of course, the bombing filled countless diaries and letters, although there was much self-censoring of the latter when they were sent to children and spouses far from home, so as not to worry them. A 'London can take it' attitude was created from the start, its chirpy insouciance rapidly becoming as boring as 'the night we nearly copped it' bore in the saloon bar.

The behaviour of blitzed Britain has been much analysed. That any future war would be a 'modern' war from the air had been an exciting though dreaded concept since the mid-twenties when the Fascist poet Gabriele D'Annunzio thrilled to the 'blacking out of the sun' with planes. He was responding to he who was to be the enormously influential apostle of mass demoralization by bombers, General Douhet, who said, 'Hammer the nation itself to make it give in. It will be an inhuman, atrocious performance, but these are the facts.' Douhetism lay behind Britain's later merciless pounding of German cities from the air and the dropping of atom bombs on Japan. Many other influences combined to cause people to believe that, when a second 'Great War' was declared, there would be a holocaust directed from the skies. There was H. G. Wells, there were the cinema news programmes showing the destruction of Chinese, Spanish and Abyssinian cities and their helpless populations. The bombing of the small Basque town of Guernica on an April afternoon in 1937 by Junker and Heinkel planes, and its deliberate annihilation by explosives and incendiaries, became a foretaste of what would happen to London should another war against Germany break out. Nobody foresaw how Londoners or the citizens of places like Coventry, Liverpool and Cardiff would behave. Churchill in 1934 was prophesying that millions of people would rush from the capital, which he endowed with bovine helplessness – 'as the greatest target in the world, a kind of tremendous, fat, valuable cow, fed up to attract beasts of prey'. So abhorrent was the bombing of open cities that many believed that, while Britain would naturally defend hers, she would not dream of obliterating the enemy's – only his factories, shipyards and so on. Picasso's 'Guernica', commissioned by the new Spanish Republican government for its pavilion at the World's Fair in Paris, was a masterpiece painted to show civilized Europe's outrage at Douhetism, or the mass demoralization of a people by bombers. It had immense influence.

Meanwhile, precautions against the effect of air raids had begun to be set in motion, some public, some highly secret. The first Air Raid Precaution committee sat in 1924, its chief aim to decide what to do with a panic-stricken city. In 1931 there was talk of evacuating schoolchildren, expectant mothers and toddlers from London. In 1935 ARP in the form it would be known throughout the war was born, its local controllers granted considerable status. Dr David Anderson designed an excellent garden shelter from fourteen sheets of corrugated iron. These would be complemented in 1941 by the indoor 'Morrison' shelter, a solid table-like structure. By now there was a vast army of some two million fire-watchers, firemen and wardens. The imagery created by blazing London raged through the poetry of Stephen Spender, T. S. Eliot, Dylan Thomas, Edith Sitwell, George Barker, Stevie Smith and Arthur Waley. By the end of 1940 many more people had been killed in air raids than in the armed forces – 23,000 civilians. There was no Douhetism – at least on the predicted scale. People were frightened and unnerved but there was the reverse of national panic. There was loss and pain and miserable discomfort, the mourning of the death of families, friends and neighbours, of the destruction of beloved homes and of noble architecture. But there was an underplaying of emotion, there was control and an awe-inspiring display of adaptation to a shattered scene. Stevie Smith summed it up:

> Yesterday morning we padded to our offices through piles of broken glass, in the sunshine the streets sparkled like diamonds with the stuff, smashed so small, looking like diamonds and frost. There is a large bomb crater in the road just outside what is left of St James's, Piccadilly, it's deep all London clay and with fountains of water cascading down into it from broken mains: smells of gas and burning everywhere ... It's bloody silly knocking each other's cities to bits like this.

The poet Alun Lewis, soon to die in Arakan, deplored air-raid brutalism:

Softly the civilized
Centuries fall,
Paper on paper,
Peter on Paul.
. . . .
Blue necklace left
On a charred chair
Tells that Beauty
Was startled there.

Dylan Thomas wrote threnodies for the bombing's haphazard
victims, 'A Refusal to Mourn the Death, by Fire, of a Child in
London', 'Among Those Killed in the Dawn Raid was a Man Aged a
Hundred'. Edith Sitwell saw it all as yet one more mindless nail
hammered into Christ. Eliot watched the Wren churches in flames and
thought of the pentecostal fire. The novelist William Golding, decades
later, would take a character from the London blitz, a boy with the clothes
burnt from his body, hairless, anonymous, his very name incinerated, and
make him challenge the rubbishy subculture of the post-war world.

In all, some 51,500 civilians were to be killed by the *Luftwaffe*
bombing of Britain – as contrasted with the 4,400 casualties of the
Zeppelin raids during the First World War. The loss of beautiful
buildings and simple, much loved homes and their surroundings was
enormous. The ruin was pathetic, sordid, sometimes magical. In
London the pubs, cinemas, teashops and dance-halls were packed with
people of many nations for whom custom had been put aside for the
duration. There was freedom and excitement, danger and adventure.
The West End was like the base of some vast maypole around which
crowds found their way in the blacked-out streets. Ribbons of
searchlight crossed and tangled overhead among the silver barrage
balloons. Below, in the basements of Oxford Street shops and along
miles of Underground passages and platforms, lay the East-Enders in
their blankets. They came up west in their thousands each early
afternoon to secure a safe hole for the night. The blitz was dramatic,
strange, monstrously uncomfortable, full of kindness, shocking, comic
– everything. It naturally filled the page.

The Chief Warden of Paddington, Mr Hull, kept a diary to 'build up a semi-official record' of what he and his men and women experienced. The borough of Paddington had begun to plan its ARP as early as 1936. A year later it divided itself into twelve areas and set up a lecture programme. Large-scale ARP exercises were carried out in Portsmouth and Southampton in the summer of 1937, and in Paddington in February 1938. 'Great doings in Paddington last night,' wrote the *Daily Express*.

Mythical enemy bombers wrecked houses, ripped 15 feet craters in the roads and sprayed the borough with mustard gas. It was the first air-raid demonstration conducted by a borough council in London. Girls who had been 'burned' by mustard gas were rushed to the first-aid station at Paddington General Baths. The first thing to do in such cases is to remove contaminated clothing. Two hundred people in the gallery saw nurses deprive the girls of their clothes. The organizers had warned 'casualties' to wear bathing costumes underneath.

Before the war Paddington's population was some 126,000. By 1941 50,000 had fled. The Warden service, 1,280 strong in 1938 and extremely well organized by the time of the blitz, like ARP organizations all over Britain, had to cope with much abandoned as well as much wrecked property. Chief Warden Hull rules his toppling province phlegmatically and describes it vividly, his prose, like Paddington at night, solid and gloomy until intermittently lit up with unexpectedly bright images.

Incendiaries

11 January 1941. Although these bombs have hitherto been no strangers to Paddington, basket-loads having fallen on the borough and been appropriately dealt with, on this night approximately 1,000 incendiaries fell over 'O' and 'P' post areas simultaneously, landing with a clatter, clutter or flop, according to the nature of the lodgement, which suddenly transformed the peaceful moonlit scene into a spluttering chessboard of fireworks.

Emerging from the shadows there immediately appeared numerous figures shaped like human beings but active as monkeys, scanning, scurrying and scrambling as best they could to reach the spots where the need was most. Streets, mews, gardens and trees were lit up on all sides, window-panes sparkled with reflections, and at least one bomb, lodged on a top-storey fire-escape balcony, showered a brilliant cascade of sparks to the depths below. Another, tucked into the corner of a stone window-ledge, fizzled itself into impotent fury because it could only break a few panes, whilst another came to an inglorious end by plunging straight through the roof and ceiling into a bath of water.

Wardens and fire-fighting parties were up against local problems concerning rapid access into various buildings, occupied or empty, a hatchet or heavy shoulder doing the trick against an obstinate door. A ladder, much too short, provided nightmarish attempts to reach a wanted spot, and what with pumps, buckets, running footsteps, toil, sweat, smoke and the smell of burning bombs and property, no wonder the feline residents on the prowl for mice or companionship felt that this war was becoming a beastly nuisance.

Fluctuating glows through top-floor windows showing spurts of activity indicated that bombs were being tackled indoors. In one instance an agile climber scrambled over the roof-tops on a perilous journey to gain access along a narrow and shaky-looking fire-escape in time to assist an elderly stirrup-pump party comprised mainly of women panting with exertion, but rejoicing in their mastery over an obstinate bomb which was trying to burrow its way into the room beneath. A momentary pause for a breather and further investigation through an open window, and the climber could see the buildings opposite silhouetted against a bluish-red background of sky. Here and there were smoke umbrellas tinged with dull red, indicating a greater hold by the fire, and tougher jobs in progress.

Soon the uncanny lights began to fade, thanks to the prompt action of all concerned, and only three high explosives caused additional damage to Paddington this night, with injury to one person. Although some 570 incendiaries were reported to Control, the remainder simply left signs of their natural death where they had fallen harmlessly in the streets or open spaces, or where the funeral pyres were more readily indicated by small quantities of sand which finally reduced their initial glare.

Warden E. Savastapulo of Post 'P', who was injured when endeavouring to subdue with sandbags an incendiary bomb which exploded, died in St Mary's Hospital, his being the first Warden fatality whilst on duty in the borough. His funeral was held at the Greek Church Aghia Sophia, Moscow Road, W2, five days later.

Parachute Mines

16–17 April 1941. On this night many parachute mines descended all over the metropolitan area. A few minutes after the alert sounded at 2103 hours it was very evident that Londoners were in for something more than a casual visit. Many planes could be heard overhead, seemingly everywhere. Occasional flares, suspended like brilliant chandeliers, appeared almost stationary in the clear night sky, to be shot out. It was difficult at first to distinguish whether bombs or semi-distant heavy gunfire were responsible for the noise and occasional tremors. Paddington 'Jim Crows' on the watch from house-tops could see a big fire, and clouds of smoke varying in colour between green and red, and drifting east. Muffled explosions reminded one somewhat of Vesuvius in mild eruption. Indoors, there were creaks and flappings of blinds and curtains. Window-frames rattled, inside-doors swung open and closed with a sighing and a soughing, as if operated by ghosts, pictures moved uneasily on the walls, a card on a mantelpiece fluttered to the floor, and the atmosphere was uncanny with a feeling not easily defined or accountable because of the lack of any nearby bomb activity. It was all indicative of big stuff being somewhere on the move.

By midnight more fires, at intervals, pin-pointed parts of Greater London receiving attention, and for quite a long time barrage balloons were clearly visible at considerable distances. Added to the continuous din of heavy enemy bombers was that of our busy fighters, who frequently signalled their whereabouts. Bombers diving to escape the fighters, or to set a more direct course for bomb or mine, zoomed through space and hurried off, followed by a rapid peal of thunder from the guns and the cracking of flak on their tails. A direct hit would send a plane in a long last drawn-out whining dive to mother earth. The spattering of spent machine-gun bullets, or of showers of shrapnel, or the lighter whine of a shellcap, joined in the music of a fascinating night. It seemed astonishing that amidst so much activity Paddington should remain unscathed.

Just before 0300 hours two parachute mines descended which gave our Civil Defence Services a packet of trouble, and work lasting several days and nights before all the casualties were accounted for. By 0430 hours aerial activity had almost ceased, but a homeward-bound Nazi plane, attracted by the glare of a fierce fire still raging in a neighbouring borough, finished up the night with a parting bomb launched from a great height. It seemed to whistle for miles before landing near Paddington. A faint waning moon now began to lose itself in the dawn of another day, whilst below the pulse of Civil Defence all over London, with that calm, heady, tireless energy which has made the attempts of the Hun to destroy the cities and morale of our people look silly and useless, began to beat faster. In every direction there were swirling clouds of dust, fronts and backs of buildings agape, some draped with drooping roofs, sagging floors, wrenched-off doors, tattered wallpapers, tossed-about furniture, broken windows, and pock-marked stone buildings which had stopped the passage of blast-driven debris. Craters in the roadways, burst water-mains and fractured gas-pipes. But although the electricity flickered now and then, during the whole of the Battle of London the supply rarely failed and left us in the dark.

London was to receive 18,800 tons of high explosive during the 1940–41 blitz. The behaviour of ordinary people under bombing, whether in Britain, Germany, Vietnam, Iraq or even in Japan, has never been as predicted. They are hurt, wearied but not demoralized. Tom Hopkinson, writing in the influential *Picture Post*, made the point that in Britain most ordinary people 'in those days were used to deprivation and lived every day with anxiety; so that side of the distress was not so much new as additional. The rich never understood this.' Hopkinson saw the inter-war theories about the usefulness of bombing cities in order to quickly win a battle as being full of contempt for the 'common man', for 'even where his courage may have faltered, his common sense – and cunning too – kept body and mind alive, with that seemingly endless capacity for adaptation which, alas perhaps for the future of the earth, has made him paramount over all other beasts'. 'You've got to forget this civilian,' said Barry Goldwater in 1967. 'Whenever you drop bombs, you're going to hit civilians.' Hit, yet mysteriously not panic them – thus making the main gist of such warfare a failed exercise. Although so badly bombed itself, there was little pity in Britain for the 'saturation' bombing of Germany, and those who protested against it, like George Bell, the Bishop of Chichester, were condemned for their lack of patriotism.

On 19 September 1942 George Orwell's BBC War Commentary mentioned that:

the British bombing raids on Western Germany continue and are now too frequent to be enumerated individually. The RAF are now dropping bombs which weigh no less than 8,000 pounds or $3\frac{1}{2}$ tons. These bombs do not penetrate the ground but burst on the surface, devastating the houses for hundreds of yards around. Aerial photographs of Karlsruhe, Düsseldorf and other places show whole areas of hundreds of acres where there is scarcely a house with its roof intact . . .

Four days ago, September 15th, was celebrated throughout this country and the world as the second anniversary of the Battle of Britain. Between August and October 1940, after the fall of France, the Germans made an all-out effort to conquer Britain by

air and loudly boasted that they would be able to do so within a
few weeks. They started off in August and September with
daylight raids aimed at destroying the Royal Air Force, and when
this had evidently failed, switched over to night raids directed
chiefly at the working-class areas in the East End of London,
aiming at terrorizing the civilian population. The whole ma-
noeuvre however was a failure.

Ed Murrow, reporting to America, said:

One bombed house looks pretty much like another bombed house.
So it's about the people I'd like to talk, the little people who live
in those little houses, who have no uniforms and get no decoration
for bravery. Those men whose only uniform was a tin hat were
digging unexploded bombs out of the ground this afternoon.
There were two women who gossiped across a narrow strip of
tired brown grass that separated their two houses. They didn't
have to open their kitchen windows in order to converse. The
glass had been blown out. There was a little man with a pipe in
his mouth who walked up and looked at a bombed house and
said, 'One fell there and that's all.' Those people were calm and
courageous. About an hour after the All Clear had sounded they
were sitting in deck chairs on their lawns, reading the Sunday
papers. The girls in light, cheap dresses were strolling along the
street. There was no bravado, no loud voices, only a quiet
acceptance of the situation.

An anonymous young fireman wrote this description of the East End
raids while lying injured in Guy's Hospital. Like so many witnesses of
the blitz, he is haunted as much by its strangeness as by its horrors.

I was on a stretcher. I could hear a pump moaning away behind
me and beyond that the sound of the fire. So they hadn't taken
us very far from the ladders. I felt weak and couldn't call out to

Mary. Then George came along and asked me how I was getting on. So I said, 'Bloody.' He said, 'You ought to be more careful, but you've got a blighty all right.'

I said, 'What's wrong with me?' He said, 'I don't know, but I just seen you looking at the Ambulance Girl, so you ain't dying.' He wouldn't believe me when I told him I and the Ambulance Driver were engaged to be married.

I couldn't move an inch when I tried to get up, so I decided my back was broken. But, of course, it wasn't. Art came over from the pump behind me, and he and George kept cracking jokes.

Then I remember the all clear going. George went over and said to Mary, 'Fireman over there says you promised to marry him . . . ' Mary didn't even look up but said, 'Tell him I'm going to marry another fireman – from 25 Station.'

George nearly jumped off the ground and said, 'But he *is* from 25 . . . ' Then it was Mary's turn for a surprise. I thought I was going to burst into tears when she saw me. She said, 'Are you the concussion case?' I didn't know what I was, but she was right enough, and here I am.

In spite of the headache I got, I must say I rather enjoyed it all. Talk about drama in real life. And what's more I'm enjoying it now, with damn all to do except lie here and write.

Mum and Dad came up to see me yesterday. They said Station Officer Adams himself got hold of the Post Office at home and told them to tell Mum that I wasn't badly hurt. That was nice of him.

Later. I feel I ought to be able to write all sorts of things about the Fire Brigade now I'm here in Guy's, but I can't think of anything to say. I've been re-reading this diary. What I've left out more than anything else is the people of the East End with whom I've been living for so long. After the Blitz in September, the way those people settled down to it was quite extraordinary. What a wonderfully adaptable animal is the Englishman or woman. But then I suppose mankind generally is fairly adaptable.

Look at the people of Madrid. They had it for four years – bombs and shells. Must have been like life on the coast.

It looks to me very much as if this bombing in modern warfare is a complete flop. You obviously can't win a war on bombing. Anyway, Hitler won't win this war on it, that's one thing certain. The way the provinces have taken it too. It's the same thing as the East End over again. I think the East End got it worse than anyone else, not because the Blitz was actually worse, but because the little brick houses fell down as soon as the German airmen looked at them. And then there weren't any proper shelters. The People's Convention have certainly a case there.

I can remember going into a house – I think it was a two-pump job in Batty Road – and we had to get the family to agree to the removal of the old father who was bedridden. It wasn't what you'd call a rescue job, because the fire itself was actually next door. But we had to get the old man out. Mother wouldn't agree. Said there wasn't any danger. Said he'd be OK where he was. It was raining bombs and incendiaries all the time, and there was precious little roof over the old man's head. And there he lay in bed listening to Adams arguing with his missus. Then suddenly he said, 'Tell 'em I've been in this bed two years. Tell 'em I'm going to die in this bed anyway, so I might as well die in it now.'

But we moved him just the same. Now, that family had the old man, mother, the three daughters and a son all living in that one room. What's more, one of the girls had a child who slept there too. They paid eighteen shillings a week for that room and use of lavatory and sink outside in the passage. They cooked on an oil stove in the corner near the son's bed. The girls all slept in one bed – together with the baby. That house was lousy, the bricks were rotten. Three hours after we'd got them out a second Red went up and an HE nearly half a mile away sent the whole lot over. I wonder what happened to that family?

The other thing that strikes me is the way I say something in this diary and then leave it, without telling what happened afterwards. I said all about the East End being knocked down in September and never went on to say how the people put up with it. I said somewhere that 'the street outside the station was a mess'. Well, it was. But the Demolition people put it right in about a month. I honestly believe an unobservant person could walk down the Eastern Way today and not know there was a war on. They might think a lot of house-building or demolition was in progress, but it doesn't look like war.

And I haven't written about the almost supernatural power of explosives. I've seen bits of bomb-splinter cut right through a steel girder. I saw a whole ten-ton girder down at the docks thrown fifty feet in the air and then come down on a row of houses and knock them flat. One of the things which astounded me at first was the way an HE on a single house in a row will take that house out as if some giant dentist had drawn a tooth. And the people will go on living in the houses on either side. There's nothing neater than the extraction of a house from a row by a bomb. They say this is due to some building act which makes it a law that the party-walls must be double between houses – against fire. Well, it works against bombs too.

I've seen some pretty miserable things since the Blitz started. What sticks in my mind more than anything else was the little boy who was fetched out of a fire and kept saying, 'My little widdle, my little widdle', and looking for it with his hands. But it had been burnt off. He died. It's extraordinary how few people get over burning – even quite mild burning. They nearly all seem to die afterwards in hospital. I suppose it's the shock.

But after a night of Blitz, when we got back to breakfast at 25 Station, I'd go up in the Rec. and sit at the glassless windows and look out on to the Eastern Way. And I'd see the milkman go by with his hand-cart.

The Deed and the Award

> How can I live among this gentle
> obsolescent breed of heroes, and not weep?

> Keith Douglas, 'I Think I am
> Becoming a God'

Many wartime novelists and film-makers struggled to capture the insouciance of heroism, only to tumble into its clichés. In the long run it was found that only the hero himself could come up with the perfectly offhand word. The distinguished Canadian artist Hugh Cronyn's account of receiving the George Medal (instituted for 'Acts of Gallantry' by George VI in 1940) is a classic example of the hero speaking. Such attitudes as his could not be faked. They had to rest on a genuinely cool ability to have done what had to be done, and on a kind of youthful amusement at life never being more crazily interesting than at the moment when it could vanish.

Cronyn was a youthful member of the artistic community which lived by the riverside at Hammersmith and Chiswick when the war began. He had earlier painted in Spain during the civil war. Hitler's war took him all over the world and also introduced him to Suffolk, where he met his wife, Jean, and where later he made his home. His friends included Julian Trevelyan, Mary Fedden, John Nash – an official war artist for the second time – and many painters living in and around the Stour Valley.

In September 1939 I had gone up to Hutton-le-Hole in Yorkshire to join Gin and Ray Coxon who were painting there on the edge of the moors. Hutton was a nice little place with a stream running down the middle, dividing one side of the wide valley into two terraces with a line of small houses along each side. They had been there about a week when I joined them. Our position there was becoming suspect because the news of the declaration of war was now likely and our painting activity was being looked on with suspicion by the older inhabitants who recalled that at the beginning of the '14–'18 war German bands were up north, playing in various small towns, and it was thought that they could have been spying. Shortly after the blackout was decreed, Gin and Ray felt we should make our way back to London for them to look after their house, and also to join Ray's friend who had a converted lifeboat which he had offered for use in the Thames in time of emergency. Gin did a marvellous feat of driving through the blackout with coffee-tins over the headlights, two-inch slits allowing only light forward.

Raymond went down to Hayling Island where the lifeboat was and found no one ready, came back and, a few days later, asked me if I would join them to get it into a fit state for the journey around to the Thames. It lay in a creek behind Hayling Island sandbar and had adequate cabins, a Vauxhall marine engine and a 'handy billy', but as it hadn't been moved for some time it was questionable whether it would be in a fit state to do what was required of it. We were told that we would need a pilot to take us around the Channel and up the river. It was another three or four days before he arrived, a Thames Yacht Marina owner, by which time we were able to lay in stores and do some paintwork which was badly needed. We saw this dapper little man coming along the towpath wearing a porkpie hat and bringing a rather pretty girl with him. We took them on board and found it was going to be a jolly party. We went ashore and 'phoned for permission to proceed to sea, only to be told that our pilot must go to the Admiralty in London to see the charts of the minefields. The Admiralty said that there were no minefields on our course and that we could proceed at the next high water, which was necessary to get the boat across the sandbar. When all was ready for sea, we hauled on the anchor rope. Nothing came up but the end of the rope. The anchor stayed imbedded in the mud, so we had to put to sea without an anchor. The sea was calm, fortunately. As we started along the coast we noticed that we were making water very badly by the sterngland and put into Shoreham to inform the authorities of this and to try and stuff up the gland temporarily. The harbour there was completely silent and closed, and the harbour-master, to whom I gave the line to moor alongside, was very sarcastic that I'd not put a bowline or anything on the line to put around the bollard. We were all very green and I think I was the only one with knowledge of sailing in the small boats apart from the pilot. We set off again, but the leaks became so bad that we put into Margate. Having telephoned the authorities, we were told to leave the boat there, return, and go our separate ways.

Some weeks later we received telephone messages from the Port of London Authority down at the Tower Pier to say that the boat had been repaired and brought round by two fishermen who were ready to hand it over to us. The pilot and I were the only members of the original crew available, so we went down with a motor mechanic brother of Gin's as engineer, and a young nephew of hers, neither of whom had any knowledge of boats. We started upstream to Lambeth Pier which was empty and to which we moored, and the pilot went ashore to get further orders and to report our arrival to the Admiralty. While he was away a large tug with barges waved us away from the Pier as they wanted to come alongside, so we had to take the boat into midstream by ourselves and find a buoy to moor to. It was an ebb tide and we got swept down towards Westminster Bridge. I had little knowledge of handling boats in a tideway so as I saw the buoy coming towards me I told the young chap to jump to it with the end of a rope. Thus we were secured stern first to an enormous iron buoy in front of St Thomas's Hospital and opposite the Houses of Parliament. I could see A. P. Herbert watching us through binoculars from *Water Gypsy* moored nearby. By the grace of God and some fiddling we got the boat turned round, the sharp end up towards the current, and waited there for the pilot to return. We then proceeded upstream to his boatyard where our boat was going to have a thorough inspection. She was declared completely useless and practically sinking. So again we were all disbanded and I went back to painting.

It was pleasant painting around the Thames at Hammersmith, where I had a studio in Black Lion Lane, an old garage which had been fitted with a balcony, a stove and everything one required. Many of my friends were already finding suitable activities, some in the forces, some doing ARP work. I applied to join the Friends' Ambulance Service as a stretcher bearer. I also applied to become a Canadian War Artist with the Canadian Forces in Europe, through my cousin General Crerar, Commander of the Canadian Forces in England, but found that I couldn't be accepted or considered except by returning to Canada. But I did get permission to go to Aldershot and there did several pastel drawings of the Canadian officers in charge of the wild troops stationed there. Nothing ever came of these drawings and I still have them.

It was about this time that I did a pastel of A. P. Herbert. We rowed across from the Houses of Parliament to an empty barge in the river, climbed into its rusty interior, where APH took his clothes off for his daily sunbathe and I did a pastel of his head.

Not long after this I got the opportunity to join one of the small boats in the Thames as crew. These were now organized under the control of the Port of London Authority at Tower Pier. We had to go and buy our 'chauffeur's' uniform from Gardner's Corner and have nautical buttons sewn on and collect passes from the Authority. Our job was supposed to be minespotting and running messages from ship to shore, or any duty for which there was no available craft. It was an ARP job, £15 a week, three days on and three days off. We were divided into groups from Westminster, Tower Pier, Cherry Garden Wharf, Woolwich, Grays, Middlesex and Canvey Island, where there was a boom-gate across the Thames. I joined a small motor cruiser named the *Winona*, well built with two Gardner twin diesel engines, powerful and comfortable. We were stationed under the bows of the *Cutty Sark* and from there we carried out patrol duties up and down the Thames from Grays to Tilbury and back again. This was the time of the Evacuation from Dunkirk. We thought we were going to be allowed to go over and help but we were retained as guardians of the Thames. We had one lone Lee Enfield rifle. One duty was to take personnel who had been brought back from Dunkirk and deliver them along the river to wherever they had come from. These were the volunteers who had been over in the small boats. They were completely done in and tired out when we took them on board. For three days they had had no sleep or rest and it was painful to see their state of exhaustion. Our patrol was called the River Emergency Service but it soon became apparent that the Admiralty wanted to take it over and we were told that at a certain time we would parade before representatives of the Board of Admiralty and either sign on for the duration or not. It had been a very relaxed sort of service so far and we were completely ignorant of the duties we would have to perform under naval discipline.

I had some weeks previously answered an advertisement requiring yachtsmen with a knowledge of coastal navigation to become officers for small boat work in the Channel. I had sailed quite a lot with friends from Gravesend and had made several trips across to France, and thought I knew the river fairly well, so I applied to be accepted for officer training. After three weeks I was called for an interview by two RN commanders and had to answer many searching questions about navigation on the river. I was then studying a yachtsman's book on navigation and sailing by Lunn and I told the commanders that I would go on doing this whether I was required to join or not.

In the meantime we had paraded on the deck of the *Cutty Sark* in front of enlistment officers who wanted to know whether we wanted to sign on as naval ratings in the reorganized River

Emergency Service, now called the Royal Naval Auxiliary Patrol. I made it plain that if I did sign on I would want to accept the call-up for officer's training if it were offered. Well, I did sign on and, of course, we were immediately sent to Portsmouth for kitting-out as ordinary seamen and came back on duty resplendent in what my mother used to call Sailor Suits. I remember taking one of A. P. Herbert's daughters to the Café Royal in my new Ordinary Seaman's uniform and having a drink at the next table to a Commander RN, who couldn't believe his eyes that a rating should be in such a place.

Our boat was then posted to Holehaven on Canvey Island, where we were to carry out the same type of duties as before, including patrolling the chain boom-gate across the river during the night. I remember my first watch ever, in complete darkness and in fog. I was keeping a direct course by compass and I was amazed when the compass started going round and round and round. I hadn't the wit or experience to know that we were caught in an eddy by the boom-gate. Fortunately one of the others rushed up, the engineer who used to be a dredger engineer. He put her into reverse and took us out of the absolutely crazy trap that I had let us get into. It was all experience but also all becoming more serious than I had imagined. We were patrolling up and down the river in broad daylight when the German bombers came over, the Dorniers coming in across the Channel and turning left up the Thames right over our heads. They came on and on. Little puffs of smoke were seen below the aircraft and we thought that these were parachutes being dropped. My legs went hollow as our only armament was a First World War machine-gun. However, these little puffs of smoke were the anti-aircraft shells failing to reach the bombers. It was on that night and during the next few days that the Germans rained such terrible devastation on the Thames shipping and warehouses. By this time we were all in uniform but we hadn't yet been issued with the White Ensign. A signal was received at the Lobster Smack in Holehaven, our HQ, which said that we were to collect the White Ensign and proceed up the river next day to take Churchill and his wife to see the ruins of the bombing. It was a great honour to us to think that we had been chosen for this duty because APH, who had his *Water Gypsy* carrying out the same duties further up river, had not yet received his White Ensign. We were the sturdier of these little boats and able to stand the current and the buffeting. We came up to Cherry Garden Pier and then to our disappointment we found that we were to take on the journalists and the food, while the PLA launch just ahead of us had been allocated to carry Mr and Mrs Churchill. We followed them round and saw the devastation and the fires that were still burning, and then we returned to Holehaven.

There are many sunny days I have left out during which it was sheer pleasure cruising up and down the river, or when we beached our ship to scrape and anti-foul her bottom and do running repairs. Then there were the continuous fire bomb attacks, as we were near the petrol tanks strewn all along the sides of the Thames. We were in the midst of this fire bomb rain. We then discovered that the tanks did not contain petrol and that most of them were full of molasses. After a few weeks of this fringe warfare I received a command from the Admiralty to proceed to HMS *King Alfred*, the old swimming baths near Brighton which were used for officer training. We had by this time taken into our little ship ordinary ratings from merchant ships, and they gave me a foretaste of the smell and the claustrophobia one would get on a mess deck with the hammocks slung across the tables, and anywhere else where there was room to sling them, so I wasn't disappointed to hand in my Ordinary Seaman's uniform and my boots, and to go out and buy a new uniform at Gieves and report to HMS *King Alfred*.

HMS *King Alfred* was actually the former Hove swimming baths and playing fields. Anything the Navy took over on land or sea came under the same naval routine, although we were billeted ashore. I was very fortunate to be accepted for the course as I found that most of the others had far more seagoing experience than I had. The Canadians, one of whom I knew, came from yacht clubs, especially the Royal Canadian Yacht Club in Toronto, of which I had been a member, and had been accepted for this course only after a stiff examination. But I had been accepted without this exam as at the time there was a great shortage of command material with small boats. Little did I know that once you got into this great machine called the Admiralty they did what they liked with you.

It was a five week refresher course in navigation, seamanship, how to erect sheerlegs, do anchor drill for HMS *Hood*, how to salute, do field drill, how to wear gaiters if you were a gunnery officer, and ethics. The latter impressed me the most and I felt I was being taken into some mystical body in terrestrial form. There was no allegiance sworn, the real Senior Service. Yet again, little did I know. One morning at Divisions the Commander called for volunteers to train to deal with the magnetic mines which were being dropped on London and around the coast. Several officers went forward to see the Commander but I hesitated, and this is a thing one must never do. It was not until after Divisions that I went up to see the Commander and volunteer.

I think we stayed on a week at HMS *King Alfred*, after which we were sent on mining courses at HMS *Dolphin*, the submarine base at Portsmouth, and then up to Campbeltown to continue our training. There I found an old friend of mine, Edward Young, in charge of the training submarine and I obtained permission to sail with him in the submarine as part of my course. I think this convinced me that I would not volunteer for submarine work. Edward Young was an author whom I had met in Hammersmith. Later on I came across – or at least our convoy came across – his submarine as it proceeded with the northbound convoy at night and was run into by a merchant ship proceeding with the southbound convoy. I had volunteered for the work on magnetic mines because as our course at HMS *King Alfred* continued I realized how little I knew about seamanship and the Navy itself. I dreaded the possibility that I might be drafted to a seagoing ship as an executive officer. This actually happened to me later on, and when I hardly knew one end from the other. So better that one should do something which no one else knew much about. And this was the reason why I volunteered – to save face! The Commander in charge of our hurried training tried to get us danger money. This was refused by the Admiralty but they agreed to give us instant promotion. So here we were after only five weeks, full Lieutenants RNVR. Quite a brassy thing to be, though for me full of consequences later on. Seniority was a prerogative in the Navy. Soon the call came for members of our group to proceed to their various appointed stations which were mostly in and around London. To my great disappointment – and this was where the hesitation counted – I, with the others who volunteered later, was deployed in bomb disposal, something I was not looking forward to.

In training for bomb disposal we were sent to an RAF camp to see what a bomb looked like, and how it was fused and detonated. This type of bomb fusing we later found was quite different from the German bombs. We then went on to a naval site to see the only German bomb and bomb fuses in captivity. We listened to the buzzing mechanism of a time fuse capable of being set between 0 and 72 hours which had been taken out by some heroic person. We burnt the interior of a bomb to show how to dispose of it because a bonfire of TNT can be made once you have picked out the picric acid. And we had a day's course at the Admiralty on electricity – just the elements one had learnt at school. We were also taught not to say 'yes' to a Commander; a Commander was always right and you must answer, 'Aye, aye, Sir.' We then collected the tools of our trade, which were very simple and very secret, and were told that from now on we were to get on with it by ourselves.

I was dispatched to Bristol as my headquarters and put in charge of the whole of Gloucestershire, including Avonmouth, and of any Admiralty property as far as Salisbury. Avonmouth docks and Bristol were the places which kept me in constant activity. I had a few weeks of quiet before it all began, and then the raids on Avonmouth started, nightly with fire bombs at first, and then the heavies coming in as the fires lit up their targets. I was billed with Captain Trewin, the captain of Bristol dockyards, and had to wait until after a raid began until I was summoned by telephone to where the incident might be. The first of these was in Avonmouth docks – right by the gates. The area had been quite heavily bombed and was completely evacuated. I was told that there were two bombs at the gate by a resolute policeman who, of course, had no option but to be on guard, and was taken into the canteen where the bomb was said to be. I looked at the fragments of the exploded bomb which were like an open cylinder. This was the first exploded bomb I had ever seen. The policeman said, 'You will see the other further along at the other end of the canteen.' I was alone in the darkness but I had a torch and shone it on the unexploded canister quietly sitting there. It didn't look much like anything I'd been told about. On inspection I started to make out a name in the ironwork, CALOR, and of course it was one of the canteen's Calorgas cylinders, unexploded. The other had exploded during the fire. So I got off pretty lightly that night.

The raids were constant after that, but the work of the dockyards went on. I think my first most unpleasant duty as an officer with knowledge of explosives was when I had to go down in the lock gate caisson to renew the demolition charge placed at the bottom of the gate at the beginning of the war. This was overdue for change and the explosive might be in a dangerous state. I went down the tube, which was very narrow, by a ladder fixed to its side. At the bottom I found two battery-like objects with electric wires fastened to them. These were to be disconnected and my Chiefie, who was up top, let down a rope to haul up the old batteries and then lower down new ones. These had to be connected to the wire making sure not to break off the little nodules of picric acid which had formed on the connections. I was glad when this was over and we could get back to whatever might be next.

I had an office by the harbour entrance and a Chief Petty Officer, retired RN, who had been recalled and was worth his

weight in gold, as most Chief Petty Officers are, also seven
ratings, mostly 'Scouses'. The raids continued and I had to visit
every hole, scrap of bomb or camouflet (as the hole underground
left by an exploding bomb which cannot be seen from the top is
called), and had to declare whether there was a live bomb or
not. Sometimes I would get mixed up with fires in the dockyard,
and with the fire engines and all the ARP people who were
working to keep the damage down, and there was always the tea
lady. Mrs Fedden of Bristol ran one tea wagon and Mrs Lennard
another. They would come down after the raid was over and
bring refreshment to all who were working in the devastation.
I was having dinner with the Lennards one night in Clifton,
and hardly had the sirens gone when a stick of bombs exploded. It straddled the house. We jumped under the table and
the dust from the vibration was falling all around. However, this
was the signal for Mrs Lennard to light the gas under her tea
urn.

One night I had taken the Surgeon Rear-Admiral's daughter
to a dance at the Assembly Hall in Bath and we got back so late
and in such darkness that I put up at the Admiral's. About five
in the morning he came in, woke me, and said that I was to
report immediately at the railway station to go to Swansea to
help in an emergency. It had been arranged already that my
group and the Petty Officer would meet me at the train. This
was to be my first defusing of a bomb. It was only a small one,
50 kg, but the officer in charge at Swansea was himself fully
occupied by a great enormous 1,000 kg bomb which he was
trying to dig out of the dockyard. These bombs usually detached
their tails when they went into the ground so that you could tell
how big they were going to be. Some of them had large papier-
mâché whistles strapped to their tails to make an eerie sound as
they came down through the air. Others were small fire bombs
which were eased into a canister and separated into small units,
only going off when they struck the ground: there were so many
of them at a time that it sounded like the beginning of a
rainstorm with the rain pattering down. But these were more the

range of activities for the ARP and the firemen, and contained
no explosive.

We had a call to go to the County Cricket ground in Bristol,
where a stick of bombs had fallen across the pitch. The ground
had been taken over by the Admiralty as a training ship so had
become Admiralty property. The bombs hadn't exploded and
had to be dealt with *in situ*. The ratings and I dug down to these
bombs, then the ratings departed while I did my little ceremony
on the fuse, which took about 40 minutes. After that we pulled
the bombs out of the ground, emptied the picric acid and the
TNT and made a bonfire of it. Those we couldn't open we
loaded on our truck and swizzed through Bristol with two red
flags flying and sirens blowing, and dumped them in a park
across the other side of the Gorge. It looked like a rogue
elephant's cemetery. However, we left one or two of the burnt-
out casings of the 250 kilo bombs in the ground of the Bristol
Cricket Club, beside the clubhouse, as souvenirs.

One morning we received a signal to proceed by tug to a ship
at Portishead harbour, a large bay where ships which were in
any dangerous condition had to anchor. It was said to have an
unexploded bomb on board. So we went out by tug, Chiefie, the
seven ratings and myself. On board the Captain was in quite a
state of fidgets but laughingly said that he had been sitting in the
bridge toilet having a comfortable one when, whoosh, like a
railway train, the whole front of the toilet and the bridge were
carried away, and the bomb fell in the water on the other side.
Also, another bomb had come through the plating into the
forward hold and was lying on their cargo of phosphate. It was in
such a position that it needed no digging out and the fuses looked
pretty harmless. I loosened the base plate and with the help of the
crew on board lowered it on to our tug and took it a quarter of
a mile away, where we rolled it into the water. There it would
be safe as the water would enter and render the explosive inert.

The next ship-going adventure was not quite so easy. Again
we were called out in our tug and went aboard a tanker full of
high octane petrol. There was a hole in its side just above the

water-line and when we looked through one of the hatches the bomb could be seen lying on the bottom like a silver fish. As the ship was still full of high octane petrol I had to go back and get instructions from the Admiralty in order to see what would happen to the bomb fuse when the petrol was taken out and the whole of the inside decontaminated with steam as usual. The reply was to proceed normally, so we spent a couple of days waiting while they got the tankers out to her to unload the petrol and were able to clean it out enough for us to go down and have a look. I think she was called the *Chesapeake*, a small American tanker. A wooden box was put on my head. It had windows into which air was pumped, like those early films of pearl divers. I got down to the bomb and found it had two fuses, so I had to do my little 40-minute ceremony on each fuse and, as I was not too sure of my bends and hitches, Chiefie, although getting very fat, went down too and put two hitches on the bomb, ready to pull it up. I think this was a very noble thing to do and I hope he got some reward. We got it up with all hands on board pulling, including myself, just to the coaming of the hatch. This coaming was 3 feet above the deck and we could not get it over, so there was the bomb swinging on its rope until one of the hands from the *Chesapeake* jumped on to the rope and his extra weight swung the 500 kilo bomb on to the deck, and we finally loaded it on to the waiting tug for disposal in deep water. For this I was recommended for a medal, but I think many other people should have got one too.

The *Chesapeake* steamed in next day past our window and you could see the hole just above the water-line where the bomb had entered. I had no more incidents on board ships but the endless boredom of digging for suspected bombs in the dockyard went on. I think the bombs retreated in the mud each day as one dug. In some cases we went down to thirty feet and I had to get the civilian dockyard men to do the shoring-up for us as it was very dangerous for our hands working through the mud at that depth. This sort of boring heavy labour was really getting me down and although the raids had stopped to a certain degree, I had applied for relief for medical reasons. But it was a while before I was relieved from the Bomb Disposal Service.

In the meantime I had been issued with a heavy motor-cycle, which was death in itself. I only rode this machine once and left it for my relief to break in. I had my own little car, a Morris Minor, and I drove back to London in it with my first 50 kg bomb in the back. I picked up a young WAAF on the way who seemed to be waiting outside an RAF station for a bus, but by the time I got to Young's Corner I thought the friendship should be at an end. I dropped her and turned right through St Peter's Square to my lodgings with the Coxons. The next day I reported back to my Commander at the Admiralty and was given a good handshake. He said he was going to give me the best posting he could. By this time I knew enough to say, 'Aye, aye, Sir.' Later on, when my citation came through, he took me into a little room over the dirty cinema in Charing Cross Road where there were two men in shirt sleeves who dealt out decorations. They said, 'We thought you would prefer the George Medal to the MBE as it is more original.' So that's what it was.

Operation

> I observed these battles partly as an exhibition – that is to
> say that I went through them a little like a visitor from the
> country going to a great show ... When I could order my
> thoughts I looked for more significant things than appear-
> ances; I still looked – I cannot avoid it – for something
> decorative, poetic or dramatic.
>
> Keith Douglas, 'Alamein'

The uncomplaining patrician Englishman, brave but anti-heroic, be-
mused but capable, witty and spiritual, attracted the post-war novelist
and film-maker. The genuine article appeared in a modest memoir called
Going to the Wars, published in 1955. The author, Sir John Verney,
had served as an amateur soldier in Somerset during the 1930s and
towards the end of the war was working, as he said, 'as a Staff Officer
planning operations for others to carry out'. One of these was 'Operation Swann', named after Proust's famous character, and here the
writer was less detached, having decided to put himself into this
particular action. His distinctly private description of Operation Swann
made at the time was to form the concluding chapters of *Going to the
Wars*, one of the finest military autobiographies. Operation Swann
sees Sir John as a parachutist being dropped into Sardinia during the
opening stages of the landings in Italy. At the heart of his account of
this adventure is his lack of conviction in the usefulness of what he is
doing. Originally, the operation was to be made by submarine, but
engine trouble prevented it at the last moment. Thus it was that on

7 July 1943 six far from sure heroes fell from the sky to attack a
landing-ground in the middle of Sardinia which might be of vital
importance to the Germans when the Allies landed on Sicily three days
later. After a few days' adventures and posings as Germans, and
exhausting wanderings all over Sardinia, they were, inevitably,
captured. It was 19 July 1943, the day Badoglio decided to arrest
Mussolini. Sir John was twenty-nine.

But in our prison outside Sassari, we had none of the facilities of
an organized *campo concentramento*, which, with Hilary, we
enjoyed later for a while; no mail, no Red Cross parcels, no
amateur theatricals, no cigarettes, no variety. Above all, no
variety. The atmosphere was not unlike that of a prep. school in
which the usual proportion of masters to pupils had been
reversed. True, we didn't play games; but we were led out for a
walk every morning in the yard.

Escape was pointless, unless we were moved towards Italy.
We lived in dread of that, and of some sudden reprisal by the
Germans for the Ottana incident. As the Captain had hinted,
our best hope for freedom was to cause no trouble and to wait
philosophically for deliverance.

But male human nature is ill-designed to support boredom.
The danger was in ourselves.

Jim and Bryan, like so many healthy and unimaginative young
men in captivity, suffered the most. They grumbled continually
about the food, the hardness of the beds, the absence of
cigarettes. Then, sinking into despair, they rotted before our
eyes.

An American pilot called Hank gave us news of the raid on
Rome and of progress in Sicily. Returning from the raid, he had
landed in the ocean, had drifted for two days in a rubber dinghy
on to the Sardinian coast and thence had been sent to join us.
We welcomed, at first, this infusion of new life into our stale
company, but after the tenth hearing of his sufferings to exposure

Amos and I silently wished him back in the Tyrrhenian Sea. A naïve character whose crew-cut extended within as well as over his head, he clearly thought us a bunch of decadent Limeys, though Kempster's tough good looks and much vociferated intention to escape impressed him.

While Jim and Bryan rotted, Kempster went mad.

He could not forgive himself, or the planners in Algiers, that his own part in Operation Swann had been unsuccessful. Reaching the airfield only to find it disused, he had marched across half Sardinia in search of another, literally dragging his patrol with him. No one could reasonably be blamed, least of all himself, for this gallant failure. But then none of us, least of all Kempster, were reasonable.

We all talked much of escape, to pass the time, but only Kempster, keen soldier that he was, had landed in Sardinia scientifically equipped. Steel files, handkerchief maps, silk cords and gold coins were sticking-plastered all over his body. Like a schoolboy showing off his treasures, he revealed this collection to us one day and we laughed so hilariously that the *carabinieri* came in before he could get dressed. They spotted the corner of a map hanging out of his shirt. We were searched from head to foot, the guards were doubled, and our walks stopped. The withered elderly Lieutenant, who had treated us well hitherto, was much shaken. He kept the *carabinieri* patrolling the wire fence round the yard, or sent them on surprise visits to our cell. And thereafter, like schoolboys, we teased them by picking noisily at the walls and floor.

Kempster, as I think I have said, was partially German and obsessed with war. Having lost his escaping tools, for which he blamed us all, he sat morosely on his bed dreaming of military exploits that might have been and might yet be. Or he concentrated on keeping fit. He walked naked five miles every day round the room. It made us giddy.

'What will you do after the war?' we interrupted him at his exercise, preferring talk to giddiness. He sat down and said defensively, 'I shall go on fighting.'

'Who against?'

'What does it matter? War is eternal. Look round you everywhere. Look at Nature red in tooth and claw, look at business, look at marriage. It's all war. Why not accept it? I do.' He rose again suddenly and stood declaiming, as if in a pulpit. He was half-terrifying, half-comic.

'I acknowledge in myself the impulses towards Death and Power which, multiplied a millionfold, seem to me to have more basic connection with the final disaster of war than all the history-book stuff about ideologies, land hunger, scraps of paper, broken pledges, and the rest. To fight is the proper state of man. In every child flourishing a wooden tomahawk, in every old man bent over his chessboard, I see the symbol of all wars that have been, the seed of all wars that are to come.'

. . . It was our duty, Kempster maintained, to make ourselves a nuisance. And Amos, maliciously amused by my dilemma, supported him.

'A disgraceful way to treat British officers,' they both said at every opportunity.

But it would be unfair to name one more than the other. We were all to blame. For the sake of peace we suppressed our private tensions, but we expressed them, in an exaggerated form, against the Lieutenant and his *carabinieri*. As the officer commanding Operation Swann, I was continually being driven to voice some general, and, to my mind, unjustified grievance. But, morally a coward, I have never found it easy to resist the demands of my friends. In this case it would have been better for us all if I had . . . In retrospect our behaviour was childish and self-destructive. Perhaps, too, we suffered a nervous recoil from the strain of the past month. Perhaps, too, we showed off a little to one another and to Hank, the stranger. However it was, our six interacting personalities produced a disastrous compound. At the end of three weeks we were no longer six grown-ups, we were a committee. Our joint attitude became, to say the least, arrogant. But we pushed our arrogance too far.

We heard of Mussolini's downfall a fortnight after it occurred.

He, too, though we did not know it, was a prisoner in Sardinia, on the island-port of La Maddalena. It may have been this irony which prompted the Lieutenant to come in and remove the picture from our wall. As a Fascist his emotions at this time must have been greatly strained. Already fed up with us, he was in no mood to be chaffed.

'Ho, ho,' we all cried; 'so Humpty Dumpty *has* had a fall.'

And we danced round the room triumphantly.

The Lieutenant walked out, beside himself with anger.

When, the next morning, I marched into his office as usual, I decided to begin, diplomatically, by thanking him for favours received.

'I want none of your thanks,' he snarled venomously. 'You're ungrateful *prigionieri*, and I'm sick of you. I've arranged for you to be sent to Italy. And good riddance!'

So after that we hated him openly and he hated us.

Little Boy

> Among clouds like antique white clay images of warriors
> were some that suggested Dragons twisting angrily and
> darkly upward. Some, as they lost their shape, were tinged
> rose. Presently, they separated themselves into bland reds
> and yellows and purples, and their stormy powers left them.
> The white shining face of the god had taken on the ashen
> hue of death.
>
> Yukio Mishima, *The Decay of the Angel*

The indignities which war imposed on the person were supposed to be
either laughed off or accepted with pragmatism. Nobody was supposed
to react as D. H. Lawrence did to his medical when he was called up. The
outrage he felt at having to parade naked before an army medical board
knows no bounds in his novel *Kangaroo*. If his protest was excessive, as
well as being clearly based on a very different kind of anger resulting from
Britain's salacious prying into his life, he does have a point. Having to
submit publicly to indecency for the sake of the common good, common
sense and so on could leave long-lasting wounds. Much of the disgusting
nature of Britain's prisons is the result of officialdom's indifference or
blindness to the suffering caused by privation. This form of hurt lies half
suppressed in wartime writing, it being thought a weakness to complain
of such matters. And there was the moment when Western reticence, a
cultural thing, was invisible to the Japanese. Such humiliations as Tosh
Kano describes during his account of what happened after the fall of
Singapore may seem trivial, even comic, in comparison with so many

of the pains which would follow that disaster, but in their own way they were all part of the dreadfulness which befalls the self in war.

Kano was a Japanese-American who served in the Imperial Japanese Army, when he had to change his name to Nekemoto. His account of what happened when, to the respective amazement and glee of the Japanese and the disbelief of the British, Singapore fell, and most of its inhabitants had to be interned, is written in English and strives to be impartial. As somebody who survived Hiroshima he is beyond criticism. A great number of prisoners had to be medicated, fed, secured, put to work, while the Emperor's forces swept forward over all Asia. One had to be sensible.

Our most difficult problem was with the clothing and the boots. I could not get any from our Headquarters supply. Each POW had two shirts, two stockings and one pair of boots. Each camp had little stock on hand. The only way we could do was not to wear them out. In regards to clothing, I suggested to the POW camps that it was a good idea to send their men out to work without shirts in order to save them. They could use them in their camps at night. The camps agreed and went out to work without shirts, which gave the soldiers good tanned bodies and made them healthy. For the boots' soles, I asked the Quartermaster for worn-out tires which were piled in the yard. These I got right away because they wanted to get rid of them. With these tires we made shoe soles. It turned out to be very good, maybe better than leather.

As for the medical problem, we had many skin diseases because of the shortage of bathing water. Thus we killed two birds with one stone by letting the POWs go out working without shirts, and got them to use the Japanese soldier's loincloth underwear. It is a piece of cloth two feet long and about seven inches wide, with straps sewn to both ends, just like an apron, only it is put on the back and tied in front. Then the hanging cloth end was brought to the front between the legs and pushed under the straps. It is much more comfortable and easier to wash. I have pictured the usage of this loincloth underwear and the treatment of the inner diseases. The patients were lined up in front of the medics who were sitting down in chairs with iodine and paint brushes in their hands. The medics would hold the patient's penis up with chop-sticks and busily paint the iodine on the diseased penis under and around the roots. After painting, you can imagine how busy the patients were fanning with newspapers and magazines. This piece of cloth became very handy because the penis could stick out through the hole made in the cloth to prevent the penis getting wet from the iodine. This rough treatment cured the skin diseases even though it burned a little.

Tosh Kano saw the rededication of Singapore according to the Shinto faith.

We named the temple 'Shonan Jinjya' as the city's name Singapore was changed to Shonan and the island's name to Shonan-to. It was the name of an old Japanese temple built before the war in Singapore. Most of the Japanese who lived in Singapore had their graves there. The meaning of Shonan meant 'the Shining South'. That was a good name and had the right feeling for the Japanese at that time when everything was so successful. The Japanese did not expect that a stronger and richer country like Great Britain would be conquered so easily. The Japanese felt that they were the Shining South and the conquerors. Everybody was very proud. All the fears and worries at the outbreak of war disappeared. Now Japan had the south in her hands. So she believed the war would be in her favor, and pretty soon Japan would be on top of the world.

Tosh Kano and his wife and children were living in the centre of
Hiroshima on 6 August 1945 when the American Army Air Force
Boeing B-29 dropped the atomic bomb, killing outright 100,000 people.
The bomb was called by the Air Force 'Little Boy'. The one they
dropped on Nagasaki three days later was called 'Big Boy'. The day
after this, 10 August, Japan sued for peace and President Truman
designated 15 August 'VJ Day'. Tosh Kano's own little boy was
eventually to die from the radiation, but Kano himself and the other
members of his family were strangely uninjured. He became a civil
engineer at the American Marine Corps Air Station at Iwakuni,
dying of cancer in 1978, a man of two worlds. An interpreter, he put
down the bombing of Hiroshima to a linguistic error.

The Japanese reply 'Mokasatsu' to the American message to
surrender was mis-translated to 'Not considering'. This mis-
translation caused the first Atom Bomb to be dropped on
Hiroshima and made history.

The 5th Engineering Regiment was located at the northern
end of Hiroshima City. My X Company was composed of five
officers and two hundred and fifty men. My Company barracks
was a two-story wooden structure nearly fifty years old, and
was the oldest building in the Regiment. The building was
closest to the main gate, about fifty yards away. Between the
gate and the building was a large camphor tree. My father and
sister returned to Japan [they had been interned in Texas] on the
reciprocation ship from America, and were living in Furuiehi,
Hiroshima. I was commuting from Furuiehi, which was about
6K north of Hiroshima. But as the air raid alarms became more
frequent, I had to stay in or move to the city to be closer to my
Company. 'If we die, we will die together,' I said. 'I will find a
house which is close to the barracks. There are many vacant
houses and I am sure I will get one easily.' I did not have any

difficulty in finding a house as many rich people's houses were vacant. The rich people were glad to have someone live in their homes, even for free. I rented the house of a rich stockbroker. So I moved to this house with my wife Shizue, my daughter Yorie, aged three, and my son Toshio, aged one. My wife was also pregnant.

The B-29s were passing over it almost every day, but not a single bomb was dropped. They flew so high that we could see the shining silver body, about the size of a matchbox, with the long white cloud tail following, and hear a humming sound, 'boom-boom'. When we heard this sound we felt safe, as the B-29 was high up in the air and not attacking us. We grew familiar with this sound and didn't get excited, just saying, 'A B-29 is in the air . . .' Once a B-29 dropped propaganda leaflets and I got one. It said, 'Springtime in March and April. The cherry blossom's season. But July and August will be the season of ashes.' That was right.

It was 8.15 a.m. when the bomb was dropped. The bomb was dropped near the center of the city. Its target was the famous large T-shaped steel bridge 'Aio-bashi'. It went off about 500 meters from the ground, in the air, and was dropped with a parachute, so the B-29 had plenty of time to be out of danger. It was 1.2 kilometers air distance from the place I was to the center of the blast. I was very fortunate to be protected by the high railroad embankment from the direct blast, as my back was facing toward the center of the bomb. I could only say that it was just like the operation of the old-fashioned photo-flash unit. When you light it, the flash first and then the explosion, the heat, the smoke, and the explosion gas. When the bomb went off, it was the same type of operation as this old-fashioned photo-flash. So the people of Hiroshima called the Atomic blast by the photo-flash nickname, 'Pika-don'.

It was 8.30 a.m. when I passed through the main gate. I saw my Company building standing. Only the south side, the side facing the blast center, was pushed in. All of the leaves on the camphor tree were blown away. I couldn't understand what this bomb was that had caused such great damage. I thought we were unfortunate to have this great bomb. I couldn't figure it out.

The Misdirected

'Now one can breathe more easily,' said the Knight, putting back his shaggy hair with both hands, and turning his gentle face and large mild eyes to Alice. She thought she had never seen such a strange-looking soldier in all her life.

> Lewis Carroll, *Through the Looking-Glass,*
> *and What Alice Found There*

Both the call-up and the various forces volunteer centres, for all their vetting of body and mind, netted some chronically unsuitable specimens. Barrack-room mates, sergeants and eventually the commanding officer himself would find themselves defeated by what at first they preferred to see as something which could be licked into shape but which, being lunacy, had no controllable pattern. Army ways came up against a powerful absence of assimilation. In the case of Gunner Sir James Stephen, 4th Baronet, aged thirty-three, Eton and Trinity, this was an unwanted clash of understanding, for he longed to soldier with a will. Instead, he was thrust where the army traditionally believed awkward squad types such as he could do the least damage, in the cookhouse. However, there was still the problem of eating and sleeping alongside the rest of the battery. Sir James, though impervious to roughing it, was bewildered by the habits and language thought normal by his companions. He was a large, fat, dirty man, and an only child. Some hereditary basis of his mental state could have been deduced from the fact that his mother, née Shore-Nightingale, had sent all her kinswoman Florence Nightingale's letters to the local salvage drive. Sir James had studied law while in residence at Toynbee Hall, had enrolled at the Royal Institute of Journalism, and liked to write songs, and knit for the forces. He had also become a Roman Catholic convert and was as fanatically moral as his total innocence would allow. As with many mad people, like Ivor Gurney when he wrote,

> Horror follows horror within me
> There is a chill fear
> Of the storm that does deafen and din me
> And rage horribly near,

Sir James understood that things were not right, were not as they were for most men, though what this 'rightness' was he could not tell. Nor could the army psychologists, for he passed through their hands uncomprehendingly. He could not fight Hitler. This much they made plain. They looked past the dreadful uniform at the 4th Baronet and were polite and kind. Gurney had written:

> Certain people would not clean their buttons,
> Nor polish buckles after latest fashions,
> Preferred their hair long, puttees comfortable,
> Barely escaping hanging.

This First World War poet had also said:

> There is a man who has swept or scrubbed a floor
> This morning crying in the Most
> Holy Name
> Of God for pity, and has not been able to claim
> A moment's respite.

Jankers for misfits, that was the army's way. Sir James, who longed to fight evil, either the Nazis or Gunner Smith in the next bed for doing what he said he had done, many times, to a girl down by the bridge, had been put to peeling spuds. Thus he cried too in 'the Most Holy Name' and skived off whenever he could to read Gibbon or sit in teashops, though always accompanied by 'the storm that does deafen and din me'. In a few months they released him. For some years he worked on the land. Then, after being certified insane in 1945, soon after Hitler had committed suicide, he was committed to an asylum. The facts of his illness were stated in *Who's Who* as starkly as those of anyone's career. His army journal could be parts of *The Good Soldier Švejk*, except any amusement or cynicism was unintentional. Nor was Sir James saying with Apollinaire, 'O God, what a lovely war, with its songs and its long leisure hours', but he could now and then meet craziness with craziness and make some sense.

2 April 1941. This morning we had the major's inspection, from which I was absent, having been told to pick up tins. This was lucky. The wind blew my overcoat over twice and twice Lewis picked it up. Then along came the major and prodded my overcoat with his stick. Over went the coat. 'That man will have to do his kit over again,' said the major. All the same, I didn't have to do it again, and the only account I heard of the matter came from Lewis. Lewis says that of course it's nothing to worry about, a man who's a major has to say something.

After the inspection, also from lunch to tea, I was prisoners' escort. Well, well, it's the way the world wags. It is a dirty job, but I have not yet been on a route march, or done fire piquet, or done a guard. The reason for all this is my bad foot. But I can't expect to spend the duration writing poetry and reading Gibbon. The prisoners cocked snooks at me, made ugly faces, giggled, implored me to lend them money, and in fact behaved like a lot of naughty children seven years old. One man was particularly irritating. He wanted me to lend him money. I pointed out that this was illegal. He then quoted St Paul on charity and said I was a sounding brass and a tinkling cymbal. The what of it was that I began to catch the infection from the prisoners and to giggle myself. I see prisoners have a bad time. When they are not on parade they are locked up in a rabbit-hutch all by themselves.

Now Fr O'Connor has arrived to hear confessions, and has heard mine. He served in the last war and has been PP of Chatham. He is a captain in the army. He has served all his life in the diocese of Southwark. He enjoys reading the Catholic press, which I don't.

Gibbon is fascinating. I observe that the Romans had PT and dug trenches. After the break I was told not to do anything so I sat in the canteen and read Gibbon. Then after dinner came spud-peeling. At 4 o'clock all the light duty men paraded in front of the canteen for an interview with the RSM. He began by asking me how old I was. When I said I was 33 he asked whether I was quite sure that I wasn't younger – as if I should tell a lie which may be so easily detected.

1 May. Yesterday two things happened. The first was that Sergeant Sharp ordered me a haircut. The second was that I went round to the Troop Office and asked if I might have a leave pass sometime soon; this was surprisingly effective and I got one the same day. So I went to Chatham and bought a ticket – price 1/3 – which entitled me to a cabin in the Salvation Army Hostel. Then I tried to get a haircut, and found the shops were shut. Then I jumped on a bus which announced that it was going to Faversham. Sittingbourne would have been cheaper, besides containing the perquisites of haircut and tea, but I don't regret having gone to Faversham, as there were plenty of cricket pitches and hop trees on the way – dark stems with glittering tops – and there was the man who provided the King's armament and was therefore called the King's Port at Faversham. There I got my haircut in a shop which was about to close down, and by a barber who is about to join the RAF – as a barber – except that he hopes they will soon employ him as a mechanic. Then I had sardines on toast for tea. Then by way of variation I came back by train from Faversham to Chatham. The train was a fine handsome train with a steam-engine, thank God – no electricity beyond Chatham. I sat and meditated a long time before it started. Then I had food in the YMCA hut and retired to roost rather earlier than I would have wished in my Salvation Army cabin. This was a rather inferior structure in which all the light came from a bulb in the passage outside, and wasn't sufficient to read by. The bed was not quite long enough for me to lie in. There was no coke, therefore no hot water. In the morning I managed to get a wash and shave in the Sun Hotel and breakfast in a shop in Military Road, some Gibbon in a chair in the Salvation Army hut, lunch in a café in the High Street and, with a bus to Strood, I was back in the guardroom at Tower Hill at precisely 2.

Casualty. The Reverend Richard Inge, whom I met once. He was at Eton and Magdalene, and a curate at Leeds, but enlisted in the RAF as an aircraftman and was killed as a pilot officer. I suppose his decision to enlist must be respected, but it looks as if he cannot have taken his duties as a curate very seriously.

In the afternoon I scrubbed the under-sides of my gaiters. As it was the first time in their history that they have ever been scrubbed, the dirt was colossal. Yesterday I completed the 'Song of a Soldier whose Leave Coincided with Kit Inspection' and put it in an envelope addressed to Bombardier Wood, enclosing a note. I hope it may bring fruit in due season. I think there must be something wrong with Bob Robertson. Yesterday evening I discovered that he keeps photographs of upwards of twenty women in his bedroom, none of the women having the slightest vestige of clothing on.

I have bought a tin mug at Woolworths. The mug is inscribed DOG, which causes amusement.

Last night there was a dive-bombing raid on Chatham dockyard, which was chiefly unpleasant because of the noise.

Last night Buffin came in a bit tipsy at 11.30, a time when he had no business to be anywhere except in bed. He came to my bed and said something affectionate to me when I was half asleep, so I clenched my fist and struck him unexpectedly on the nose. The result was that he set up a wail of 'Hit me on the fucking nose, he did!' which he repeated over fifty times, thereby causing much amusement. I expressed regret that I had not broken his neck.

Mass at Strood: before going I spent 25 minutes peeling spuds, the first time I have worked on a Sunday since I have been here. Most of the men in my barrack-room come from Nottingham, which is much better than Wales.

A bowdlerized version of Hašek's anti-military satire *The Good Soldier Švejk* had appeared in English in 1930. Although still not widely read during the war, its theme of what happens when a questioning misfit gets caught up in the military works had become familiar to many a civilian-soldier. Discipline was much the same as it had been during 1914–18 and had taken little or no account of the fact that the outlook of those called up to fight Hitler was not at all the same as that of those who had been conscripted to fight the Kaiser. Worse, some of the King's Rules and Regulations devised to cope with the drilled rabble of Wellington's day were still being devoutly enforced.

Gunner Sir James Stephen had a way of confronting absurdity with absurdity. Unlike the wily Švejk, his challenge was non-deliberate. Sir James admired the way the army did things even if, as he looked round his barrack-room, he had to admit that it had a poor judgement where its recruits were concerned. So it was a great blow to him to be invalided out. What he longed for was to put a marker in his *Decline and Fall of the Roman Empire* and do battle against the Hun. The Austrian army did its best to get rid of Private Švejk by putting him in a bin, but he manages to join up again during a moment of national danger and wild patriotism, much to its distress. From now on it has a real fight on its hands. What hope has an entire army against a Švejk? None at all, Sir James would have said, and would have cracked this unholy fool one on the nose.

There'll be a very good harvest here after the war,' said Švejk after a while. 'They won't have to buy bone flour. It's a great advantage for the farmers when their fields are covered with the dust of a whole regiment; in other words it's a very good means of livelihood. The only thing which worries me is that the farmers shouldn't let themselves be cheated and sell these soldiers' bones unnecessarily for bone charcoal in the sugar refineries. In the barracks at Karlín there was a lieutenant called Holub. He was so learned that everybody in the company thought he was an idiot. You see, because of his learning he never learnt to swear at the soldiers and considered everything only from the academic point of view. Once the soldiers reported to him that the army bread which they had drawn was not eatable. Another officer would have flown in a passion at such insolence, but not he. He remained quite calm, didn't call anybody a pig or a swine, and didn't sock anybody on the jaw. He only called all his men together and told them in his pleasant voice: 'First of all, my men, you must realize that the barracks aren't a delicatessen shop where you can choose pickled eels, sardines and sandwiches. Every soldier must be intelligent enough to swallow any ration he draws without complaining about its quality. And he must have enough self-discipline not to make a fuss about the quality of what's put before him. Just imagine, my men, if there were a war. The soil in which you'd be buried after the battle wouldn't care a hoot what kind of bread you were gorged with before you died. Mother Earth would decompose you and eat you up boots and all. In this world nothing is allowed to vanish completely. Out of you, my men, there'll grow new corn for bread rations for new soldiers who again like you perhaps won't be satisfied, will start complaining, and then come up against someone who'll clap them in gaol until kingdom come, because he's got the right to do that. Now, my men, I've explained everything to you nicely and I believe I need not remind you again that whoever comes and complains a second time will thank his lucky stars later when he's allowed out again into God's light.' 'If he'd only swear at us,' the soldiers said to each other, and they didn't at all like all those refinements in the lieutenant's speeches. And so once they chose me from the company and asked me to go and tell him that they all liked him but it's not the army if people don't swear at you. And so I went to his house and asked him to cut out all this refinement; that the army must be as tough as nails and soldiers are used to being reminded every day that they're bastards and swine. If they aren't they lose respect for their superior officers. At first he defended himself, spoke about intelligence and said that the times had gone by when the birch rod ruled, but in the end he accepted it, gave me a sock on the jaw and threw me out of the door so as to bolster his prestige. When I told the others the result of the negotiations they were all very pleased, but the very next day he went and spoiled it all. He came to me and said in the hearing of all of them: 'Švejk, I lost my temper yesterday. Here's a guilder for you. Go and drink my health. One's got to know how to treat the men.'

Flare Path

> Of us all, I think Noel was the most elated. His face wore a
> permanent fixed grin which nothing could wipe off.
> 'Spitfires at last,' he kept repeating.
> 'Spitfires or Hurricanes,' I said meanly.
> He continued to grin.
> 'Don't give a damn. They're both good enough for me.'
>
> Richard Hillary, *The Last Enemy*

Flying created a new concept of being immortal. The release from the
pull of the earth and the entering into a blue for so long associated with
the after-death experience, between them carried the airman into a
heady continuity. Added to which, in both world wars the airman's
life was a short one. Also a disappearing one. There was a taking off
and a total vanishing, an ending not without its appeal. Few had
flown since the invention of the plane at the beginning of the century
and the aviator was aware of seeing what few had seen. Successful
flyers were a combination of skilled driver and exhilarated spirit, full
of daring and fright. It was not long before the amorphous physical
and spiritual feelings which flying aroused began to take literary form,
most influentially in the novels and essays of Antoine de Saint-Exupéry.
Born in 1900, he would have been a sailor had he not failed the French
navy's entrance exams. So he learned to fly and became first a civil
pilot for his Empire's desert routes and ultimately a Free French
airman attached to the American Forces in North Africa, failing to
return on 9 July 1944. Saint-Exupéry's semi-mystical and intensely

practical writing, *Night Flight* (1931), *Flight to Arras* (1942) and most of all *Wind, Sand and Stars* (1939), taught the airmen of the Second World War how to die. Saint-Exupérian sentiment so often comes into their letters. He was forty-four and battered by many flying accidents when he died, or was claimed by the element of air.

This final transcendence marks so many last letters to parents and friends. Often the attempt to comfort and console is overtaken by a kind of exultation, as the writer becomes unable to hide his interest in this going on and on which to him clearly is not death as the non-flyer knows it. Just before taking off from RAF Wattisham, Suffolk, on his first operational flight on 24 May 1941, Flying Officer Michael Scott wrote a farewell letter to his 'Dear Mother and Daddy'. The war, he told them,

> has shown me new realms where man is free from earthly restrictions and conventions, where he can be himself playing hide-and-seek with the clouds, or watching a strangely silent world beneath, rolling quietly on, be touched only by vague unsubstantial shadows moving placidly but unrelenting across its surface. So please don't pity me for the price I have had to pay for this experience. This price is incalculable, but it may just as well be incalculably small as incalculably large, so why worry?

And in a previous 'last letter', written a few months earlier, he had told his father, 'Now I am off to the source of Music . . . I have no belief in a personal God, but I *do* believe most strongly in a spiritual force which was the source of our being, and which will be our ultimate goal.'

Michael Scott had taught at a preparatory school in Cheam, Surrey, and had loved the work. He was also training himself to become a writer, taking a postal course at the then popular Regent Institute, and sending his short stories to magazines. He was killed a few weeks after his twenty-fifth birthday. His stories were all about children and one of them, 'Firelight', about the death of a little brother long ago.

I have a solitary life. When my day's flying is ended, I like to sit in my comfortable armchair, before a blazing coal fire, and read or write. Sometimes I do neither, I simply sit looking into the plumbless depths of my fire, whose sullen red coals hold so many of my memories, and dream.

The other evening I dreamed of a garden. It was a big garden, walled on all four sides, and with three magnificent walnut-trees raising their proud heads to a July sky. The way into it led up through a green gate, up some stone steps and through an orchard of apple-trees. In the middle of this garden there was a summer-house, whose green paint was flaking off from exposure to every variety of Gloucestershire weather. Its front was shaded by a rickety contraption on hinges which could be let down to keep out the rain, or opened up to welcome the sunlight. Through this could be seen the three walnut-trees across the tennis court, and behind them, the placid outline of Cleeve Hill, peeping over the wall.

A child was sitting in this summer-house to escape the hot July sun. I am not sure what he was doing, but that doesn't matter. Perhaps he was whittling down a hazel shaft to make an arrow for his bow, or making a rope ladder from string purloined from the kitchen dresser. He often used to make rope ladders to aid him in his fantasy of running away at midnight with his sister, although he had never got past his bedroom door.

As the child sat playing, a shadow was thrown across the floor. He looked up and saw his mother in the doorway. She seemed to be laughing in a queer sort of way, with her face screwed up into a grimace which made him want to laugh too. 'I've got something to tell you, darling,' she said. 'David's gone.'

... After a while the woman and the child went out together. They went to the bed of sweet peas outside the summer-house and picked the finest bunch that they could find. 'We'll give this to David to take away,' said the woman. 'He'll like that, won't he?' The child had dried his tears by now, and he thought it a very good idea. When the picking was over, the woman pointed to the biggest walnut-tree, the one which overlooked the road.

'That's going to be cut down,' she said, 'to make his coffin.' And the child did not grudge it, though he was very fond of his friends the walnut-trees. 'That is a good idea, too,' he said.

Flying Officer Scott worried about his parents seeing this story after his death in case it upset them. His sister discovered it and was startled that he should have been haunted by a death which took place when he was four. 'No one knew that he had been so affected. I had been sent away to boarding-school because the eighteen-month-old brother had been fatally ill for a long time. My poor mother! Both the next two boys were killed in the war.'

Antoine de Saint-Exupéry's last but one book was not about flying but was a very adult tale about childhood – 'Grown-ups never understand anything for themselves, and it is tiresome for children to be always and forever explaining things to them.' Michael Scott made low-level flights over Cheam School to delight 'my boys'.

He was the almost classically courageous and efficient young airman who believed that you could not have good times without bad times, or bliss without some kind of struggle. 'There can be no winter without a spring . . . this spring will come and, until it does, we must hibernate under the anaesthetic that our work provides.'

> Just sing a little song to help the boys along,
> The airmen with the golden eagle's wings.

This 'little song' was a Flying Diary for the last five months of his life. It is an eloquent exposition of Bomber Command training and private emotion, practical and honest.

1 January 1941. A New Year. Winter's first snow, and shining through a veil of diaphanous snow-clouds, a crescent moon. I would like to know where I was going to stand on December 31st 1941. Let there be no retrospect of the maelstrom of 1940, but let us look forward to 1941 in a spirit of hope. In twelve months I hope to be back home, with 500 flying hours, a demobilized FO about to return to schoolmastering. To have flown is one of the greatest joys of my life, but I want to return to my life's work.

I hope to have 30 short stories in my notebook, two or three published, and a novel half-finished. Finally I hope to have a diary which is worthwhile; a chronicle of impressions rather than events. It will be interesting to see how many of these bear fruit.

Today was a good flying day. My final Nav[igation] test [from Thame to Buntingford and Grantham] well carried out, I think, thanks to Arthur Read's piloting. I ask for no better pilot or companion than Arthur; he is utterly reliable, and words of wisdom escape at the oddest moments. He notices everything that I love, birds circling the 'drome at dawn, fiery sunsets, light effects in the mist.

2 January. More snow. 3″ of it. The earth looks strange and unfamiliar from the air, a white sheet dotted with man-made ugliness. I had a grand time at 6,000′ playing hide-and-seek with the clouds. Got lost in a snowstorm coming down and hit the Great North Road, and followed it up to Grantham. Being alone, I was not very anxious though it was IF most of the way. I am seldom nervous alone, but I depend too much on the opinions of others to make a success of that.

Final Nav. test a success. 88% Pilot, 77% Observer.

I must be a better pilot than I thought.

4 January. The snow is second-hand, tarnished stuff, but still looks good from up here. I went to Great Heywood this afternoon, and circled there, and everything looks neat and tidy. A lazy evening writing, and talking to John Barrett. The Western Brothers on the wireless. As caddish as usual.

5 January. Orderly Officer, which is a soft job on Sunday. It was bitterly cold today, and more snow in the offing. Night flying was cancelled, and I flew back in the gloom of 5.30. I feel much more confident in the air now, and really think that I may make a pilot one day.

7 *January*. I have sent up two stories to the Regent School, namely 'Burning Coals' and 'The Tale of a Walking Stick'. I also tried *Lilliput* with 'Two Critics'. My writing is too immaturely romantic to succeed yet, I fear, but I would love to get my name into print, even in a paper like *Lilliput*, which I affect to despise.

8 *January*. I found the wistful 5/4 movement of the Pathétique as moving as ever. It is so peaceful, yet so despairing. 'We can do nothing,' it says. 'We can only sit and think.'

I have started a story about a boy waiting for the appearance of foxcubs, as I did once at Cheam. They never come, but he is satisfied by what he sees besides. The influence of H. E. Bates is very strong but I hope not too obvious. I am reluctant to go to bed, having a good fire, although I have finished Daphne du Maurier's *Come Wind, Come Weather*, propaganda for Moral Rearmament, and which was more convincing than such pamphlets usually are. One of these days I shall be a Grouper, though my intellect tells me that they are all wrong (or is it my pride?).

9 *January*. Rumours of departure mean nothing. The Course has been extended to another week. CFI Test today. Not so good, I attempted to make a forced landing in a field full of pylons. Otherwise a day of waiting. 'Foxcub' finished. It goes rather well, I think, especially the last sentence.

10 *January*. A mist-drenched thaw, damp fingers everywhere, reaching into every corner of an ice-cold building. An odourless fishy atmosphere everywhere. I was stranded over Harlaxton with Louis Gunter and Esplin. The latter was a trial cap and Rhodes Scholar at Oxford. Intelligent and pleasant to talk to.

A new battery has given my wireless-set a fresh lease of life. The early Brahms Trio sounds lovely. A beautiful second movement in Scherzo form with one of Brahms's broadest tunes in the Trio.

I won 7/- at poker tonight in fifty minutes, and then left to listen to the Brahms. Two sides to my character!

12 January. I actually had an hour's flying this morning! A bit of solo flying, for which I really haven't the nerve.

13 January. Night flying finished at last. A hectic last circuit; having drifted on to the flares, I came in across wind, went round again, lost the flare path, mistook the leading lights for flares, came down the flare path at 200' downwind, did a steep turn round, and so in. Was glad to get down to terra firma again!

I seem to have finished my flying and hope to get leave shortly.

26 January. I have got my wings, and am expecting my commission through at any time now. I had a filthy journey yesterday, with a temperature and incipient 'flu, which has luckily died away today. I passed out 13th at Grantham, Arthur being 14th! He and I tied for our Navigation Test, which was very satisfactory.

24 February. The Course has started at last. Two hours' cockpit drill on the Blenheim. Everything is so inaccessible that it is very hard to place one's hand on the right knob at the right time. I seem to have lost none of my old skill on the Link, in spite of being so out of practice.

25 February. More cockpit drill and Link. Also Snooker, which I enjoyed for three minutes, and then loathed more and more for the rest of the game.

27 February. Twenty-five! But I don't feel any older than I did yesterday. Thank God we have finished lectures and start flying tomorrow, though the thought of flying a Blenheim terrifies me.

3 March. Over four hours in the air. Solo after 2¼ hours, which
is satisfactory. Blenheims are very nice to fly, though I find the
landings very tricky, holding off too high, I think, and getting
the stick back too far. I went over Newbury yesterday and bust
up a game of football. The boys were much impressed – by
nothing, I'm afraid.

15 March. More flying at last. 1½ hours instrument finishing up
by trying to land wheels up! I felt as if I had never flown a
Blenheim and was completely ham-handed. Dirty-Dog Houlston
put up the Hydraulic Selector Lever, which foxed me completely,
BF that I was. Blast!

   Yesterday Fl/Lt Hill wrote himself off shooting up the 'drome.
He hit a tree on the boundary, probably not seeing it until too
late. A sad end to a DFC. I expect I shall do plenty of low flying
myself, but not with a crew on board.

18 March. Over three hours in the air. A cloudy day with wisps
of mist below 3,000'. I went up to 11,000' to look at the sea over
Cromer way and then descended in spirals over Blocking Lake.
A grand life.

21 March. ¾ hour IF (Blind take-offs). Quite successful. I seem
to have no trouble with the instruments now. 100 mins. solo, a
deplorable effort. I tried a one engine circuit without success,
and made a very shaky landing. Then I went up above the
clouds and lost myself. What an aviator! I am hoping that one
day I shall not frighten myself too much, especially for the sake
of the crew.

   I hope to get back to Bicester soon, possibly before the end of
term at Cheam. I want very much to see the boys again before
the end of term.

25 March. The long nose is a delight to fly – much easier than
the short, and freer in the controls. It is steadier and easier to
keep at a constant A/S.

30 March. A trip with a staff-pilot to bomb. Julian did very well; average error 77 yards, much the best of the day. We had a trip together in the afternoon, with no success, as the bombsight was WS. A snappy landing at 45' to the landing T finished a satisfactory day. We shall go to the OT [Officer Training] flight soon.

8 April. A bit too much flying. A 4½ hour trip in the morning, Kettering – Doncaster – York – Lincoln – Royston – Kettering – Bicester – Upwood – Henswell – York – Henswell – Melton – Mowbray – Bicester. Then no lunch and an hour's map-reading in the afternoon which resolved itself into a trip to Aylesbury, and then to Newbury, where I shot up WJM and family, who were waving in his garden. We returned via Henley, and I was too tired to land properly, and had to go round again twice. Poor Julian. Photos of Lincoln Cathedral and Shefford Junction.

20 April. Low bombing level 250'. Not a bad effort. Average error 65–55 yards. Red landings in a cross wind.

21 April. More low level bombing. Much better. 35–30–34–18 yards average error. The last was the pilot's best so far (11 yards!). Landings good.

26 April. Operations loom on the horizon, but I have hardly realized their imminence yet. I would cloud-cover to low level at present, so I am praying for cloudy weather.

1 May. Wattisham. 1 van-load take-off with +9 boost. They are very heavy to land with such a weight, and I had to go round again once.

17 May. Got up at 2.30 to do a night cross country. Unfortunately we fouled the landing T on the way out to take-off, and so our early rising came to nought. Formation in the afternoon. This was quite good for a first effort, though I got rather close once or twice! On the battle order for tomorrow.

18 May (Sunday). A very heavy day, all formation flying. I found this very hard work at first, but it came a bit easier toward the end. We went over to Watton to join up with 21 and 89. Apparently we are to do a show on Tuesday morning with fighter escort. May the gods be with us! Formation flying is the most companionable of pursuits. Twelve dots in the sky linked by a spirit of fellowship and each dependent upon the rest. What more could a man ask! Today is the first day of Summer.

24 May [In his sister's hand]. Did not return from first operational flight. Aged 25. FS.

One of the lessons of war is how to say goodbye, though few attempted to learn it. Death in battle was not like death in old age or by execution, or like knowing that one was terminally ill, and deliberated last words were comparatively rare. Usually, the official notification of death while on active service was followed up by personal letters from officers, clergymen and close friends. Strangely yet understandably, when a last letter was consciously composed it often lacked the intimacy of those sent by comrades to the killed man or woman's family. The best last letters are from those who still eagerly await a reply. The sudden snapping of communication at a commonplace moment is often more poignant than the valediction of the measured farewell. Best to have gossip and grouses, love and kisses, and then not another word.

The war had only just begun when an RAF officer sent his mother what was to become the pattern of the measured farewell for the rest of the duration. She was a widow and he her only son, and he clearly dreaded the exceptional devastation which his death would cause her. So he shapes their intimacy and interdependence into a formal pattern of religion, patriotism and philosophy on the meaning of life. He has to convince her that his death was worthwhile. In doing so, he cannot avoid making himself appear noble and heroic, though this was not his intention. This making his loss bearable was also to make Flying

Officer Vivian Rosewarne's private farewell the most public of the war. For his mother was persuaded to print it in *The Times* eighteen days after his death and later issue it as a booklet. It was widely read but not emulated. The King praised it and it was discussed in pulpits and anthologized. In some ways it could have been written during the beginning of the First World War. No one seems to have asked if Rosewarne would have liked his letter to be in everybody's hands. Born the year of the Somme, he died on 31 May 1940, the week which saw the evacuation of Dunkirk. He was twenty-four. A Stock Exchange clerk, he had every kind of difficulty in getting into the Royal Air Force. It was thought that his Wellington was shot down in flames over the English Channel. He was an inventive yet partly mystical person. At first he was known simply as 'An Airman' but by the close of 1940 his identity was as famous as that of the first VCs of the war. His letter was displayed at the fund-raising 'Wings for Victory' rallies up and down the land, Frank Salisbury painted his posthumous portrait and the simple openness of his faith and character made it possible for leader-writers as well as leaders to use an old brave language to describe Britain's role in the war. Yet what he wrote was for a woman who would be alone in the world should he die. The widespread fame of the letter turned her into a heroine for having borne such a son.

An Airman to His Mother

Dearest Mother,

Though I feel no premonition at all, events are moving rapidly and I have instructed that this letter be forwarded to you should I fail to return from one of the raids which we shall shortly be called upon to undertake. You must hope on for a month, but at the end of that time you must accept the fact that I have handed my task over to the extremely capable hands of my comrades of the Royal Air Force, as so many splendid fellows have already done.

First, it will comfort you to know that my role in this war has been of the greatest importance. Our patrols far out over the North Sea have helped to keep the trades routes clear for convoys and supply ships, and on one occasion our information was instrumental in saving the lives of the men in a crippled lighthouse relief ship. Though it will be difficult for you, you will disappoint me if you do not at least try to accept the facts dispassionately, for I shall have done my duty to the utmost of my ability. No man can do more, and no one calling himself a man could do less.

I have always admired your amazing courage in the face of continual setbacks; in the way you have given me as good an education and background as anyone in the country; and always kept up appearances without ever losing faith in the future. My death would not mean that your struggle has been in vain. Far from it. It means that your sacrifice is as great as mine. Those who serve England must expect nothing from her; we debase ourselves if we regard our country as merely a place in which to eat and sleep.

History resounds with illustrious names who have given all, yet their sacrifice has resulted in the British Empire, where there is a measure of peace, justice and freedom for all, and where a higher standard of civilization has evolved, and is still evolving, than anywhere else. But this is not only concerning our own land. Today we are faced with the greatest organized challenge to Christianity and civilization that the world has ever seen, and I count myself lucky and honoured to be the right age and fully trained to throw my full weight into the scale. For this I have to thank you. Yet there is more work for you to do. The home front will still have to stand united for years after the war is won. For all that can be said against it, I still maintain that this war is a very good thing; every individual is having the chance to give and dare all for his principle like the martyrs of old.

However long the time may be, one thing can never be altered –
I shall have lived and died an Englishman. Nothing else matters
one jot, nor can anything ever change it.

You must not grieve for me, for if you really believe in
religion and all that it entails that would be hypocrisy. I have no
fear of death; only a queer elation . . . I would have it no other
way. The universe is so vast and so ageless that the life of one
man can only be justified by the measure of his sacrifice. We are
sent into this world to acquire a personality and a character to
take with us that can never be taken from us. Those who just eat
and sleep, prosper and procreate, are no better than animals if
all their lives they.are at peace.

I firmly and absolutely believe that evil things are sent into the
world to try us; they are sent deliberately by our Creator to test
our metal because He knows what is good for us. The Bible is
full of cases where the easy way out has been discarded for
moral principles.

I count myself fortunate in that I have seen the whole country
and known men of every calling. But with the final test of war I
consider my character fully developed. Thus at my early age my
earthly mission is already fulfilled and I am prepared to die with
just one regret, and only one – that I could devote myself to
making your declining years more happy by being with you; but
you will live in peace and freedom and I shall have directly
contributed to that, so here again my life will not have been in
vain.

Your loving Son
   Vivian

Acknowledgements

The twin sources of these letters and journals from the Second World War are a number of old friends and the Department of Documents at the Imperial War Museum, London. I am immensely indebted to the kindness and generosity of both.

First the friends. I thank Mrs Diana Collins for allowing me to include letters from her brother Captain David Elliot; Mr Hugh Cronyn, GM, for a passage from his privately printed monograph, *Steady as You Go! A Canadian at Sea* (1990); Mr R. N. Currey for an extract from his *Troopship Journal*; Mrs Stella Martin Currey for letters written to her husband; Mr Christopher Elliott for letters written by his brother, Donald, and sister, Jean, and for much expert advice and permitting me to quote from his schoolboy diary; Mrs Juliet Laden for her letters from a pen-friend; Mr John Guest for letting me quote from his classic memoir, *Broken Images* (Longmans Green, 1949); Mrs Diana Hopkinson for letters written by herself and her husband David during 1939–45, and subsequently included in her memoir, *Love in War* (unpublished MS, Imperial War Museum); and Sir John Verney for passages from his *Going to the Wars* (Collins, 1955), for me one of the last war's finest personal statements.

I am most grateful to Mr Roderick Suddaby, Keeper of the Department of Documents at the Imperial War Museum, for his help and advice, and great kindness. My thanks, too, go to the copyright holders of the following documents deposited at the Museum for permitting me to include them in my anthology. These documents are:

The Bells Go Down: The Diary of a London AFS Man, author unknown

Diary of a Conscientious Objector by F. B. Breakspear
Diary of Private A. Brook
The Diary of a Desert Rat by Private R. L. Crimp
Sumatra Diary by Miss M. Dryburgh
Letters of Gunner F. C. Hawkridge and Mrs Joan Cheeseman
Stepping Stones to Austria: Or a Circumstance of War by Miss
    Margaret Heard
Journal, September 1941 by Lieutenant Bruce Hollingsworth
Civil Defence Goes Through It by Mr W. E. Hull
Memoir by Tosh Kano
What More Could a Soldier Ask of a War? by Sapper A. J. Lane
A Metal Man's War-Time Diary, August 1939–February 1941, edited
    by John Lassington
A Wartime Log by Captain J. S. Naylor
Diary of Sergeant L. D. Pexton
The Private Journal of a War Cameraman by Mr David Prosser
Letters to His Wife of Sergeant C. F. N. Louis Rose
An Airman to His Mother by Flying Officer Vivian Rosewarne
The Diary of Flying Officer Michael Scott
Letters of Private T. N. Seckle
Memoir by Sir James Stephen
The One That Didn't Get Away: Memoir by Gunner James Witte

I would also like to thank the following publishers and literary
executors for permission to quote from:

The Cage by Dan Billany and David Dowie (Longman, Green and
Co. 1949). *British Soldier in India: the Letters of Clive Branson*
(British Communist Party, 1944). *Collected Poems of Keith Douglas*
(Faber and Faber, 1966). *New and Collected Poems, 1934–84* by Roy
Fuller (Secker and Warburg, 1985). *The Good Soldier Švejk* by Jaroslav
Hašek (Penguin Books, 1973). *The Collected Poems of Sidney Keyes*
(Routledge, 1945), BBC Broadcasts by Ed Murrow and George Orwell.
Selected Poems of Alun Lewis (George Allen and Unwin, 1981).
Journal by Keith Vaughan (Alan Ross, 1966). *The Phoenix Generation*
by Henry Williamson (Macdonald, 1965).

READ MORE IN PENGUIN

In every corner of the world, on every subject under the sun, Penguin represents quality and variety – the very best in publishing today.

For complete information about books available from Penguin – including Puffins, Penguin Classics and Arkana – and how to order them, write to us at the appropriate address below. Please note that for copyright reasons the selection of books varies from country to country.

In the United Kingdom: Please write to *Dept. JC, Penguin Books Ltd, FREEPOST, West Drayton, Middlesex UB7 0BR*

If you have any difficulty in obtaining a title, please send your order with the correct money, plus ten per cent for postage and packaging, to *PO Box No. 11, West Drayton, Middlesex UB7 0BR*

In the United States: Please write to *Penguin USA Inc., 375 Hudson Street, New York, NY 10014*

In Canada: Please write to *Penguin Books Canada Ltd, 10 Alcorn Avenue, Suite 300, Toronto, Ontario M4V 3B2*

In Australia: Please write to *Penguin Books Australia Ltd, 487 Maroondah Highway, Ringwood, Victoria 3134*

In New Zealand: Please write to *Penguin Books (NZ) Ltd,182–190 Wairau Road, Private Bag, Takapuna, Auckland 9*

In India: Please write to *Penguin Books India Pvt Ltd, 706 Eros Apartments, 56 Nehru Place, New Delhi 110 019*

In the Netherlands: Please write to *Penguin Books Netherlands B.V., Keizersgracht 231 NL–1016 DV Amsterdam*

In Germany: Please write to *Penguin Books Deutschland GmbH, Friedrichstrasse 10–12, W–6000 Frankfurt/Main 1*

In Spain: Please write to *Penguin Books S. A., C. San Bernardo 117–6° E–28015 Madrid*

In Italy: Please write to *Penguin Italia s.r.l., Via Felice Casati 20, I–20124 Milano*

In France: Please write to *Penguin France S. A., 17 rue Lejeune, F–31000 Toulouse*

In Japan: Please write to *Penguin Books Japan, Ishikiribashi Building, 2–5–4, Suido, Tokyo 112*

In Greece: Please write to *Penguin Hellas Ltd, Dimocritou 3, GR–106 71 Athens*

In South Africa: Please write to *Longman Penguin Southern Africa (Pty) Ltd, Private Bag X08, Bertsham 2013*

BY THE SAME AUTHOR

Akenfield

'One of the most absorbing books that I have read in the last ten years. A penetrating, extraordinarily unprejudiced, yet deeply caring account of modern rural life in England' – Angus Wilson

A huge bestseller, Ronald Blythe's close-up of a Suffolk village has, for most readers, justified C. P. Snow's forecast that it would become a classic of its kind. Only a man born and bred in the county could, one feels, have extracted the confidences and revelations that fill these pages as a soldier, a farm labourer, a district nurse, an ex-army officer and other typical figures tell their personal stories.

'It seems to possess an appeal far beyond its immediate subject matter for a variety of readers' – *The Times Educational Supplement*

and Selected by Ronald Blythe

The Penguin Book of Diaries

Ronald Blythe introduces this wonderful anthology with an essay on the diarist's ambivalent art. He gives us gems from the journals of the famous and the unknown, personalities as various as Johnson, Darwin, Hardy, Evelyn Waugh and Virginia Woolf. His selection spans four centuries, and each contributor is introduced with a witty and scholarly portrait. They all share a passionate curiosity about the world and a particular genius for writing that catches the magic of the moment.

'Blythe's admirable selection provides a splendid introduction to a body of literature that can become an addiction. Those already smitten will be stimulated to return to old favourites and to break new ground' – *Sunday Telegraph*